CIVILIZATION
AND THE
TRANSFORMATION
OF POWER

CIVILIZATION
and the
TRANSFORMATION
—— *of* ——
POWER

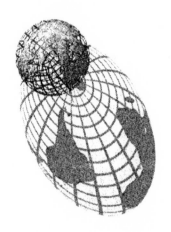

by
JIM GARRISON

PARAVIEW PRESS

NEW YORK

T.S. Eliot quotations are excerpted from *Four Quartets,*
first published in 1944 by Faber and Faber Limited, London.

Book and cover design by Tom Joyce

Cover photo illustration by John Lund

Library of Congress Cataloging-in-Publication Data
has been applied for.

ISBN: 1-931044-00-7

PRINTED IN THE UNITED STATES OF AMERICA

This book is dedicated to my grandmother,
Carmela LaRocca, who at one hundred and two
still inspires me by her delight and wonder
at the simplicities of life.

CONTENTS

ACKNOWLEDGMENTS   ix

FOREWORD   xv

INTRODUCTION   xxiii

  1. THE MOTHER GODDESS   1

  2. THE EPIC OF GILGAMESH   29

  3. THE BUDDHA   45

  4. EVE, MOTHER OF ALL LIVING   55

  5. APOCALYPSE   79

  6. THE TRIALS OF JOB   117

  7. SOPHIA   123

  8. MARY   143

  9. THE JUST MAN   155

 10. THE PARADOX OF POWER   175

 11. THE BLACK DEATH   187

 12. NOTRE DAME   211

 13. OUR GOD COMPLEX   227

 14. NUCLEAR WEAPONS AND THE HOLOCAUST   271

 15. THE FEMININE   287

 16. FAUST   309

 17. THE ARRIVAL OF BUDDHISM IN THE WEST   331

 18. WANDERING IN SINAI   339

EPILOGUE   349

ABOUT THE AUTHOR   353

INDEX   357

ACKLNOWLEDGMENTS

A BOOK THAT TAKES FIFTEEN YEARS TO WRITE compels many acknowledgements. It arose out of my doctoral dissertation at Cambridge University (1975–1982), the focus of which was the question: Why is it that, after several billion years of evolutionary life, our species, in our generation, has brought the entire life process to the brink of extinction through thermonuclear war? This seemed to be the greatest and most important question that I could ask. Everything I have done since then has in some fundamental way been framed by this exploration.

I could not have come to ask this question without a life oriented by deep inquiry. To this I owe my father a profound debt of gratitude, for his first and most enduring teaching to me was that I would never find peace until I found my peace in God, thus sculpting my young life around a pursuit of the Absolute. I also owe my mother deep gratitude, for it was she who framed our family with ceaseless nurturing. My Aunt Sally has also been an extraordinary embodiment of constant giving and self-sacrifice over the years. These experiences confirmed my original intuition that, ultimately, the universe is benign.

When I was five, I chanced upon a Buddhist priest in a temple in Taiwan, where I was growing up (my parents were Baptist missionaries). Bearing witness to him sitting absolutely motionless before a statue of the Buddha made an indelible impression on my young soul and provided me with my first encounter with the numinous. From that point onward, I carried with me, in dialectical tension, the Christ and the Buddha as co-equal lights of human consciousness. I believe them to be the most profound human beings to have ever lived. Even today, I sit in Buddhist meditation and write Judeo-Christian theology.

During my university and graduate school years, my immersion in the works of Sigmund Freud, Martin Buber, Teilhard de Chardin, Dietrich Bonhoeffer, Alfred North Whitehead, and Carl Jung deepened my sense of the intricacies of the human psyche and the complexities of the life process. My greatest teacher and mentor at Cambridge, Erick Hutchison, led me then, as he does now, into an exploration of the antinomial complexities of reality and an ever-deepening awareness that maturation comes only slowly and painfully as we journey through life, making mistakes and using them as opportunities for growth. Whatever depth I have gained has come at great cost to myself and many around me, for which I feel great sadness at times and also a deep sense of vulnerability to life's contingencies. We are in what we know not, yet we must act; though to act is to suffer.

In the last decade I have learned much from an immersion in the works of the great lights of Greco-Roman antiquity:

Plato, Aristotle, Aeschylus, Euripides, Sophocles, Plutarch, Tacitus, Levy, Herodotus, Thucydides, and Plotinus. Among my contemporaries, the works of Carlos Castenada and Ken Wilber have been of profound influence. Reading the histories of Will Durant and Arnold Toynbee helped provide context to our place and time, as has reading the foundational texts of the major world religions. All these have been my teachers.

It should be noted that this book was not written in the quiet of a university library or on retreat but at a dead run: in airplanes, at hotels, early in the mornings, along the edges of a very busy life. It has very much been a reflection of my life process.

To my friends and colleagues at the Christic Institute, the Clamshell Alliance, the Sunbelt Alliance, the Radiation and Health Information Service, the Esalen Institute Soviet American Exchange Program, the Gorbachev Foundation/USA, and, now, the State of the World Forum, I owe deep thanks. They have been extraordinarily generous as I have expressed my theological convictions through political activism, especially Alan Cranston, Chad Dobson, Steve Donovan, Joe Firmage, Jim Hickman, Michael and Dulce Murphy, Sara Nelson, Jim Primdahl, Tom Rautenberg, Danny Sheehan, Linda Taylor, and Amy Vossbrink. Mikhail Gorbachev, with whom I founded the Gorbachev Foundation/USA and the State of the World Forum, has been both mentor and friend, as have Jane Goodall, Ruud Lubbers, Wally N'Dow, Marian Wright Edelman, and Jose Ramos Horta, several of the Forum Co-Chairs.

The friends I have made along the way have been like jewels found along the seashore, especially Richard Baker, Koji Biosi, Jean Houston, Audrey Kitagawa, Sam Keen,

John Naisbitt, Martin Palmer, Steven Rhinesmith, Rupert Sheldrake, Bob Schwartz, and David Whyte. In one way or another, all have helped give my thinking and thus this book their shape and texture.

My wife, Claire, and our sons, Luke and Zachary, have been sources of stability, challenge, and reflection, and I love them dearly. They have absorbed many manifestations of my shadow and my exhaustion along the way. Children make one's life immediate, calling into question all our flights of abstraction, which this book certainly is. In and through the interplay of the immediate and the abstract, somehow—often just at that point of either exuberant joy or total despair—life is lived and maturity emerges; and families are shaped as roots are deepened. For those like myself who are restlessly active, the wisdom of limits that family life bestows is learned slowly.

As I was crafting my final reflections on the paradox and transformation of power—the essence of this book— my friendship with Carman Melendrez provided a profound deepening to my experience of and appreciation for the antinomial polarities of life; namely, that the opposite of a great truth is not necessarily a falsehood but can often be another equally great truth. For those seeking to live fully, the light and dark dimensions are often sharply dichotomized and yet intimately intertwined. They are embedded in one another, and both serve the needs of the life-force, which is to say that pathos has its own logic, its own mysteries, and its own reasons, along whatever pathways life compels it to take.

I am honored that Caroline Myss, my dear friend for whom I have felt deep love and respect for nearly twenty years, has written the foreword to this book. She is the most incisively clear person I know and full of compassion for human frailty. She has taught me much about the power of forgiveness.

Lastly, without Sandra Martin, my literary agent and good friend; Tom Joyce, who designed the book, the extraordinary cover, and coordinated publication; and Sam Matthews, my extremely meticulous and thorough editor, my labors would not have produced the book you hold in your hands.

My thanks to all.

One word about footnotes. We have tried to minimize their use in the text by noting the first time a book is cited with a footnote. Subsequent references provide page or line numbers in parentheses at the end of the quote.

I HAVE ALWAYS HELD THAT POWER IS THE fundamental ingredient of the human experience and that paradox is the primal language of God. Not one word we script, not one word we say, not one action we determine is without an inherent capacity to reshape this world and all of life, and that is a fact of creation, and thus of power. The agreement to manage this force of life, and of death, is our covenant with creation itself. The entire history of humanity is a study of what we have learned about our relationship to and with power, recording the consequences of its potential to destroy or rebuild civilizations. In truth, we are addicts to the shadow side of power, and we thrive and heal when we absorb its nectar. We cannot deny our addiction because power is the substance that has the alchemical force, an inherent spiritual electricity, that is required for us to come to know the nature of God, the Being who has created us to be dependent upon this substance for our existence and the care-taking of its potential for our survival.

Power, survival, the nature of the feminine, and the relationship of God to evil as revealed to us through the archetype of destruction and rebirth is the theme of this superb and spiritually thought-provoking book. Jim Garrison has undertaken an examination of the masculine and feminine polarities of the human psyche, presenting the thesis that without the unity of these two vessels of the life force, we can never accomplish the integration of our psyches, much less hope for a successful awakening of this civilization. And in the process of this transformation, we must address the reality that God permits unreasonable, if not cruel, acts of evil to occur, and not necessarily as punishment for wrongdoings, for that would make these actions humanly righteous.

But God, as Garrison is quick to note, defies human reason. The story of Job teaches us that, for it is witness to the fact that God is free of the restraints of the rational human mind, and it is for us to cope with this paradox. The fact that we would even allow ourselves to openly consider that God has a random, if not wild nature, is yet another indication that we are exploding with the energy of transformation because within the paradigm of reward and punishment, this profile of God could never be introduced into mass consciousness. Now it needs to be made public, as Garrison suggests, because it speaks of a transformation taking place within us that is consciously, if not unconsciously, directing us to live with a more authentic recognition of the personality of God. But what is to be gained by looking into the eyes of a God that admits to a love for evil? How is that to bring us comfort, when it is this Being who we turn to in order to receive grace in times of pain and distress?

And along with this profound shift in our theologies, we must recognize, and respect, that the underlying force of the Divine that is demanding we transform our relationship to power for the sake of survival is the feminine psyche of God, the Mother force, and not the Warrior God. With or without the crises that determine the majority of political and social actions taking place in our global community, we would come to this stage in our awakening that requires we welcome in the next paradigm of our evolution, in conscious realization that the masculine is to the process of transformation what the feminine is to the process of integration, and that achieving any degree of wholeness requires their union.

How do we even hope to achieve this Divine call to dismantle our relationship to this ironclad power that has provided us with so much on our investment? Our economics rely upon the masculine, as do our systems of protection and defense. We rarely had to fear the feminine nations of the earth for they are no competition on the battlefield, ironically becoming a serious threat only upon learning how to manufacture an artificial representation of the male phallic in the form of a nuclear missile. And then there is the matter of Mother Nature herself, and how the masculine power of the psyche made it possible to sample what it would be like if it could finally dominate the one power it desperately relied upon but never before controled: Her natural cycles of life. Achievements abound that allow the masculine psyche to force Mother Nature to grow her seeds and produce life from Her belly long before Her wisdom would have it so. Symbolically this achievement for the male psyche meant that the masculine had finally committed a rape that could only be called archetypal. The masculine had stolen Mother Nature's ability to birth, protect, and nurture life according to her internal laws. Now, even her precious rapport with her lunar self had been subjugated to the rulership of the masculine.

Part of the genius of this text is that Garrison speaks for the feminine, serving as a channel for Her voice and Her wisdom. There can be no transformation of this civilization into one that can survive, he urges, unless we come to know the feminine nature of the Divine once again, for our integration of our own psyches depends upon it. Why has the masculine feared the feminine? Garrison addresses this question, offering us a map that leads us first into the historical psyche of the feminine and Her many manifestations, from Sofia, to the Virgin, to the Divine Mother. Further, through uniting the psyches of the feminine and the masculine, we are then in a position to approach an unthinkable possibility that may well be the most hidden truth in all of human experience; that God embraces evil, creates evil, allows evil to exist. How can this be? How can pure and perfect Divinity seek to destroy the life that it has so lovingly created? What sort of God is it that would send the Devil to tempt His most perfect human, Job? Yet, according to Garrison, without pursuing these questions that so richly express the paradoxical nature of God, we cannot even afford to hope that the paradigm of unity that we are attempting to animate for this next stage of human evolution will materialize.

To begin this examination, we must address the God we have always wanted, and therefore have always sought, and place that profile next to the God that is, the God we write about in our fears. The God that we want is one that has been sculpted by the rational mind of the masculine. Ordered, logical, reasonable, and rational, this is the God we have long desired because this is a controllable God, one whose actions can be predicted because He is bound to the rules and honor code of human justice. This God would never act without reason, or just cause. This God would have to explain Itself to our human courts were it to permit a Holocaust, allow a Flood, or turn Its back on a Hiroshima, as Garrison is quick to point out. This cannot be our God, the behavior of the controlled masculine. What, then, is the cause of such irrational, chaotic behavior? Surely some form of power is at fault. Indeed, said the masculine voice, it must be the feminine which so offends God. It must be Her force, and so the Goddess was silenced.

But, as with all of the paradoxes that characterize the personality of God, the feminine was in fact far more ordered and logical than the masculine, only Her order relied upon lunar forces, and its logic was one based upon how to balance and provide for life rather than devising means to take from it. The directives of the feminine come from an inner knowledge of the psyche, the force that mothers our emotional and psychological fragments, always seeking ways through the unconscious to bring them to unity. The rational nature of the masculine fears these fragments, and to quell that fear, separates them as a means for maintaining control. Unity for the masculine introduces emotion and intuition to the intellect, a threatening partnership to be sure.

Now the feminine lunar nature is making Her prone to generating an ever-increasing number of floods, famine, and every form of life force catastrophe. Her emotional rages have increased because She can no longer endure, nor forgive the rape of her offspring. Clearly, the Goddess Demeter has descended once again, threat of destruction in hand. She showed civilization once before that She is capable of creating famine, and erasing the love She carries within Her to provide for all life. And this time, as before, a bargain with Hades, Her masculine aggressor, needs to be reached for He holds Persephone, the virgin offspring of Demeter, captive once again. The transformation and the survival of life depend upon what takes place at their bargaining table. We must consider the question, "Can we transform our separation of power and create a single productive force, or must we risk living within a civilization in which survival remains a day-to-day challenge?" The choice of the word "productive" is deliberate, because it is foolish to speak of harmony or to use any word that reflects a desire for creating a perfect society. If nothing else, the Divine would not allow such a place to exist because, as is so well known, Moses did not make it to the Promised Land, not because he offended God, but because there never was and never will be a Promised Land on this earth. But we can hold to the possibility that we can lay the groundwork for a society that is productive based upon the fact that the masculine needs the feminine, and vise-versa. It is not that the masculine is to be blamed for the crises facing humanity. Rather it is simply that the time has come when the masculine and feminine aspects of the psyche must share in nurturing and protecting all that is life.

Given this effort to mediate a peaceful merger of the masculine and feminine aspects of the psyche, we must add to the equation yet another Divine paradox, which is that these two faces of the Divine--the masculine and the feminine— when combined create the alchemy of choice. And as Garrison so intriguingly examines in this text, choice, the greatest of all powers that exists within the human experience, is both a blessing and a curse--a spiritual necessity, as are all Divine paradoxes. We are, all of us, seated at the bargaining table of Demeter and Hades. Only this time, Persephone cannot be split in half, ruled partly by Hades, and nurtured partly by Demeter. She must be cared for equally by both the masculine and the feminine psyche, the new archetype of partnership. This is the choice we face. Can we integrate these polarities that have represented domination or cooperation with life, and perhaps transform this ancient myth to include their having a mutual offspring that makes an integration of both their forces of the psyche possible?

Even with such a union of the masculine and feminine

psyches of God, however, we still must recognize and contend with the fact that God allows evil to exist within the human experience. We cannot pray for God to change, or for life to be other than what it is, an experience of polarities ruled by a paradoxical God. And we will always have choice—our blessing and our curse—and our God will never succumb to our pleas that He become a rational and controllable force that plays by the rules of human justice. The desire for this paradigm is nothing more than spiritual madness. But we can respond to the manner in which life speaks to us. We can choose to respond to Mother Nature's call to allow Her to emerge once again into the psyche of the Divine so that She can participate, if not lead us, into an era whose fundamental commitment is to transform a civilization into one in which survival is no longer a hope, but a given.

No easy way exists to walk a path that has yet to be built. But there are leaders, and Jim Garrison is one of them. In *Civilization and the Transformation of Power,* he gives voice to the feminine, to the Goddess, to the Virgin, to Demeter, to Sophia because it is their power that illuminates our new direction. He takes on the exploration of God's relationship to evil, an examination that pushes the envelop of one's spirituality because it would seem so opposite to the Divine design to include in that portrait a God who cannot be trusted because of a precarious nature, yet demands faith at all times. In this exceptional text, Garrison is carving a path that is not leading to our transformation, but is the process of transformation itself.

CAROLINE M. MYSS
Author of *Anatomy of the Spirit* and *Why People Don't Heal*

INTRODUCTION

I can do without answers to all my questions except

the one question, What questions should we be asking

in a world that is burning? —ANON.

AT THE TURN OF THE MILLENNIUM THE world is burning. Transformation is occurring in every sector, at every scale, in every dimension. Nothing we have inherited from the past is able to withstand the accelerated pace of change; everything from the future remains a perpetual possibility. Society has become completely malleable to the power of science and technology; our mind, continually susceptible to novelty; our relationships, opened to new configurations and meanings.

It is almost unbelievable that 90 percent of everything that has been discovered or invented in the entire history of civilization has been invented or discovered in the past seventy-five years. Explosions in science and technology are creating opportunities that stagger the imagination. Revolutions in biotechnology, nanotechnology, digital technology, and information technology are reshaping human society and offering us essentially unlimited power over ourselves, over nature, over life itself.

Yet all these achievements have not made us more ethically balanced or more wise. Upwards of two hundred million persons have been killed in this century alone for reasons of war and ideology, more than have been killed in all of recorded history combined. The advent of nuclear weapons in 1945 made possible for the first time the annihilation of all life. Chemical and biological weapons, other products of this century, could also do irreparable harm on a scale heretofore unknown.

Ironically, the incidences of natural disasters—earthquakes, floods, famines, tornadoes, hurricanes, and drought—are occurring with a frequency without modern historical parallel.

In social terms we are witnessing an equally powerful force. After millennia of male domination, women are rising to positions of leadership in virtually every sphere of endeavor. In the process we are completely reforming gender relationships and our inherited beliefs concerning governance, community, family, hierarchy, and spirituality. This is giving rise to extraordinary possibilities in our appreciation of human potential and societal values.

Equally fundamental, a global consciousness, spawned by economic globalization and mass communication, is for the first time uniting all of humanity into a single unit, bringing the six thousand discrete cultures and societies now existing around the world into sustained interaction. Nation-states, the mainstay of commerce, government, and culture for centuries, are rapidly giving way to networks empowered by information and communication technologies. Human civilization is being reborn on a global scale.

Such are the transformations occurring in the world that President and poet Vaclav Havel suggests that

There are good reasons for suggesting that the modern age has ended. Many things indicate that we are going through a transitional period when it seems that something is on the way out and something else is painfully being born. It is as if something were crumbling, decaying and exhausting itself, while something else, still indistinct, were arising from the rubble.[1]

At the onset of a new century and the third millennium, propelled forward by change, we find ourselves in the space between epochs. We are being torn from the past and yet the future is indistinct. With unimaginable power at our disposal, with transformations occurring in every sphere, we are strangely unsure of where we now want to go. To use a Biblical image, it is as if we were delivered from the bondage of Egypt but have not yet entered the Promised Land. We are thus wandering lost in the wilderness of Sinai, full of potential but without clear direction.

Sinai bespeaks a time when the old is gone, but the new is not yet fully discerned. It is a time of transition, a time of hope and preparation in anticipation of the new, as well as a time of disorientation and confusion, emanating out of the passing of the old. All our inventions and discoveries, even our deliverance from the grip of the Cold War, have brought not utopia but turbulence, not a new world-order but uncertainty and chaos.

Being lost in Sinai, the world around us burning in transformation, compels us to ask whether we are caught up in a random accumulation of events that are sweeping the world into an unknown reality beyond anyone's control, or are deep patterns of history operating that can be discerned in

1. Vaclav Havel, in a speech given at Liberty Hall, Philadelphia, July 4,1993.

our present moment? Are we in a time of unprecedented newness in which everything is being reinvented, or are we in the grip of déjà vu in which the past is mysteriously present and framing our future?

May I suggest that the answer to both alternatives is yes? We are in a time of novelty, *and* we are experiencing the repetition of very deep historical patterns. Everything is completely new, *and* we have all been here before. We are marching relentlessly into the unknown, *and*, if we look deeply enough, we can discern that this unknown is undergirded by the knowable. To be able to discern both alternatives, separately and together, is to be able to come to terms with the paradox of power, which characterizes our age.

I use the term "paradox of power" very advisedly. Things seem as confusing as they are because everything seems paradoxical. New inventions and discoveries abound to raise standards of living, eliminate certain diseases, and make life more comfortable worldwide; *and* thousands of plant and animal species are made extinct every year as a result of this technological progress. Multinational corporations sell their products in every corner of an increasingly prosperous world, *and* new diseases and refugee migrations sweep the earth. We are comforted with myriad accouterments of technological progress, *and* we are confronted by multiple crises in human relations. We continue to foul our nest, even as we build better ones.

At a time of unparalleled expansion at the scientific and technological levels, we participate in and give witness to unimaginable destructiveness. The generation of humanity that put a man on the moon and developed a cure for polio produced the Stalinist dictatorship and shoved millions of Jews into gas chambers. The companies that manufacture the consumer goods we all enjoy slash rain forests to the ground and adhere to minimal environmental standards only by force of law. In the name of progress we destroy; through destruction we "progress." The more we know, the more destructive we seem to become. The more power we exercise, the more power we seek.

This is a universal phenomenon, affecting the entire human race. Whether from Japanese, European, or American corporations, technological developments are generated to satisfy consumers while their ethical, social, and environmental implications are left essentially unexplored; and whether in the Balkans, Africa, or Tibet, peace is discussed while violence abounds. Human technology and human relations everywhere reflect this paradox of progress and destructiveness, altruism and greed. Human life is played out on the anvil of tragedy and hope.

This paradox undergirds human historical, psychological, and spiritual life. The polarity of opposites within the context of life, death, and renewal constitutes a basic matrix of human existence itself. Carl Jung called this the *cruciform nature of reality:* Everything in our experience is comprised of opposites, and all things evolve through time within a pattern of life, death, and renewal. Moreover, these opposites are not simply neat pairs of polarities, such as light and dark, male and female, which are easily identifiable and understood. Rather, the cruciform nature of reality describes existence as comprised of *antinomies:* internally consistent, mutually exclusive truths, which to our conscious mind seem totally *disconnected* but which are inseparably *interconnected* within our psyche and in the realm of Spirit.

It is almost impossible to grasp an antinomy intellec-

tually because an antinomy cannot be explained rationally. That not withstanding, the subject of this book is the
antinomies that make up human history, that shape and,
paradoxically, redeem our life. The best way to understand
them is through stories, which I will recount as we proceed. A way to think about antinomies is to reflect on the
notion that the opposite of a truth does not necessarily
have to be a falsehood. The opposite of one truth can be
another equally profound truth.

Paradoxes and antinomies are played out not only in
the life of individuals but also in the life of civilizations, a
fundamental point to observe when one considers that it
is largely Western science and technology, Western practices
of democratic governance, Western theories of free market
economics, and Western culture that are pervading and
dominating the rest of the world. In many ways the
triumph of globalization is the triumph of the West
over the globe. Western antinomies have become global
antinomies.

European military and economic power from the
fifteenth through the nineteenth centuries compelled the
rest of the world to enter various Western dominated
military, political, and economic spheres. European
culture and religion followed its soldiers and traders.
European wars have been fought on the world map. The
two major European conflicts of this century were the two
"World Wars." Nuclear technology, which has brought the
world to the brink of the abyss, arose and expanded
primarily among countries dominated culturally and
religiously by Judeo-Christianity. Only later did the Asian
nations embrace this technology, seeking to keep pace
with this Western definition of ultimate power.

It must be one of the supreme ironies of history that, by the twentieth century, a religious culture founded on the Torah and the great commands of Jesus to love God and one's neighbor as oneself was dealing with neighbors only from behind nuclear shields, motivated by a mind-set that projected fear, mistrust, and, at times, veritable hatred. Had the Soviet and American blocs gone to war, as almost happened on several occasions during the Cold War, both superpowers would have been destroyed along with their European allies. Although fallout and the predicted nuclear winter would no doubt have carried radiation over much of the earth, it would have been largely those nations comprising Christendom that would have annihilated each other.

We must allow this paradoxical fact to confront us with all its starkness. Europeans and Americans, Christians and Jews are the principle developers of the fundamental forces transforming our world as well as the great crises challenging it. Put simply, Judeo-Christianity and Western civilization have become addicted to the acquisition of power: not power for service, but power for-and-of-itself.

This is a harsh statement; nevertheless, it is my contention that, in order to discern what has engendered our remarkable advances in science and technology on the one hand and our weapons and policies of unimaginable destructiveness on the other, we must go to the roots of our Judeo-Christian tradition. This will allow us not only to understand our predicament more clearly, but also to activate the resolution of the global crises we have engendered. These opportunities and crises are not being forced upon us from without; they are welling up from within.

As paradoxical as it may seem, we must contend with the issue that the power drive that motivates us to advance technologically and obsesses us to destroy incessantly is rooted in some mysterious way in the very depth of the human soul and lies at the heart of Western civilization's religious tradition.

That the present triumph of science and challenge of crisis is exemplified most strongly within Western civilization is not an accident of history. Judaism and Christianity, which form the foundational religious matrix of Western civilization, are religions that arose out of crisis and have historically been concerned with the exercise and transformation of power. The temptation to misuse power is a principal focus of both traditions. It is illuminating of the central enigma of Western civilization that it has produced such scientific advances, has become the channel of such destructiveness, and has within the past century conquered the world.

There is a parable that brings this point into focus. A man was thirsty and, finding a Buddhist monk, asked him what to do. "Meditate and detach yourself from your thirst," the monk replied. The man asked the same question of a Christian priest. "Go dig a well," the priest replied.

To detach oneself from thirst entails meditation upon the unity of existence, the suffering that accompanies all attachment, and the emptiness of all form. Enlightenment comes from within. To dig a well requires action: property must be obtained, water found, tools utilized, work done. It is an event that happens *within* history rather than an awareness that comes *about* history. To dig a well is to exercise power; to exercise power is to make history. Judeo-Christianity and Western civilization have dug many wells. This is their principal achievement; it is also their central predicament. Paradoxically, the Eastern mystics, meditating upon water, have equally much to say about well digging, a point that will be further developed as the book unfolds.

Judaism and Christianity are religions embedded in history. Both religions were founded upon specific historical events, and their focus has always been on the unfolding of history, the realm in which God and humankind enter into relationship, into covenant.

The foundational events of Judaism and Christianity occurred at points of historical crisis. Judaism was born with the Exodus; Christianity, with the Crucifixion. Both events were violent, overpowering, cataclysmic. The Exodus involved Israelite enslavement in Egypt, the ten plagues sent by Yahweh against Pharaoh, the crossing of the Red Sea, the giving of the Law in the wilderness of Sinai, the entering into the Promised Land. Out of this cauldron of contradictions, this cruciform polarity between enslavement and deliverance, monotheism was refined; the Ten Commandments, proclaimed; and the religion that became Judaism, generated.

Christianity arose out of an intense struggle between Jesus and the religious leaders whose response to his life and message was to kill him. Christianity was born at the Cross. Paul, who proclaimed Christ crucified to the Gentiles and shaped the charisma of Jesus into the religion of Christianity, was also killed, as were most of Jesus' disciples and thousands of other early believers. Christianity was empowered by the blood of its martyrs and within three centuries became the official religion of the Roman Empire.

The power of Judaism and Christianity derives from the intense convergence of violence, darkness, and judgment on the one hand, and triumph, light, and deliverance on the other. The Exodus culminated in the entry into the Promised Land; the Crucifixion was empowered by the Resurrection. The cruciform structure of reality and the question of power are given their deepest revelation in these two events. It is the cruciform structure of reality and the transformation of power, as revealed in the Exodus and the Cross, that undergird the West's historical, psychological, and spiritual foundations.

The Exodus and Crucifixion thus provide the widest context within which we are given clues to the deepest possible interpretation of response to the immense movements that have surged through human history and confront us still. It is grimly ironic and profoundly illuminating that Judeo-Christianity, which seeks the transformation of power through humility, obedience, and self-sacrifice, has fortified our insatiable power drive as a civilization.

The ultimate symbol of power is the possession of nuclear weapons. Their advent is humanity's greatest contemporary crisis and is thus a major rite of passage for the human race. Humanity, at risk of destroying itself, is being given insight into the mystery of power. It is tempting to put aside the nuclear issue because a few treaties have been signed and the world is preoccupied with other concerns. This would be utter folly. From the dawn of humanity until 6 August 1945, every human being has lived with the awareness that he or she would die. Since that first atom bomb burst over Hiroshima, every human being has had to live with the certainty of not only his or her own death but with the possible termination of the entire human race. Every future generation will live with this knowledge and thus with this threat. Nuclear weapons are the lasting curse this century has perpetrated on the development of humanity. That the major nations of the world, led by the Untied States, remain obsessed with their possession and continued refinement makes their possession and eventual use by additional nations and terrorist groups inevitable.

The vision of a fiery end to history has always been a powerful one in Judeo-Christianity, a point that will be further explored in Chapter 6. During the second and first centuries B.C.E., lasting until approximately the first century C.E., Jewish and Christian prophets believed they were witnessing the end of the world. Their apocalyptic visions foresaw that only God could save them from an evil world and would do so by destroying the world and then recreating a new heaven and a new earth.

The Bible ends with the apocalyptic visions of Saint John, foretelling in gruesome imagery the destruction and transformation of life on earth. It is a vision of historical culmination, which has been embedded in Western civilization for two thousand years. It should give us great pause that the fundamental religious mythology under-girding Western civilization is the fiery end of history at the hands of a wrathful God.

What the ancient prophets believed only God could do, human beings can now do. If the end comes, it will be a human finger that pushes the button, for it will be human ignorance, human wrath, and human stupidity that creates the context within which the only "rational" option in some leader's mind will be to wage nuclear war. In this sense Hiroshima has *humanized* the apocalypse, even though God is not thereby left behind. Divinity is at work in all things, including the most profoundly good and the most barbarically evil.

It behooves us to examine the ancient apocalyptic visions of the Jews in light of what it is now possible for us to do two millennia later. What we shall discover is that during their time of great crisis, when the orthodox believers looked above to what they perceived as a God of power to end it all in order to begin again afresh, there was, in fact, a dramatic outpouring of a subtle, feminine energy —called *hockmah* by the Jews, translated "Sophia" by the Greeks —which transformed their life.

Paradoxically, while looking above to a masculine God to save them, their path of renewal was discerned by a feminine presence within. This energy had been present in the world since creation but arose with particular intensity during their time of trials, enabling them to reorder their life with a new sense of proportion and creativity. In Sophia the Jews discerned the ordering principle of creation, an ordering principle that they discovered to be not simply a boundary but the paradox of power.

The God of power above never did break through the clouds and destroy the world; rather Sophia, rising up from within, affected that ancient community profoundly and was largely responsible for the psychological receptivity in the ancient Near East to the phenomenon of Jesus, who, among other names, was called the "Sophia of God."

That a profoundly subtle and sensitive feminine consciousness should arise in the ancient apocalyptic era to empower humanity to reorder itself at the moment of deepest despair is quite compelling, as is the virtually simultaneous advent of women's liberation and nuclear weapons. Just when human hands fashioned the technology of destruction, human society, initially in that nation first to develop and drop the Bomb, dramatically revolutionized the relationship between the sexes.

Even as nuclear technology revolutionized strategy, energy production, and politics, so the liberation of women has initiated a democratizing impulse throughout human culture that is transforming the world in every sector women are entering. Additionally, the arrival of Eastern spirituality to the West has brought with it a metaphysic of interdependence and wholeness, which is providing a new framework for value.

As Hiroshima has humanized the apocalypse, the rise in feminine consciousness and the emergence of a spirituality of wholeness has manifested new dimensions of Sophia. If nuclear technology is the lasting curse we will leave to our progeny, the equalization of the sexes will be our enduring blessing.

Like the Exodus and the Promised Land, and the Cross and the Resurrection, nuclear weapons and the liberation of women form an antinomy. As with all antinomies, they seem completely disconnected. What could the evils of nuclear technology possibly have to do with something as sublime as the empowerment of women? They seem to be diametrically opposed and fundamentally *unrelated*. Yet they are, in fact, deeply and inseparably *interrelated*. They form the dark and light dimensions of a single event. History will record them as this generation's most enduring legacy.

These parallels and interrelationships take on added significance when one examines another point of great crisis in the human story: the Black Death of 1348, the most lethal disaster in recorded history. This was the bubonic plague, which, in about a decade, wiped out a quarter of the human population between Iceland and India. As the plague spread throughout Europe the Christians again looked to the One they had seen as the God of power above to deliver them. Fear was again mixed with a desire for vengeance, this time against the Jews believed by many Christians to be responsible for their affliction.

At the same time, there was the most massive out-pouring of adoration for Mary in all of European history. This confluence of deepening crisis and awakening feminine consciousness was followed by fresh energy among Europeans, enabling them to move beyond the strictures of medieval Catholicism. The Black Death signaled the end of medieval society and was followed by the three great movements of the modern era: the Renaissance, the Reformation, and the Enlightenment.

To speak of the cruciform structures of crisis and the mutual significance of these great events is not to equate them in either substance or importance. Hiroshima, the Black Death, and ancient apocalypse are not the same as the Exodus or the Crucifixion; nor should Sophia be equated with the adoration of Mary or with the liberation of women. Fundamental distinctions exist and must be delineated.

These phenomena shed light *upon* one another because, though they are very different *from* one another, they deal with the *same* fundamental themes. They all reflect the cruciform nature of history and human life. They all contain enormous contradictions and embody the pattern of life, death, and renewal. As such, they point back and give further meaning to the Exodus and to the

Cross, and they point forward to illuminate our own path as we move into a new millennium and a new world.

I realize that I risk oversimplification in stating this. History and human life defy generalizations and confound those who seek consistencies. Exceptions seem to prove the rules as well as destroy them. Nevertheless, in examining the Black Death and the Jewish apocalyptic period in parallel with the nuclear crisis, one can begin to perceive the outlines of the internal structures of the overwhelming crises and shattering transformations of today.

In all three instances the communities were caught completely unaware by a megadeath experience. They reacted by blaming another group for the crisis and prayed to their God of power above for redemption. Simultaneously, there was an outpouring of a subtle, yet compelling, feminine energy, which intermingled the darker dimensions of the crisis with its own shadow-side, and which was followed by an impetus toward a new order.

Recalling how human beings reacted to the great crises of the Apocalypse and the Black Death will help us know how best to respond to our own situation. What we shall discover is that it is in times of great crisis that enormous creativity is unleashed and the cruciform nature of history is laid bare. Great cosmic forces come together—darkness and light, power and sensitivity, violence and non-violence, despair and redemption—to bring about a new way of being in the world. Darkness intensifies so that grace can abound; grace abounds so that darkness can be transformed.

Reflection upon these momentous events compels us to see that forces that we may ordinarily think of as being opposite or irrelevant to one another, in fact, belong together in a living tension as antinomies. Paradoxically, the antinomies of history and the human heart are not all in equilibrium. There are tremendous asymmetries. A fundamental truth about the cruciform nature of reality is that reality is not simply an "either/or" proposition. It is also not a "both/and" unity either. The cruciform nature of reality points to a great mystery: Life is comprised of "either" *and* "or" complexities with which we must grapple at the very core of our being. Life is filled with internally consistent, mutually exclusive, and yet inseparably interrelated realities. This is why little in human life is straightforward.

To recognize antinomies and the cruciform nature of reality is to embrace the mystery that, even in what appear to us as patterns of history, disjunctions, contradictions, and imbalances abound. Truths collide, and history is broken up to reveal even deeper truths. To live out the disjunction of the polarities means that we will suffer, even be rent asunder, but as paradoxical as this may seem, only through this can we be transformed. Thus during the twentieth century, as during the fourteenth, the world is broken up so that a new world-order can be born.

Only in the willingness to be broken at the hands of the opposites within can we be redeemed. When opposites are split, a struggle for dominance results. But when they are brought together, even if in a violent way, the transformation of power can result. This is the profundity at the heart of the Exodus and the Crucifixion; it is the crucial insight to explore in a world that is burning.

In the end we shall discover a moral chaos theory. We shall discern that at the point of our deepest despair, when all seems to be chaotic and destructive, when our pride and wickedness consume the world, there are forces operative that are serving a divine will within and through the very darkness that is precluding our capacity to see. Blinded by our shadow, we are given the strength of faith and the capacity to believe. Thus we can gain insight into the words the Greek poet Aeschylus uttered nearly two thousand five hundred years ago:

> ...drop by drop,
>
> pain that cannot forget
>
> falls upon the heart
>
> until in our despair,
>
> against our will,
>
> comes wisdom
>
> by the awful grace of God.[2]

This excruciating antinomy of which Aeschylus speaks—this despair, this wisdom, this grace—are all found in the heart of what we experience as pain. Yet the heart of pain, in the end, is framed by the "awful grace of God," used by the Divine Spirit to break up our conventionalities and instill within us a deeper sense of humility in the face of the great mystery that is the Universe we inhabit. This is the context for pain, the paradox of power, and the strength of grace.

To take up questions of historical paradox and the reality of evil is to take up issues against which all systems, all dogmas, all neatly arranged paradigms break up and shatter. The truths to which these paradoxes point cannot be viewed directly, only indirectly through stories, myths, and legends. Paradoxes cannot be dissected through logic; they can only be intuited after wrestling with the

2. Aeschylus, as inscribed on the wall of the tomb site of Robert Kennedy, Arlington, Virginia.

paradoxes themselves and allowing the collision of unknowns to open oneself up to greater awareness of a deeper unknown.

The issues presented in this book reside deeply within the core of human experience but are far beyond the grasp of our intellect. Because of this we seldom consider them in our normal life, dominated as we are by the demand to be rational and conventional. Indeed, we go to great lengths to smooth the edges of our life to ensure that we do not have to encounter these paradoxes.

Yet time and time again, just when we seem to have nearly complete control of who and what we are, something erupts—sometimes catastrophically—from an unexpected quarter that disrupts our neatly arranged lifestyle and relationships, and we are forced to come to terms with what we have attempted to ignore.

I ask the reader's forbearance as we proceed, for the issues we will be dealing with are complex and must be dealt with indirectly and with great circumspection. Mostly I will explore these issues through a series of stories—some legendary, some Biblical, some historical, some poetical—all of which seek in their own way to come to terms with the paradoxes of life and the mysterious presence of pain and power. They seduce us and mysteriously transform our very soul.

This book is about God and history, which necessitates a definition of "God." In using the term I realize I am using a word and a concept that in the modern world is fraught with meaning and with meaninglessness, with profundity and with elusiveness. I do not intend to use this term in any sectarian sense. I use it to name that awareness that knows and unites the entire universe in a harmonious whole. All we see around us is harmony, a great ecology of being in which we have arisen and back to which we all return. This is the great Tao, the great Brahma, the All Encompassing within which everything, including human history and human destiny, finds its place.

God is that Will that intends connections between the different entities comprising the universe. Without God there would be no cohesion, no creativity, no energy; all would be Void. It is with the Void that God begins, and out of the Void that God creates something from nothing. And yet, in some mysterious way we cannot comprehend, God is before nothing; God is before the Void. God is Creator and Sustainer, that Presence, that Awareness that brings life into being and unifies all the various components of the vastness of the universe into a singularity. God is the great Creator, the everlasting Sustainer, the final Destroyer.

A very rough analogy of what I mean is the human being. We can roughly say that God is to the universe what each of us is to our body. As one is aware of oneself, so God is the Awareness that is aware of the totality of everything. As one knows and directs one's body, so God knows and directs the universe. As one exercises will and expresses emotions, so God expresses divinity in different ways and at different times in the universal process.

We are alive because, in some mysterious way, the spirit of life activates our body. Each of us possesses a consciousness, an awareness of "self being alive." This awareness directs what we think, what we say, and what we do. At the core of this awareness is will, the capacity to intend. Our life is the sum of our intentions. This mysterious essence leaves suddenly when we die, and our body—a

moment ago breathing, feeling, functioning, thinking—
becomes inert and lifeless. Our "awareness", our "aliveness,"
is the phenomenon of "God."

Paradoxically, if a scientist were to dissect a body, he or
she would find various organs, bones, muscles, a brain, and
so forth but would not find a soul, a will, or an awareness.
Aliveness cannot be either quantitatively or qualitatively
measured. Yet it is as real as the physical aspects; indeed,
without this invisible consciousness a body cannot move
and will decay and waste away. Just so is God's relation to
the universe. Scientists scan the heavens for far-off galaxies
and plumb the depths of the atom but do not discern the
consciousness instilling the whole cosmos with life, intention,
and harmony. Thus they say God does not exist, cannot be
proved, and is only a consequence of religious belief.

In ordinary life we live unaware of either the totality
of the universe or the consciousness that sustains it as a
harmonious whole. We live as if only our personal concerns
were important. As the fish in the ocean are unaware of
the water that surrounds and sustains them, so we, for the
most part, live life unconscious of what surrounds and
sustains us.

Using one's consciousness to connect with Cosmic
Consciousness is the ultimate act of human integrity and
courage, for to do so is to identify not with oneself but
with the Totality. Just imagine how one cell in a body
would be affected by becoming fully conscious of and in
tune with the totality of that body. Moreover, if this cell
became conscious of and in tune with the reality that this
body was on a planet hurtling through space, the cell
would probably "blow its mind," for this "enlightenment"
would make it either hyperfunctional or completely

dysfunctional. It certainly would never again be the same.

Seeking "God," trying to grapple with the Totality of the universe, is similar for us humans who are far less proportional in relationship to the entire universe than one cell is to a body. Connecting with Cosmic Awareness is not something to be taken lightly. The Will that intends the universe, the Consciousness holding infinity, including the earth and each one of us, is the Holy, the Mysterium Tremedum, the great I AM. We cannot interact with It without being changed fundamentally and indelibly.

We have immense difficulty maintaining a positive relationship with our own body. We abuse it, and we are essentially unconscious of what is happening within it. Just imagine what it must be like to be holding the entire universe together. What subtlety of intent, what refinement of awareness must be required to keep the whole cosmos running in complete harmony every instant of every day for all of eternity, knowing that the movement of any part will be felt and will have influence on all the other parts. It is no wonder that when God came to Elijah in the wilderness, God came as a "still small voice." Given the totality of what God is taking care of, the miracle is not that God exists but that the Cosmic Awareness pays any attention to us at all. Perhaps this, finally, is what makes God, God.

The ultimate assertion of religious reflection, East and West, is that, in whatever form and by whatever path, our insignificant points of personal awareness can connect with and be guided by Cosmic Awareness. All the great mystics of every tradition have essentially had the same experience. They discover that when "God" is experienced, they feel united with the Totality; indeed, at the highest level, their individual awareness fuses with Cosmic Awareness; the drop melts into the Ocean, and the Ocean fuses with the drop.

In contemplating these realities words and concepts can only fail. In the face of Totality there is nothing that can be said, giving great truth to the insight of the ancient Chinese mystic Lao Tzu, that "The Tao that can be told is not the eternal Tao."[3] But it is equally true, in the spirit of antinomy, that the Tao that *cannot* be described is not the true Tao. It is in this spirit that I dare speak of God and our awareness of and connection with the divine.

To pursue the question of God is the task of theology. Theology is thus rightly called the "queen of the sciences." The hard sciences seek to know the material universe and measure its physical manifestations; the soft sciences seek to understand the phenomenon of human beings and the relationship of the individual with society. Only theology seeks to know that "something" in and through which all things cohere and find meaning. Theology seeks to know the Knower, that Awareness, that Will, that Totality in which all things great and small find their place and attain their value.

The direct implication of this notion is that our greatest challenge is to walk in alignment and in harmony with the whole. To the degree we can do this we walk "in God." This alignment becomes apparent when, in full consciousness of who we are as part of the whole, we say "Not my will but thine be done." In this great act we discover freedom.

This is not an easy task. For as we live, as we contemplate God, history, and destiny,

3. Lao Tzu,
The Enlightened Heart,
ed. and trans.
Stephen Mitchell
(San Francisco:
Harper and Row,
1989),12.

we have at least three different ways of knowing and experiencing reality. The first way we perceive is *rationally,* gathering the data of our physical senses and analyzing life objectively and logically. It is the way we understand the world of time, space, and causality. It is the world that we discover through the morning newspaper and television news and that is recorded in our history and science books. It is a way of knowing that is relative, transitory, factual.

In this world we exercise pragmatic choices about our life: the clothes we wear, the schools we attend, the political parties we support, the places we live, the books we read, the work we do, and the places we go for holidays. In this realm we experience and exercise freedom in the narrowest sense. Pragmatic choice constitutes our *sensibility* of freedom.

The second way we perceive and experience the world is *psychologically.* Although our pragmatic choices are decisions essentially about external affairs, they are determined largely by inner complexes and drives, which are often not understood and rarely acknowledged but which exert profound influence on our everyday choices, nonetheless. In addition to measuring things scientifically, we perceive the world subjectively, meaning that all our complexes, neuroses, and biases influence what we perceive and how we behave. Modern psychology has described in profound detail this type of epistemology and the effect of the subjective powers at work in our inner world on our perceptions of the outer word and on our behavior. The disposition of our psyche affects our pragmatic choices significantly.

Our psyche is constituted and governed by our unconscious, by the collective unconscious, and by archetypes, which, although inaccessible to our conscious ego, have enormous impact upon our perceptions of reality. Our psyche is as objectively real as our body and is profoundly influenced at every level by our own personal past and by the millennia of collective experiences that lie behind us. The psyche is also the gateway to an even deeper and more powerful realm, the reality of Spirit.

The third way of knowing is *spiritually*. In this epistemology we know only through revelation. It is a knowing that breaks in and through the psychological and commonsensical ways of knowing, infusing everything we think, say, and do with divine presence and will. Though the realm of the divine Spirit cannot be evaluated rationally, it is no less real than is the rational and the psychological. The great mystics have lived and the great religious books of human civilization have been written in the power of the Spirit. It is a way of knowing that is final, holy, and eternal. It is the epistemology of the Unseen, the Unkowable, the Unbegotten.

Only through the inspiration of the Spirit can one see the hand of Providence operating in one's psyche and affecting one's everyday choices. Only in the Spirit can one know freedom in its deepest and most expansive sense. Paradoxically, freedom at this level is not about the exercise of pragmatic choice in one's life but is a gift that leads to an inner obedience to a will not one's own.

Whereas pragmatic choice on the first level concerns itself with externals, freedom on the third level concerns itself with the inner disposition of the heart. Whereas pragmatic choice gives us the feeling of control over the details of our life, freedom at the level of Spirit submits to the will of God in our life. As we shall discover, real freedom is not the power to choose but the willingness to obey.

This is the paradox at the core of freedom: In thinking we are free, we are controlled; in choosing the path of submission, we experience authentic freedom.

These three levels of knowing and experiencing co-exist in dialectical tension. They are neither symmetrical nor equal. The first level seems to give us the most conscious control, but it is the weakest and smallest in scope. We have choice but no freedom. We have power over external details but are driven by internal impulses.

The second level emanates out of our psychic depth and carries the memories of life since creation. The psyche is the receptacle of life's accumulated experiences passed down from generation to generation. It impinges upon our conscious self, framing and governing our pragmatic choices in creative and destructive ways, but has no final autonomy in and of itself.

The most fundamental way of knowing is in the realm of the Spirit. It is invisible, but all-powerful. God created and sustains us but remains invisible to human eyes. Divinity, like our psyche, undergirds our existence and impacts our life but is not amenable to any of our ordinary common-sense or psychological categories. It comes simultaneously from the future, the past, and the present as the Creator and Sovereign of all dimensions of time, space, and causality. The Creator of the universe is free of the universe. Our freedom in the universe can only come as we acknowledge the divine will in our pragmatic choices. The revelation that comes from the Spirit through grace can only be appreciated through our heart; it remains forever elusive to our intellect.

We live our life mostly in the realm of the first and second levels, the rational and the psychological, acting as if the realm of Spirit either did not exist or were synonymous with the psychological dimension. We repeat in our present the patterns of the past. But the Spirit is not the psyche, and the psyche is not rationality. All three categories interact but must be kept distinct.

These three levels form an antinomy: They are internally consistent individually and are often treated as though they were mutually exclusive. The historical, psychological, and spiritual realms seem to exist independently and to operate according to laws and to patterns unique unto themselves. Yet the three ways of knowing are inseparably interconnected beneath the surface of life; that is why our surface layers must be penetrated for this interconnectedness to be felt and lived.

Because these three realms seem disconnected superficially but interact deeply within us, the harder one is hit on the historical level, the greater the opening is for the psyche and Spirit to enter our everyday existence. The more completely one's superficialities are broken up on the surface of life, the more one can be filled with the Eternal from the depths of life.

This is why history, psyche, and Spirit are fundamentally important to one another. Each of the three is essential to the operation and manifestation of the other two. Being totally distinct and yet completely integral, they must operate concurrently to be real experientially. In fact, what we shall see is that the moment of the most intense historical disjunction, when violence, wickedness, and destruction seem to abound unimpededly, is precisely when Spirit has optimal opportunity to rework the psychological and historical realms with the power of transformation. Human life is shattered so that humanity can be redeemed. Pragmatic choices are disrupted so that freedom can be experienced.

In this manner the Torah was delivered to Israel, not in the serenity of peaceful meditation in a bountiful garden, but in the aftermath of the cataclysm of enslavement and deliverance from Egypt that left Egypt decimated and the Israelites expelled, wandering lost and confused in the wilderness of Sinai. The birth of Christianity came not in the academies of Athens after sustained philosophical reflection but in the wake of a torturous Crucifixion and amid the blood of martyrs fed to the lions for the pleasure of the Roman masses.

The great challenge all of us face is to live our life as openly as possible to the discontinuities between our common-sense way of knowing and the psychological and spiritual ways of discernment. We must live with the awareness that when the psychological and spiritual realms move, normalcy is shattered. In this movement the finite is infused with the Infinite, the transitory with the Eternal, the mundane with the Holy. The challenge is to embrace this shattering and risk tragedy, knowing this is the only path to wholeness.

Our confidence must come from knowing that without the shattering there is no experience of grace; without threat to or disruption of personality there is no movement of the psyche; without enslavement there is no deliverance; and without suffering there is no spiritual obedience. In the end we are always confronted by antinomies: Without the Exodus there is no Promised Land; without the Crucifixion there is no Resurrection; and without the development of nuclear weapons there is no dramatic impulse toward the liberation of women.

The essential message of this book is that in facing the future we must release certainties concerning any dogma, particularly dogmas we claim as our own. Rather, we must embrace multiplicity and selectivity, subordinating the dictates of our ego to the Self under the guidance of the Spirit. We must engage anew with our religious traditions with an attitude of reverence. We must respect the cruciform nature of reality, which unites the disparate aspects of the world in a purpose that redeems. Above all, we must not give up our roots. All roads, even our own, can lead to Rome.

For all our advances in science, we are in what we cannot fathom; we are of what we do not know. We must proceed into the future more with awe at the Unknown than with certainty of the known. All our answers, even if they come through science, only exist in the light of consciousness, for only in this light we can measure and quantify existence.

Beyond the light lies the vast expanse of the Unknown, the borderless frontier of darkness where no measuring rod, no plumb line can discern beginning or end, above or below. For all our technological advances, we have, as Saint John of the Cross said, "nothing to guide us but that fire which in our heart is burning."[4] In the face of the darkness beyond our light, we cannot know; we can only feel the "fear of the Lord."

As we increase our scientific and rational knowledge and the circumference of our light and hence our power expands, so, too, the circumference of the darkness expands, ever silent, ever full of the Holy. The greater the light, the more

4. Saint John of the Cross, *Dark Night of the Soul,* trans. Allison Peers (London: Burns and Oats, 1935), 28.

facts we can know and the more power we can wield. Yet
with the light comes an equal measure of darkness to confront our certainties and to challenge the very power created by the light.

In the face of the Holy, in the face of each other, we
must be bold enough to be truly humble, to be open to
feelings of awe: awe at the ground of our being, which is
beyond understanding; awe of our past, which has brought
us to the present, step by step, mistake by mistake, inspiration
by inspiration; and awe at our future, which holds out to us
the perpetual possibility of fulfillment.

To attain this humility, to experience this awe, we
must not hold on to the conventional wisdom of the
world, rather we must allow ourselves to be transformed
by the renewal of Spirit. This calls for nothing less than
questioning the established patterns of thinking used to
protect ourselves and our power. We must be open to a
constant transformation and renewal by the Spirit, which
is seeking ceaselessly to draw us into painful encounters
with the cruciform nature of reality in order that we may
be redeemed.

Our task in this critical hour is simply to touch the
earth again and, having touched it, to say, "Not my will but
thine be done." It is through such humility that grace slips
in from the darkness beyond and within to transform our
life and thereby our exercise of power for selfish ends into
an instrument of divine service to others.

It is within the context of the reflections above that
this book traces the interior story of humanity from the
dawn of civilization to the present time, using legends,

myths, and archetypes to challenge humanity to view itself in new ways and to understand our place in history.

The story begins with the strands and patterns of the rise of civilization during the Neolithic revolution, with an emphasis on the role of gender in humanity's beginning. I then tell civilization's foundational story, the Gilgamesh epic, coming from history's first civilization in ancient Sumer, dating back to the third millennium B.C.E. In powerful and poignant ways, this epic encapsulates humanity's achievements and predicaments as we begin our recorded history.

In the aftermath of the rise of civilization in Sumer come two very divergent responses to the stresses of civilization: one from the East, distilled most profoundly by the Buddha; and the other from the West, begun with the amazing odyssey of the Jews. Buddha's story and perspective frames the Orient; that of the Jews, the Occident. The insights of the East will be described and then left in the reader's mind, not to be revisited until the present time when they are proving essential to the newly emerging cosmology and culture.

The profound contribution of the Jews to Western civilization is traced from their great creation myth of the Garden of Eden, to their triumph in the Exodus from Egypt, to their loss of nationhood and their inability to cope with the forces of Hellenism, to the agony of their Diaspora under the Romans. In these latter times, when history seems to forsake the Jews, a dramatic pattern unfolds: the anomie of apocalypse and the powerful wisdom of a feminine presence they called Sophia. This is a foundational pattern in our collective history and requires careful study and evaluation, for it is shaping our present hour.

It is out of the maelstrom of Hellenism, *pax Romana*, and Jewish apocalypse that a new world-order arises. Out of the contradictions of the old regime, a new synthesis and new commandments emerge: Jesus of Nazareth captures history and changes fundamentally how we think about ourselves, such that we even begin our calendar with the date of his birth. When this new impulse co-mingled with Greek philosophical thought and Roman political power, the two-thousand-year trajectory of Western civilization was established.

The story of the West is then traced briefly and thematically, first focusing on events of the first millennium, then concentrating considerable attention on the Black Death, the most lethal event in recorded history. In and through it institutions are shattered, just as they were in Judaism under the impact of Hellenism and of Roman occupation, and a new feminine presence emerges in the adoration of Mary, just as the phenomenon of Sophia appeared in the in the middle of the Jewish apocalypse.

Again, the intermingling of devastation and the feminine ushers in a new order. The Black Death signals the beginning of the modern era: the Renaissance blossoms, followed by the Reformation and the Enlightenment. These events are the pillars of modernity, the foundations of our rational, scientific approach to the world. Until the Black Death, humanity was enveloped by faith, as sculpted by medieval Catholicism; with the Enlightenment the mind replaces faith, as demanded by the new scientific method.

This advance provides the West with enormous technical and political power, and by the end of the nineteenth century, the West controls the entire world. It also releases enormous anxieties, creating the long, dark shadow-side of modernity. As we became obsessed with technical and scientific developments, we negated the feminine and denied the sacred. This is the essence of the Enlightenment.

The notion of progress originating with the Enlightenment culminates in the twentieth century with all the technical achievements that define modern living. The twentieth century will also be remembered for the advent of nuclear weapons and the terror and destruction that sacrificed more human lives because of war and ideology than the rest of recorded history combined.

In and through this turbulence the same historical pattern—devastation, the rise of the feminine, and human renewal—is replicating itself. Concurrent with the development of the technology that can destroy the earth has been the liberation of women and the unprecedented democratization of human relations. The advent of nuclear weapons and the rise of the feminine, like the Jewish apocalypse and Sophia, the Black Death and Mary, are interconnected and will usher in a new renaissance, as the pattern suggests.

Our task is to realize that we stand in the crack between the worlds and that the greatest challenge is submitting to and following the feminine presence within each of us. Although the feminine is not the sacred, only the feminine can lead us to the sacred. The sacred cannot be approached by the masculine. In our darkest hour it is the Great Mother, Eve, Sophia, Mary *recidivus*, and all the great feminine archetypes and energies, emerging out of the depths of our soul, who will once again guide us onward along our journey.

CHAPTER 1

THE MOTHER GODDESS

At the still point of the turning world.

Neither flesh nor fleshless;

Neither from nor towards; at the still point, there the dance is,

But neither arrest nor movement.

And do not call it fixity,

Where past and future are gathered.

Neither movement from nor towards,

Neither ascent nor decline.

Except for the point, the still point,

There would be no dance, and there is only the dance.[1]

H
UMANITY'S STORY BEGINS WITH THE MYTHS before history. I say myths because all that is available to us are stories and various fragments found in archaeological digs scattered across Europe, Africa, and Mesopotamia. These are all we have to work with as we conjecture the beginnings of human culture, the origins of wisdom, and the foundational relations characterizing human society.

1. T. S. Eliot, "The Four Quartets," in *Collected Poems 1909–1962* (London: Faber and Faber, 1963), 199.

Nothing much distinguished human beings from the higher primates in the early phases of the Pliocene epoch except the very rudimentary use of tools. Evidence unearthed near the Gora River in Ethiopia suggests that humans of this time used sharp-edged flakes of rock for cutting. That was some 2.6 million years ago when humans, like the apes, lived in forests and were principally tree dwellers.

Toward the end of the Pliocene, when the forests began to disappear and the savannahs began to expand, the stronger primates expelled the weaker ones to protect diminishing ecological niches. Coping with the dangers of the open savannah was the genesis of humanity. The evidence suggests that, unable to retreat to the higher branches of the trees, our forebears had to band together and use rocks and sticks as primitive tools and as weapons against the predatory beasts of the plains. Holding weapons and tools with hands allowed mouths to be used for communicating warnings and issuing commands.

There were other profound changes in early humanity, the principal one being that the females shifted from the estrus cycle to the menstrual cycle. This changed the nature of sexuality from one of specific, periodic availability to being sexually available essentially all the time. Weapons and tools revolutionized human power; the shift in female sexuality revolutionized human relations. Gone was the momentary coitus of animals in heat; begun was human sexuality with all its passions, complexities, and extravagances.

This is an important point. Right at the beginning of human development it was a change in the female, not in the male, that gave impetus to the next phase of growth.

This memory may be what is behind the Genesis account we will explore later in which it is Eve, not Adam, who is the primary actor. Deeply embedded in our collective unconscious is the memory that at critical moments the feminine, the female, is catalytic and instrumental in originating something that transforms female and male relations and creates a new basis for human interactions.

Nature enveloped the early human communities with her cruciform patterns and cycles of life, death, and renewal: The weather was extreme and unpredictable; the animals were large and predatory; the resources available for shelter and protection were limited. Adversity challenged every dimension. The principal resources available to our forebears were their wits and a few tools and weapons. We are here because they survived. In our collective unconscious is the memory of how they survived.

When our forbears left the safety of the trees there emerged an interrelated complex in which the elements of weapons and tool utilization, food sharing, and communication reinforced one another to empower the otherwise small, unspecialized primates. Primitive home bases were established, which allowed for storage of food and implements, protection of the young, and refuge from the extremities of the elements. The use of weapons and tools necessitated communication and education.

Grouping the females and young within the safety of the home bases allowed for more intensification of communication and the generation of a number of domestic arts. Evidence suggests that fire was discovered approximately six hundred thousand years ago. Almost all activities during this period were in some way related to the acquisition and sharing of food. The men hunted; the women gathered herbs and seeds. Whatever the source, food-sharing allowed for communication and for the beginning of ritual.

The taking of life for food, particularly through the hunt, provided the impetus for appreciating the religious dimensions of the cruciform structure of nature and thus for establishing the first religious rites. To kill was to break the cycle of life, yet killing was necessary for the tribe to live. The death of one part of life for the sustenance of another created a separation and a bonding. Wounding and killing required expiation. The animal was treated as a brother or sister to the men hunting it. Prayers were invoked to ask for the cooperation of the animal. It was thanked for giving its life for that of the tribe. Rituals were developed that restored unity after the sacrifice. Hunting was the impetus for humankind's first rites of worship.

The identification of primitive peoples with the animals and plants they consume is a universal response, observed in almost all such cultures. Shamanism and totemism originate in this mystical participation of humans with the natural order. Even contemporary society, in rituals immortalized by the Seder and Eucharist, consecrate the consumption of food. We still celebrate eating together as if we were somehow remembering and needing to revere that primal point when gathering food enabled us to survive.

Approximately three hundred thousand years ago, we took another step forward. The first engraved tool found comes from this Acheulean period of *Homo sapiens neanderthalensis*. Christened *le bâton de commandement* by Abbé Breuil, the first expert of renown to examine Paleolithic art, the object is simply a bone with various markings. Yet it signals a fundamental advance in human consciousness and offers us a significant insight as to how our earliest ancestors first interpreted reality.

Most specialists believe the bone to be either a hunter's tool or a shaman's ritual object. The term *bâton de commandement* suggests a masculine and military connotation, probably because military officers carry batons to this day. Although it is impossible to know with any certainty who fashioned this ancient bone and why, there is another interpretation I will explore and use as a gateway to begin the discussion of the power of the feminine in the ages before history was written.

I would like to join with those who suggest that the *bâton* was probably used as a primitive lunar calendar. Such an interpretation means that humanity would have had to observe a basic periodicity of nature in order to construct a model of natural processes. The human being was no longer simply living in nature unawares; whoever fashioned the *bâton* was miniaturizing the universe and carrying a model of it in his or her hands in the form of a lunar calendar. It should be noted that the Greek word *mene* means moon; in Latin, *mensis* means month and *mensura*, measurement. Tracking the waxing and waning of the moon allowed our forebears the earliest measurement of time longer than a day.

That woman and the moon are interconnected is recognized by all human cultures and forms the basis of conceptions concerning lunar goddesses. This is not surprising given the cyclic patterns of a woman's menstrual cycle and the harmonizing of menstrual cycles within groups of women. *Menstruation* is derived from the root words just mentioned.

As the first observers of the basic periodicity of their body, women were in all probability the first observers of the periodicity of nature, beginning with the most obvious: the phases of the moon. Women must also have been the first to recognize the relationship between their own inner processes and the external processes of nature. Though the *bâton* could have been a bone used as a masculine ritual weapon or as a rod to command, it could just as easily have been a feminine measuring device. Its owner could as easily have been a midwife as a hunter.

Imagine the awe prehistoric communities must have felt when they understood that the moon waxed and waned, that women bled but did not die, and, when they did not bleed for nine lunar cycles, that they brought forth life. In the face of nature they stood in wonder. In the face of woman's interconnectedness with nature, particularly her ability to bring forth new life, they grappled with a fundamental mystery. Upon this mystery, in conjunction with the rituals associated with the hunt, they based their first religious cosmology.

Any cosmology developed in relation to the *bâton* those three hundred thousand years ago must have been extremely primitive; nevertheless, it formed the foundation for what we now believe. This was the period of the Ice Age. Neanderthal communities had to contend with bitter weather and were forced to hunt large and dangerous beasts: the woolly mammoth, the woolly rhinoceros, the bear, and the reindeer.

It was a time when survival depended upon physical prowess, and the physical strength of the male was essential to the safety of the group. Hunting was necessary for life, and, as far as we can tell, the bands of humans moved with the great herds and lived principally off the kill. Weapons and tools were the male symbols of power against the external world, and the rituals of the hunt were atonements for disrupting the Whole. Propitiation for killing became the bedrock of men's mysteries.

Women's mysteries were the gateway to religious reflection concerning nature and life as a whole. The internal relation between the woman's menstrual cycle and her capacity to bring forth life was the *symbol of harmony* with the mysteries of life and the foundation for rituals consecrating the Great Spirit that sustained the Whole.

Approximately one hundred thousand years ago, the archeological evidence suggests that our forebears began to bury their dead ceremoniously. Bodies dating back sixty thousand years found in Europe indicate that they were buried in the fetal position, facing east, and were sprinkled with red ochre dye and flowers. It is probable that as the men were developing weapons and rituals for the hunt the women were developing rituals and burial rites to return the dead relative or friend to the greater whole out of which they all had arisen, in which they all lived, and to which they all were destined to return.

Approximately fifty thousand years ago, just as the Ice Age was drawing to a close, *Homo sapiens sapiens,* our immediate forebears, emerged. For the next twenty thousand years, human society continued to hunt and worship as Neanderthal society had for hundreds of thousands of years. Approximately thirty thousand years ago the last of the glaciers retreated northward, and the frozen tundra that covered Europe and Asia transformed to steppe. Temperate climate replaced frozen wasteland, and the woolly mammoth, woolly rhinoceros, cave lion, and cave bear disappeared. A host of smaller animals, such as deer, horse, bison, and wild oxen began to migrate throughout

Europe and Central Asia, followed by increasingly skillful and diversified human communities.

Human communities began painting the sides of their cave dwellings in northern Spain and southwestern France. Discoveries at sites such as, Lascaux, Altamira, Les Trois Frères, Ariege, and La Pasiega, indicate a human response to nature that is imaginative, complex, sophisticated, and exuberant. At Les Trois Frères, there are hundreds of paintings of animals; at Lascaux over two thousand paintings of animals and men in various stages of the hunt have been found. Some paintings date as far back as thirty thousand years, although most come from the period circa 15,000 to 10,000 B.C.E.

In over one hundred sites where cave paintings have been discovered, the themes expressed revolve essentially around the hunt. Depictions of animals and hunters abound, and there are clear representations of shamans, of imaginary beings comprised of animals and men, and of men covered with various animal skins. The pervasive motifs are those of the kill and of men planning and executing the hunt—sometimes themselves being wounded or killed but invariably conquering their prey.

The caves were probably where the first shamanic identification between the warrior and the hunted animal were ritualized. The caves were also probably the places of initiation for young boys, a place where they were taken from their mothers and initiated into the rituals and stratagems of the hunt.

These caves must have been exclusively male preserves. There are numerous depictions of animals and birds that paleontologists categorize as female, as well as composite figures of human and animal features, but no explicit paintings of human females have been found on the walls of any of the caves discovered so far.

Approximately twenty thousand years ago sculpted figurines of females began to appear, more or less simultaneously, in the area from the Pyrénées in Spain to Lake Baikal in Siberia. Over one hundred thirty figurines of women have been found; none, of men. Many are rotund figures with protruding breasts, depicted either as giving birth to or as holding an infant. Many are graceful figures. Others are covered with various lines, circles, triangles, zigzags, or spirals. As far as we know, these are humanity's first images of the female.

In a cave not far from Lascaux, a rotund female sculpture chiseled out of limestone was discovered. A woman is holding in her right hand a bison horn shaped like a crescent moon and notched with thirteen lines, signifying presumably the thirteen days of the waxing moon and/or the thirteen months of the lunar year. Her left hand points to a protruding womb.

Women in these early sculptures were also associated with birds, eggs, water, and a host of animals, such as bison, antelope, deer, cows, and sheep. Females were shaped like circular, triangular, and oblong, rounded beings. They were represented as giving life and taking it back into themselves. Any males depicted with them were small and dependent.

The most predominant theme of these earliest depictions of the female is that of fecundity. The lunar motif is also pervasive. Women were understood as the Life-Givers; they were also understood as being interconnected with the cyclic pattern of nature.

Two conclusions can be drawn from the evidence

gathered from these earliest strata of human self-reflection. The first is that from the earliest reflections of the human community, men and women diverged fundamentally in how they acted in and understood the world.

The men were concerned with the strategy of survival, with taking life, with protecting the group. Their instruments of choice were the weapon and the tool; their drama was that of conflict, victory, and defeat. Their arena was that of the hunt, playing the role of a part against other parts of the whole. Their rituals involved sacrifice and atonement for the separation that always comes with killing. From this, it was a natural development for masculine consciousness to draw distinctions, emphasizing intellect, and to concentrate on the ability to command, emphasizing the will to power. Thus, one finds cave paintings of men with weapons, pursuing game.

Women were depicted invariably as life-givers, as life-sustainers, holding the moon, protecting the child, blessing the dead. Their instrument was the measuring stick. Their preoccupation was with the meaning and rhythms of the processes of nature. Theirs was the drama of relationship. They focused on the whole, nurturing all the parts. Theirs was the wisdom of limits. Their rituals involved expressions of gratitude for life itself. From this, it was natural that female consciousness resonated with the Whole, emphasized intuition, and appreciated the cycles of nature, waiting for the "fullness of time."

The second conclusion is that in both modalities, whether that of the hunter going in for the kill or that of the rotund mother giving birth, there is a pervasive sense of connection with the natural order. In this most primitive phase of existence our forebears saw themselves as integral to something alive, something in which their individual and communal relationships were interconnected with a larger process, a totality that encompassed them, and for which they felt reverence and awe. Even the taking of life was understood to be an act within life. For them fate was nature, and nature was feminine.

No evidence has been found of organized hostilities of one human community against another during these thousands of centuries of nascent human life. One should not assume from the lack of any evidence that this was in some sense a golden age of human existence, as many commentators do. Quite the contrary, as the film *2001: A Space Odyssey* depicts, when there was competition for limited game or limited water, there was probably conflict and bloodshed at levels initially similar to those of the higher primates from which humanity evolved. Cooperation then was as it is today—limited essentially to cooperation within one's own group and often motivated by competition and conflict with other groups.

The novelist T. H. Whyte makes the point that human beings are the only creatures on earth without built-in weapons. All other animals have natural offensive and/or defensive facilities, whether in the form of beaks, claws, talons, horns, teeth, coloration, smell, or speed. Whyte calls humans the "naked tool," observing that we of all creatures must fashion our weapons with our hands. Paradoxically, the animals with built-in weapons kill, as far as we know, without malice, only to protect territory, for survival, and for food. Humans, without built-in weapons, are the only creatures that kill, not only for these imperatives, but also for a range of dark emotions, even for pleasure.

Weapons and tools have been found with the remains of the earliest humans. Unlike contemporary society, however, the use of weapons and tools then was considered to be an organic part of life. Their weapons did not condemn Paleolithic humanity to the "death dominated life" to which we of the nuclear age have subjected ourselves. For them, life was understood to be interrelated within an endless series of natural cyclic patterns. Life was treated with reverence, whether their hands were holding weapons, tools, lunar calendars, or paintbrushes, or whether they were delivering an infant or burying the dead. A pervasive sense of the sacred characterized our forebears, an overwhelming sense that they lived and breathed within a great mystery. Today, the mystery remains but is unrecognized. Though we are naturally weaponless, our violence knows no bounds.

Approximately fifteen thousand years ago the glaciers made a final retreat, the oceans rose several hundred feet, the forests returned, and the great herds of bison and reindeer migrated to the regions of the Arctic north. Human life settled in the fertile river valleys where smaller game could be found, and the temperate climates allowed all kinds of grains and fruits to be cultivated.

By this time, human culture had become somewhat differentiated and increasingly accentuated. The hunt had become more sophisticated as the weapons had improved, and the cunning and communication of the men had deepened and expanded. With the changes in the climate, it became necessary to travel farther and be absent from camp longer. Men's rituals and bonding became deeper and more pronounced.

This was equally true with the women. The gathering

of herbs and plants by women gave rise to the beginnings of herbal medicine and a growing awareness of the functions and purposes of the different fruits and grains. The first healers were women who no doubt combined healing with the religious functions they were continuing to develop. Left alone for long periods when the men were out hunting, the women bonded with the children and with each other in ways that took little account of the absent males.

With the advent of the Neolithic period circa 10,000 B.C.E. time and life quickened along the eastern Mediterranean. The quantitative developments accumulated over the tens of thousands of years of Paleolithic culture led to qualitative shifts in technology, social functioning, and religious interpretation.

A broad spectrum of food gathering had been going on for thousands of years. When wild cereals were included in the human diet is uncertain. But when it occurred, gathering was transformed into gardening and, eventually, into agriculture. Woman had taken "nature into culture," to use the social philosopher William Irwin Thompson's phrase, and developed a source of food hundreds of times more plentiful than anything possible through the hunt.

The Mistress of the Plants joined the Great Mother. With this advance into over-abundance, an inventive woman was probably the first to develop the pottery needed to hold the grains that had to be stored somehow. Pottery was also useful in carrying grains and other items to neighboring settlements, for with the beginnings of agriculture came the beginnings of trade.

Men still hunted, of course, as they had for the past three million years or so since coming out of the trees. With the transformation of food gathering into agriculture, however, the hunt ceased to be critical for the survival of the group and became what it has been ever since: a ritualized activity important for male bonding and for strengthening a sense of masculinity. But for the most part it had ceased being necessary for survival.

Hunters and gatherers had little or no property, and there is little evidence of them trading; they moved self-sufficiently with the herds, which they used for food as needed. The skills learned from the hunt, therefore, could be redirected. The beginnings of agriculture brought about a sedentary existence with fields and storage sites, which required protection; the bow and arrow and the spear were needed at home. The discovery of cereals by women was followed by the development of the art of war by men. Rituals of the hunt were subsumed within rituals of war.

The period from 9000 to 7000 B.C.E. is a period of momentous transformation in human affairs. By 6500 B.C.E., agriculture, property, trade, and war had become institutionalized and had given rise to a renaissance of thought and myth reminiscent of the Upper Paleolithic. This can be seen most poignantly in the remains of the Anatolian ceremonial center of Catal Huyuk. Even as Florence enjoyed a revival of Greco-Roman philosophy and art during the Renaissance five hundred years ago, so Catal Huyuk, eight thousand years ago, enjoyed a revival of the religion of the Great Mother. What was implicit in the cave paintings at Lascaux became explicit in the wall paintings at Catal Huyuk. What could only be inferred at Lascaux became literal at Catal Huyuk. In this sense Catal Huyuk serves as the Rosetta Stone for the early cosmology of the first humans.

Catal Huyuk is replete with shrines and temples, suggesting that it served as a ceremonial center where traders and travelers from diverse backgrounds gathered. The dominant motif is overwhelmingly feminine; images of men are almost nowhere to be found. When they are, they are always in relation to a larger female figure. The findings at Catal Huyuk suggest that what were only scattered images of the goddess in the Paleolithic period provided the cultural and religious unity of the Neolithic period.

The Great Mother of Catal Huyuk was expressed in three archetypal dimensions: as voluptuously large, she called the community from the womb; as seductively beautiful, she took males to her bed to impregnate her; and as old and wise, she governed the tombs. The predominant motif is that of the Great Mother with large stomach, wide hips, and heavy breasts. Sometimes, as Madonna, she is holding a child; sometimes, as Mistress of the Animals, bull's horns protrude from her womb. As Maiden, she is depicted alone, not as a rotund figure of plenitude but as a sexual partner for the male. Finally, as Crone, she is depicted as old, thin, and wizened.

The burial rites offer insights into her power. The dead were buried underneath the floor of their home. Women were buried with jewelry and other luxury items in a large hole in the center of the floor. Children were always buried with the women. In contrast, the men were buried in the corners in much smaller spaces and with no accouterments other than their weapons. Women took expressions of beauty to their grave; men took their tools for killing.

The artifacts of civilization at Catal Huyuk suggest a social reality where men were dominant in the political and military sectors and women were recognized as powerful forces in dominions men had little control over: birth, growth, death, renewal. Nature was overwhelming to early humanity; therefore women, who were cyclically oriented as nature was, and, even more, were capable of giving life, were held in the same high regard as nature.

Concurrent with the fall of Catal Huyuk in 5200 B.C.E., when all its temples were destroyed, came the establishment of the first known civilization. This occurred about two thousand miles to the east of Catal Huyuk at Sumer, on the alluvial plains between the Tigris and Euphrates Rivers in upper Mesopotamia. It is here that history begins. Ironically, Mesolithic society began with the domestication of animals, and Neolithic society, with the domestication of plants, but civilization began with the domestication of women.

Cultural historians and anthropologists generally point to the admixture of irrigation farming, writing, and technical specialization as the practical developments that allowed civilization to develop. What occurred socially was that men gave up the hunt as their primary focus of activity in order to protect their agricultural lands and to trade their herds and food. In making this shift they subsumed roles long considered to be within the domain of women.

This came about because, to a fundamental degree, the shift from hunting and gathering to agriculture required a heightened measure of physical strength. Digging fields, pulling plows, and harnessing oxen was back-breaking labor and therefore required the strength of a man; women could suffer miscarriages doing such work and, in any event, could not be away from the children and homes all day, which agriculture, like the hunt, demanded. This was a ubiquitous shift. There is not a single agricultural society known anywhere in the world where the natural egalitarianism found in hunter-gatherer societies did not evolve into a more male-dominated order.

Gardening had always been the work of women; the domestication of animals, that of the hunters. But when men led their cows into the fields and began to till the fields with the newly developed plow, a whole new way of life emerged. Soon there were dikes, canals, bridges, walled cities, storehouses, record keeping, well trodden trading routes, the deployment of armies, the buying and selling of slaves. Women's work and women's mysteries soon became simply a component in a male-dominated technological process and way of life. Patriarchy arose along the Fertile Crescent coterminous with civilization.

This transfer of power to the males shifted the emphasis in sexual relations away from fertility to erotica. The power of the Great Mother had originally been derived from her capacity to give birth. Now, women had to develop power not over the child but over the lover. The Great Mother had been depicted as a rotund figure with bulging breasts and protruding stomach. Now, the goddess is depicted principally as a sleek, seductive maiden, luring the man to his destiny and/or his doom. Females-as-erotica transformed women from being holders of mystery into objects of pleasure.

This was a profound transformation. As mentioned, the depictions of the Mother Goddess and her male consort during the Paleolithic and early Neolithic periods were almost exclusively those of a rotund, all-enveloping mother giving birth to a son. He had no real identity apart from her; no purpose other than being an object of her power; no existence separate from her womb and breast, the first symbols of nurture and trust humanity depicted artistically. In the earliest representations of humans the male existed within the parameters set by the Mother Goddess; he was nothing in his own right.

The principle god image then was that of the bull, one of the first renderings humans made of the god, as opposed to the goddess, although at Catal Huyuk the bull and other male images are depicted invariably as extensions or manifestations of the Mother Goddess.

Beginning with the Bronze Age circa 3500 B.C.E., the goddess becomes separated from her male consort who dies and descends into the nether world where the goddess is compelled to go to retrieve and to regenerate him. In Sumeria the goddess Inana has a lover, Dumuzi. After Inana goes to the underworld to meet her sister, Ereshkigal, Queen of the Underworld, she returns to the earth above and sends Dumuzi down to replace her as lord of the Abyss. In Babylonia Ishtar has a son-lover, Tammuz, who dies each winter and descends into the underworld. Each spring Ishtar descends to retrieve and to regenerate him. In Egypt Isis is married to her brother, Osiris, who is killed by their brother, Seth. The whole earth is barren until Isis restores Osiris to life.

In Canaan the god Baal goes down to the underworld to confront death, personified by his brother, Mot. Mot kills Baal, and their sister, the goddess Anath, goes down to take his body for proper burial. She kills Mot and scatters his body like grain in the fields. In Greece Demeter loses her daughter, Persephone, to Hades, god of the underworld. Demeter strikes the world with famine until she retrieves Persephone. This retrieval allows spring to come and the crops to grow.

Later in Greece the stories of Cybele and Attis, and Aphrodite and Adonis carry these themes forward. Cybele falls in love with Attis, the son of a king. He instead falls in love with a nymph and is driven insane by the jealous Cybele. Finally he castrates himself with a stone and dies. Cybele mourns him and a pine tree emerges from his body, and flowers spring from his blood. Aphrodite loses her lover, Adonis, who is killed by a boar. She asks Zeus to call him back to life from spring to autumn, the time of the earth's fertility.

Like the notions of sacrifice and atonement, the motif of a young god dying, descending into Hades, and rising back to life seems to be as old as human religious reflection itself. Judeo-Christianity reworked these themes for its own purposes; it did not invent them. From the earliest hunting expeditions and preparation of food, to the male/female pairings in the earliest expressions of art, to the consecration of the cycles of death and rebirth, humanity sought through its religious cosmologies and rituals to commemorate and give reverence to the cruciform dimensions of the spiritual, psychological, and mundane aspects of life.

The early Christian Church reworked the life and death of Jesus of Nazareth around most of these ancient motifs. Christian tradition proclaimed that he was born of the Virgin Mother at the winter solstice; was crucified at the spring equinox; descended into the underworld for three days; and was brought to life again by his Heavenly Father. Even today, some two thousand years later, Christmas is celebrated just after the winter solstice; Easter is celebrated according to the lunar calendar on the first Sunday following the first full moon after the spring equinox. Christ's resurrection reflects the transformation of the death of winter into the life of spring. The Exodus and the Cross are profound and powerful events not because they are exceptions to life but because they are life's chief exemplifications and are drawing upon and holding as central life's oldest traditions and rituals. They utilize the aspects of the cyclical flow of nature observed since human religious reflection began to express the ultimate purpose of God in creation and history.

Towards the middle of the Bronze Age, the Mother Goddess receded into the background as father gods began to ascend. The power of the goddess to inspire began to wane, as the energy of the gods was activated with the power of conquest. This can be seen most explicitly in the creation myths of the emerging civilizations. The emphasis is no longer on creation emanating from a mother goddess but on a god separating his parents and so initiating the process of creation.

The creation myths of Sumer and Egypt, the oldest myths for which we have actual written texts, depict this transformation. The creation myth of Sumer, the *Enuma Elish*, tells the story of the goddess of the primeval waters, Nammu, who created the heavens and the earth, An and Ki, as a single unit. The heaven god and the earth goddess in turn brought forth the god of air or breath, Enlil. It was Enlil, the young god, who separated heaven from the earth and carried off the earth, his mother, to be his bride. With Enlil, creation is no longer envisioned as a birthing from the Mother Goddess but as the result of an action taken by a young warrior-god who creates through an act of violence.

The Egyptian creation myth is somewhat more complicated. As in all ancient cosmologies, the Egyptians believed that life emerged out of the Primeval Waters, although in contradistinction with the Sumerians, they understood the Primeval Waters to be the god Nun. The god Atum arose as the Primeval Mound out of the Primeval Waters, and then, either by spitting or ejaculating, created the god of the air, Shu, and the goddess of moisture, Tefnut. Shu and Tefnut gave birth to the sky goddess Nut and the earth-god Geb. Shu, like Enlil, then separated the sky from the earth. In this act Shu personifies light and space as well as air.

Perhaps the most profound and provocative Egyptian creation myth involved the god Ptah whose divine essence was believed to permeate the entire creation. He "thought in his heart" the entire universe and created it by speaking the sacred Word in accordance with his thought.

When the Hebrews developed the Biblical doctrine of God bringing creation into being through the divine Word, they drew upon extremely ancient traditions, including those first given expression by the Sumerians several thousand years previously. The Hebrews, however, radically reworked these traditions to convey the unique witness they bore to monotheism rather than to the polytheism that characterized the older traditions.

The theological demise of the goddess came concurrently with the political invasions of the Aryans and the Semites. From the fourth millennium B.C.E. onwards, Indo-European tribes swept from the northern steppes near the Caspian and Black Seas into the alluvial plains of Mesopotamia and on to the Indus River valley in India. Semitic tribes invaded from the Syro-Arabian deserts as well, having mastered the camel as the Aryans had mastered the horse.

The Aryans swept through Mesopotamia and settled in India. Their language, Sanskrit, is considered by some linguists to be the mother tongue of all Western languages, even though the early Aryans placed such emphasis on oral transmission that writing was forbidden. They were highly disciplined warriors, herded cattle, and invented the spoked wheel and light chariot circa 2000 B.C.E. Like the Kurgans before them, they buried their leaders with sacrificed attendants beneath a mound and worshipped sky gods in particular, especially gods of the sun, wind, storm, lightning, and fire. A Sumerian scribe, witnessing their carnage circa 2100 B.C.E., described them as "a host whose onslaught was like a hurricane, a people who had never known a city."[2]

While the Aryans swept in from the northern steppes, the Semites infiltrated from the southern deserts. One tribe, the Akkadians, under king Sargon, consolidated the late Sumerian Empire circa 2300 B.C.E. The Amorite Babylonians also originated in the deserts and were later to establish that empire. It was the great Babylonian King Hammurabi who codified laws that laid the basis for much Western jurisprudence.

The influx and domination of the Fertile Crescent and Indus River basin changed the course of history and the evolution of consciousness and religion. What happened in the Bronze Age laid the matrix for today's societies and religions. Because of the dominance of patriarchy, many contemporary feminist observers view this time with foreboding and regret, believing the marauding tribes with their warrior-gods and patriarchal systems

2. Anne Baring and Jules Cashford, *The Myth of the Goddess: Evolution of an Image* (New York: Viking, 1991),156.

upset and destroyed what was basically a good matrilineal—
if not matriarchal—system where everyone got along with
basic equanimity. The suppression of the great Mother
Goddess traditions is viewed as the passing of a golden
era: men, bent on dominating everything, proceeded to ruin
the very fabric of society.

Life, as usual, is much more complex than that.
Something profound occurred in the countless millennia
before history when the Great Mother Goddess traditions
gave expression to the human awe at the universe; to the
human sense of connection with the totality of Life; and to
the human realization of the cyclic patterns and progressions
inherent in nature. Appreciation of the Mother Goddess
was personified perhaps the most poignantly in the
early civilization of Crete, a beautiful island in the
Mediterranean Sea where the climate was moderate,
nature beneficent and bountiful, and all neighbors were
across the sea. No depictions of war and battle have been
found during the Mesolithic period of Crete's history.
Everywhere, images of the Great Mother abound.

The pre-eminence of the Great Mother expressed
beautifully in Catal Huyuk and in Crete bespeaks a time
when humanity, in its infancy, stood in awe at the universe
it was just beginning to understand. Even as a baby spends
time in the womb, surrounded and sustained within the
Mother, and in its infancy receives its sustenance and love
at its mother's breast and in her arms, with the father
providing in the background, so humanity as a whole
experienced life in this way. The pervasiveness of images
of the natural world and the pre-eminence of the Great
Mother attest to this.

Humanity's time enveloped in nature, as expressed by

the religions of the Mother Goddess, was a time when the cruciform structures of nature completely surrounded humanity. In nature all polarities, all patterns, all cycles, however contradictory or predatory, are harmonized in a continuous, living flow.

But babies leave the womb, and humanity left nature for the cities and civilization. The relative ease of hunting and gathering in small groups was replaced with the rigor and discipline of farming, trading, building, warring, and protecting. These were developments requiring new exertions of strength, on the part of the male particularly. The Neolithic period and the Bronze Age were thus the weaning of the baby. This involved the assertion of a masculine impulse and a more dimensionalized female, giving rise to the emergence of the individual self apart from the collective whole. Individuality began to emerge as a legitimate point of focus. Though the Mother Goddess was still honored, countless gods and goddess, demigods and spirits sprang up, each expressing unique aspects of the natural order and the differentiating human psyche.

The hunter became the hero as humanity, formerly overwhelmed by nature, now attempted to dominate it. Masculine control mechanisms replaced the feminine sense of interrelatedness. The wisdom of limits, as personified by the Mother Goddess, was supplanted by the lust for the limitless, as personified by the warrior king. In so doing, humanity left the cyclic order of the natural world for the patriarchal order of the urban world, preferring human order to natural cycles and the capriciousness of the king to the capriciousness of the elements.

In leaving nature for the cities, in replacing the natural order with civilization humanity rent asunder the polarities, patterns, and cycles of nature. In nature power was harmonized; in cities power contradicted power, natural patterns broke down, natural cycles were disrupted. Urbanization signaled the point of transition when humanity collectively forgot it was of the earth and began to think it was simply on the earth.

Thus came separation between heroes, tribes, cities, and civilizations; between gods and goddesses; between humanity and divinity; between good and evil; between life and death; and between male and female. Large-scale cooperation and organization within one group for competition and conflict with other groups became the dominant modality of human existence. The cities, the farms, the trading routes, the new modes of transportation, the new weapons, the new mythologies, the myriad languages, all expressed a burst of creativity that has been rivaled only by our generation. Through this, humanity lifted itself out of primitive existence into civilization, and masculine consciousness began to dominate the earth.

It was creative; it was exuberant; it was painful. The terrible two's are like that. In every way it was profound, leaving humanity with a great sense of accomplishment and a deep sense of loss. When we broke from the Great Mother, we shifted from the static feminine and masculine modalities of being to their active aspects in all their positive and negative manifestations. We became conscious instead of unconscious, discriminating rather than harmonizing, differentiated as opposed to undifferentiated.

Our triumph was that we established civilization. Our tragedy was that we used consciousness to divide what was unified. We used our power of discrimination to subordinate what was existentially equal; and we exercised our increasing differentiation to divide and control what was, in fact, interrelated. In the process we wounded ourselves.

Our maturation demanded separation, but this act of separation created alienation. The cruciform structures, which harmonized us with nature under the auspices of the Mother Goddess, began to victimize us as we split asunder the polarities and pitted the elements against one another in order to dominate and control.

Religious rites of propitiation appeared as the intuitions of Paleolithic humanity concerning separation, sacrifice, and atonement crystallized into religious doctrines during the Neolithic period. To quote Hesiod, "When gods and men parted, sacrifice was created."[3]

Paradoxically, it was often the very hero who led the forces of separation who was sacrificed in order to bridge the very gap he had created. Sometimes he was assisted by a feminine figure, sometimes not. Sumerian, Babylonian, Egyptian, Greek, and Roman mythology is replete with examples of the king being sacrificed, either actually or symbolically, in order to re-create a sense of unity with nature or with the deities.

The Aryans and the Semites developed extensive sacrificial rites. The *Rig Vedas* and *Mahabharata*, the *Iliad* and the *Odyssey* are full of depictions of sacrificial rites, as are thousands of written tablets and documents discovered in the ruins of the great cities of Babylon, Ur, Ninevah, Damascus, Jerusalem, Memphis, and Thebes. All echo the themes of domination, separation, woundedness, sacrifice, and forgiveness.

Again, Judeo-Christianity simply re-worked these ancient motifs. The Hebrew high priest placed all the sins of Israel on the head of a goat and drove the goat into the wilderness on the Day of Atonement. Jesus was crucified, buried, and

—————————
3. *The Myth of the Goddess*, 162.

arose on the third day, according to Christian belief, to redeem all humanity from sin. The disjunction as well as the redemption emanating out of the cruciform nature of reality was ritualized to express the unique act of redemption God worked through in these distinct yet interrelated events of the Exodus and the Cross. The king is dead; long live the king.

What emerged during the late Neolithic period and the Bronze Age was not a perversion of humanity by patriarchy but a development of humanity through masculine and feminine differentiation. Humanity was growing up, maturing painfully from an infancy that had lasted hundreds of thousands of years. In so doing, the universal masculine impulse to separate, to define, and to rationalize was given dramatic expression. The static-feminine aspect of the Great Mother gave way to the transformational-masculine aspect of the hero and further differentiation of the feminine archetype. This shift generated the first civilization and a quest for knowledge of the workings of nature in order to exercise control over nature. The exercise of power rather than the harmony of interrelatedness became the focus of human society, resulting in the creation of hierarchical organization and the domination of women.

It is only now, some five thousand years later, that this predominantly masculine impulse, crystallized into patriarchy at the very beginning of civilization, has run its course. Its obsession with knowledge in order to exercise power has culminated in the Age of Overkill. Its despoiling of nature in an attempt to control it has led to the extinction of tens of thousands of plant and animal species. The prospect now facing humanity is renewal or catastrophe.

CHAPTER 2

THE EPIC OF GILGAMESH

Do not let me hear

Of the wisdom of old men, but rather of their folly,

Their fear of fear and frenzy, their fear of possession,

Of belonging to another, or to others, or to God.

The only wisdom we can hope to acquire

Is the wisdom of humility: humility is endless.[1]

T O UNDERSTAND THE MAGNITUDE OF THE shift from the Paleolithic power of the Mother Goddess to the patriarchy in the late Neolithic period, one must look beyond the conclusions drawn from artifacts unearthed by archaeologists. One must turn, finally, to how the human community living then gave voice to their situation, how they made sense of the enormous transitions in thought and myth that arose out of the staggering transitions in technology and power.

Fortunately, we have such a story: the Gilgamesh epic. It summarizes the pathos of the transition, bears witness to the disjunctive aspects of our cruciform nature, prophesizes the consequences of the rise of patriarchy, and in the process becomes *the* foundational story for the human race as it makes the transition from primitive society to civilization. It will not be until *Faust*, some four thousand years later, that

1. Eliot, *Collected Poems*, 199.

we come again upon such a monumental literary depiction of the human predicament.

Although the version of the epic I will refer to is in Akkadian, inscribed on eleven tablets of clay dating from 1800 to 1600 B.C.E. at the end of the Old Babylonian Period, fragments and variants found by archaeologists go back much earlier and are written in Sumerian, the language of history's first civilization. The translation I have drawn upon is Maureen Gallery Kovacs' *The Epic of Gilgamesh.*[2]

Gilgamesh was king of Uruk, a city situated along the Euphrates River in lower Mesopotamia and the capitol of Sumer. He reigned circa 2700 B.C.E. According to the myths that grew up about him, the "Lady of the Gods," the mother goddess Aruru, who had fashioned humankind at Creation, also fashioned Gilgamesh. For her pleasure, she created him two-thirds god and one-third human, such that he "walked around in the enclosure of Uruk like a wild bull...beautiful, handsomest of men...perfect" (tablet 1: lines 46–50).

As part of his royal prerogative, Gilgamesh considered it his right to take for himself any woman in the city. Women were not Great Mothers to Gilgamesh but simply objects for sexual pleasure. Groaning under this bondage, the other men prayed to the sky-god Anu, the Father of the gods and the most ancient deity of Sumer, to create an equal to Gilgamesh who could divert his attention. Anu took this request to the mother goddess Aruru.

Aruru heard the prayers the citizenry and conceived a double of the sky-god Anu. She then "pinched off some clay, and threw it into the Wilderness and

2. *The Epic of Gilgamesh,* ed. and trans. Maureen Gallery Kovacs (Stanford University Press,1989).

created valiant Enkidu, born of Silence, endowed with strength by Ninurta, god of war (1: 82). Enkidu was covered with shaggy hair and grazed with the gazelles. If Gilgamesh was two-thirds sky, Enkidu was two-thirds earth.

One day, a trapper observed Enkidu feeding with the animals and reported the event to his father. They decided to entrap the wild man. The son went to Uruk and petitioned Gilgamesh for a harlot of the temple of Ishtar (daughter of Anu). Gilgamesh granted the petition and the trapper and a harlot named Shamhat traveled to the watering-hole where Enkidu was last seen.

Of all the ancient goddesses, Ishtar most powerfully personified the new powers of the feminine to emerge out of the ashes of the Mother Goddess religions. Ishtar was the goddess of war and erotica, the seductive whore who was also the perennial virgin. She destroyed as easily as she created, driving men mad with lust, only to dispose of them after they satisfied her plans. As the Mother Goddesses had manifested the feminine in its static dimension, Ishtar symbolized dramatically the feminine in its transformational dimension, positively and negatively. It was Ishtar's role to transform Enkidu from a beast into a human.

When the trapper spied Enkidu, he commanded the harlot:

"Release your clenched arms,
expose your sex so he can take in your voluptuousness.
Do not be restrained—take his energy!"
...Shamhat unclutched her bosom, exposed her sex, and he took in her voluptuousness.
She was not restrained, but took his energy.

She spread out her robe and he lay upon her.

She performed for the primitive the task of womankind.

His lust groaned over her;

for six days and seven nights Enkidu stayed aroused,

and had intercourse with the harlot

until he was sated with her charms (1: 163–169).

Enkidu then turned his attention back to the gazelles, but they ran away; "the wild animals distanced themselves from his body." Feeling "utterly depleted, he suddenly drew himself up, for his understanding had broadened" (1: 175–184). He returned and sat down at the harlot's feet. "Becoming aware of himself, he sought a friend" (1: 194).

Under the spell of Ishtar, Enkidu had separated himself from nature. Sexuality—"the task of womankind"—was the cause for this momentous shift. No longer was sexuality a natural function of the Great Mother as she created and nurtured. In the world-view of the Bronze Age, Ishtar's power was to take women's subordination, symbolized by women being objects of pleasure, and use it for the transformation of the male. Thereby, Enkidu was empowered to make the leap from animal wildness into human culture.

Echoing the words of the serpent to Eve, the harlot said, "You are beautiful, Enkidu, you are become like a god" (1: 188). She offered to take him to Uruk, an offer he accepted gratefully. Shamhat then "pulled off her clothing and clothed him with one piece while she clothed herself with a second."

Shamhat led Enkidu to a hut beside a sheepfold on the outskirts of the city. In the Sumerian language "sheepfold" is synonymous with vulva, signifying that in this humble meeting place of sheep and shepherds Enkidu was to be reborn. Enkidu could not go directly from the wilds into the city; he had to go through the domestication process first by witnessing the domesticated sheep and by eating and drinking with civilized humans.

The sociologist Claude Lévi-Strauss makes the point that cooking is the transformation of nature into culture. Enkidu needed to experience civilized eating as well as seductive sexuality before he was ready for civilization. One parallel account in Old Babylonian states explicitly that after eating and drinking, Enkidu "turned into a human."[3]

Transformed, Enkidu chased the wolves and the lions so that the shepherds could rest at night. He also heard about the outrages of Gilgamesh and vowed to bring him to justice. He entered Uruk to the acclaim of crowds who marveled at this wild man's similarity to the king.

Enkidu met Gilgamesh as the king walked toward the house of a bride preparing for her wedding, intending to rape her. Enkidu bared the door to the marital chamber, presenting himself as a protector for the helpless maiden inside. In so doing, Enkidu protected the old order; he became the Mother's brother, the champion of nature and the matrilineal order of the Mother Goddess against the lustful encroachments of the domineering male. Transformed by Ishtar from beast to human, Enkidu's instinct was to protect the bride. Gilgamesh enjoined him in battle, praising the rights of kingship and the preroga- tives of the warrior. This battle at the bridal door symbol- izes the painful experience of the Neolithic hunters and gatherers as they made the transition to farming and to walled cities.

"The doorposts trembled and the wall shook" (2: 102)

as the two titans fought like bulls. Eventually, Enkidu triumphed and Gilgamesh was chastened. The two became fast friends. Their love for each other is reminiscent of David's love for Jonathan, which was described as being greater than his love for any woman.

Though sexual prowess was their initial bond, the deeper bond between Gilgamesh and Enkidu was their common quest for more knowledge and increased power. Gilgamesh proposed a journey into the sacred Cedar Forest of Lebanon to slay its guardian, Humbaba. Civilization implies the subjugation of nature. For Gilgamesh, the enemy was the very environment that served as the first home for our ancestors—the forest.

The two warriors set out to conquer the sacred grove, travelling for six days and seven nights. Each evening, Gilgamesh made offerings to the sun-god Shamesh and with each offering requested a favorable omen. Each night he had a dream, urging him to desist and warning him of grave consequences if he did not. After each dream, Gilgamesh awakened Enkidu immediately and recited the dream. Enkidu interpreted all of the dreams in a positive light, urging Gilgamesh onward.

Gilgamesh prayed to a masculine deity for a good omen but received in his dreams—the gateway through which the feminine speaks to us—warnings that his lust for knowledge and power will inevitably lead to destruction. Though he saw females only as objects of sexual pleasure, the feminine within his own soul—his anima, in Jungian terms—sought his transformation but had no effect. The king ignored all seven dreams and proceeded with the task of reaching the sacred forest in order to destroy it.

Finally, the two men reached the Cedar Mountain, the

Dwelling of the Gods, the throne-dais of Irnini (the name for Ishtar in her ferocious aspect). Where they sought to vanquish nature they found the transformational-feminine in its negative aspect. In this place, protecting nature, Ishtar was her most terrifying.

At the sight of Humbaba, Gilgamesh lost courage and hid because the face of Humbaba kept changing from one horrific form into another. Enkidu encouraged Gilgamesh onward, and together they engaged Humbaba in a mighty battle. They won only through the intervention of the sun-god Shamesh. Gilgamesh moved in for the kill, and Humbaba pled for his life. Again Enkidu urged Gilgamesh on. Then together, they transgressed the wisdom of limits and slew Humbaba. With Humbaba dead, the warriors "cut through the Cedar" (5: 324). They sailed back down the Euphrates to Uruk with a barge full of felled trees, Enkidu steering and Gilgamesh holding the head of Humbaba.

Back from their expedition, the two men caught the attention of the goddess Ishtar in her seductive aspect. She came to Gilgamesh in all her resplendent, seductive beauty and offered to become his lover. He repulsed her with the question, "Where are your bridegrooms that you keep forever?" and then recited all her past lovers who came to ruin, beginning with Tammuz, "the lover of your earliest youth."

> You loved the colorlful "Little Shepherd" bird [Tammuz]
> and then hit him, breaking his wing, so
> now he stands in the forest crying, "My Wing!"
> You loved the supremely mighty lion,
> yet you dug for him seven and seven again pits.
> You loved the stallion, famed in battle,

yet you ordained for him the whip, the goad, and the
lash....
You loved the Shepherd, the Master Herder,
who continually presented you with bread baked in
embers,
and who daily slaughtered for you a kid.
Yet you struck him, and turned him into a wolf,
so his own shepherds now chase him
and his own dogs snap at his shins....
And now me! It is me you love, and you will ordain for me
as for them! (6: 40–77)

Civilization was humanity's attempt to create heaven
on earth, to bring to the earthly realm and under human
control the blessings of the gods. Ishtar, as the feminine
does always in the face of such arrogance, insisted to
Gilgamesh that love of her—love of the active feminine
spirit, which points away from the earth toward the eternity
of the spirit world—may begin with passion but must end
with the reality of our limited human condition. Failure to
recognize this invites destruction. By rejecting Ishtar,
Gilgamesh rejected the cruciform reality of nature and the
limits it imposes on human existence.

Humans can never cross the chasm separating the
created from the Creator. We are created by God and
fashioned in the divine image. But it was from dust we
were sculpted and to dust we shall return. We may have
dignity but, in the end, we are mere moles, blinking at the
sunshine of a universe whose majesty was here long before
us and will endure long after we draw our last breath. The
epic questions why, when all our religious mythologies are
constructed to show the difference between gods and

human beings, we try continually to extend ourselves beyond these distinctions and become what we know we are not.

Rejected by Gilgamesh and enraged, Ishtar retreated to heaven, demanding that either the great sky-god Anu send the Bull of Heaven to earth to destroy Gilgamesh or Ishtar would spread famine on earth and raise the dead. The sky-god conceded and sent the Bull.

Anger caused Ishtar to forget that the domestication of cattle is the domain of men; the two warriors destroyed the Bull without effort. They ripped out its heart and presented it to the sun-god Shamesh, bowing humbly before him. Enkidu then wrenched off the bull's hindquarters—presumably including his sexual organs— and flung it in Ishtar's face, while Gilgamesh made a trophy of the horns and placed them in his bedroom. In the old order the sexuality of the bull was sacrificed at the altar of the Great Mother. In the new order men enshrined the horns, a symbol of power and might, in their rooms. When hunting is not for survival but for sport, hunters love to make trophies of their kills.

Ishtar and the gods retaliated by striking Enkidu with a fatal disease, marking the first time in literature where overweening pride is linked with tragic consequences, a theme the Greeks developed with their notion of hubris, and which has been an integral part of literature ever since. As he lay dying Enkidu "spoke to the door as if it were human" (7: 33), regretting that he had chopped up the cedars instead of fashioning them into doorways for the palace. He then cursed and blessed the harlot, underscoring the fundamental ambivalence in the relations between the sexes and the agony of the civilizing process.

As Enkidu breathed his last, Gilgamesh raised a loud lament, realizing,

I am going to die! Am I not like Enkidu?
Deep sadness penetrates my core,
I fear death and now roam the wilderness... (9: 2).

For six days and seven nights he mourned, until maggots began to drop out of Enkidu's nose. Gilgamesh then vowed to confront death itself. Refusing all limits, he determined to break the final boundary and marched off to the edge of the earth.

On his way he climbed the great twin-mountains of Mashu over which the sun rose; conversed with the menacing scorpion-beings guarding the passes; journeyed along the Road of the Sun where he walked for eleven leagues through the deepest darkness. Finally, dawn broke, and he came to a garden of trees filled with jewels.

Next, Gilgamesh found himself at an inn near the seashore and stopped for food and directions. The innkeeper sensed that Gilgamesh was a murderer and covered her face with a veil. She counseled him to cease his quest to conquer death, saying that to die is human and that no one can contravene that limitation, even if all others could be overcome. Once again, in a display of incredible compassion, the feminine spirit came to Gilgamesh, even after all he had done, to plead with him to discern the cruciform nature of life and the wisdom of limits.

Gilgamesh brushed her aside and boasted of the very things that she had begged him to reconsider: he had destroyed the spirit of the forest, slaughtered the sacred bull, traversed the steppes, climbed the highest mountains, and gone through the darkest tunnels. He then pushed on until he reached the edge of the waters of death.

He looked for the boatman who alone could ferry him across the waters. He was unable to find the boatman, only stone images, which he smashed in a fury. When he finally found the boatman, he was told that he had destroyed the very secret of crossing the waters: the cedars of the sacred forest. Having destroyed the cedars for sport, Gilgamesh was now ordered, as an act of penance, to cut down three hundred trees to be used as punting poles. The corrosiveness of the water destroyed each pole after a single punt.

Gilgamesh crossed the Waters of Death and at last found himself at the feet of the great sage Utnapishtim who knew of the secret of immortality. He told Gilgamesh "No one can see death, no one can hear the voice of death, yet there is savage death that snaps off mankind" (10: 290–294). It is the Mother Goddess Aruru who "fashions destiny" but who never makes known "the days of death."

Utnapishtim confided that he had been given immortality because he had accepted the limits the gods imposed upon him and had done exactly as they commanded. The key to transcending human limits is keeping divinely imposed limits. He recited for Gilgamesh the story of the Flood, how he was commanded to build an ark by the trickster-god Ea who was trying somehow to save at least one human being from the wrath of the gods. When given the orders, Utnapishtim obeyed explicitly, saying to Ea, "My Lord, thus is the command which you have uttered. I will heed and will do it" (11: 33–34). Not until the Virgin Mary do we hear again such humble submission to the divine will.

Utnapishtim is clearly a Noah figure, although his

narrative of the Flood was much more esoterically recounted than the Biblical account and was replete with sacred geometry and numerology. The ark he constructed was not a boat but a seven-story, perfectly-squared cube, and the flood lasted seven days and seven nights. By the seventh day, says Utnapishtim, "the flood was a war, struggling with itself like a woman writhing in labor" (11: 130). Its intensity terrified even the gods; Ishtar "shrieked like a woman in childbirth." Through it all, Utnapishtim did exactly what he was told and was blessed with the gift of immortality.

Utnapishtim challenged Gilgamesh with a deceptively simple task: to stay awake, examining his own mind, for six days and seven nights. Gilgamesh was snoring after only a few moments and stayed asleep for six days and seven nights. Utnapishtim remarked to his wife, "Look there! The man, the youth who wanted eternal life! As soon as he sat down with his head between his legs, sleep, like a fog, blew upon him" (11: 206–208). Utnapishtim commented to his wife, "Mankind is deceptive, and will deceive you" (11: 217), and asked her to bake a loaf of bread for each day Gilgamesh stayed asleep.

When Gilgamesh awoke, he was astonished, for he thought he had shut his eyes for only a few seconds. Shamed by the moldy loaves before him, Gilgamesh admitted he could not traverse the limits of death. Utnapishtim commanded the boatman to take Gilgamesh to the place where he could wash himself of his journey. The wife pleaded that Gilgamesh be given a special gift: a plant for invigoration and rejuvenation—almost immortality but not quite.

To obtain the gift, Gilgamesh had to tie weights to

himself and sink to the bottom of the underground waters where the plant resided. Such a test was easy for the hero, and he took the plant and hid it in his garments. Ironically, the woman, not the great sage, gave the plant to Gilgamesh, and his final test was conducted in the primordial maternal waters, not in the mountains or in the sky. Constantly ignored and violated by him, the feminine was forever present to guide him.

On his way back to Uruk he stopped to bathe at a pool. From the depths of the pool, a serpent arose, "smelled the fragrance of the plant, silently came up and carried off the plant. While going back it sloughed off its casing" (11: 296–298). Gilgamesh witnessed the whole transformation and for a brief instant was given to see the cruciform pattern of life, death, and renewal. Realizing his loss, he sat down and, for the first time since the death of Enkidu, wept.

The hero returned to Uruk, proud but defeated in his ultimate quest. The epic ends with Gilgamesh commanding the ferryman who had accompanied him home to survey the dimensions of Uruk, the walls, the foundation, the circumference, the height. The great warrior speaks about limitation through the metaphor of the walls that surround the city. He ends his exploits by taking the measure of what he has built, intuiting the wisdom of limits but in his undying pride not quite accepting them.

At a deep level, Gilgamesh understands that the human community has always defined itself within walls: the walls of the womb from which we all come, the walls of death to which we all are destined, and the walls of civilization within which we contextualize our journey between the womb and the tomb. In transgressing all limits he is forced, in the end, to accept even the most mundane limits: those of the mother, those of death, and those of the community.

It is clear in the epic that on the surface of life the power of the goddess has given way to the ferociousness of the warrior, but in and through all of the hero's adventures, the feminine never ceases the task of transformation. Sexuality and combat combine in the goddess Ishtar as women transition from Great Mother to cunning seductress and men leave off the hunt for survival in order to fight other men and conquer nature. Male power seems unlimited, empowering men to defy all limits, even death. Power for-and-of-itself becomes the goal in the new order of things. Although the Great Mother dominated the old Paleolithic order, nature is now vanquished, and the feminine must use all the subtleties of charm, sexuality, and intrigue to protect nature and to carry on the task of human transformation.

In the end the hubris of Gilgamesh precluded him from surpassing death or from obtaining wisdom. He could not stay awake, nor could he prevent the snake from taking the plant. His power controlled but did not enlighten; it served merely to deepen his yearnings for atonement. In rejecting the cruciform nature of reality, he was victimized by it.

The tragedy of Gilgamesh is that he never developed his relationship with his feminine side. The feminine, whether expressed in mortal women or in immortal goddesses, was only an object for him, merely a place to relieve himself. When he returned to the safety of the city walls, he was still strong, but he realized he was not omnipotent; and though still courageous, understood that he was not yet wise. Disconnected from his feminine, he remained obsessed with sex but was unable to experience wholeness.

Thus the beginnings of human civilization.

CHAPTER 3

THE BUDDHA

In order to arrive there,

To arrive where you are, to get from where you are not,

You must go by a way wherein there is no ecstasy.

In order to arrive at what you do not know

You must go by a way which is the way of ignorance.

In order to possess what you do not possess

You must go by the way of dispossession.

In order to arrive at what you are not

You must go through the way in which you are not.

And what you do not know is the only thing you know

And what you own is what you do not own

And where you are is where you are not.[1]

CONCURRENT WITH THE RISE OF SUMER and Babylon, marauding tribes of Aryans swept south from the Caspian Sea to trade, plunder, and expand their lands. They pillaged Babylon, and though some stayed in Mesopotamia, the main armies moved east, sweeping into the

1. Eliot, *Collected Poems*, 201.

Indus and Ganges River basins in India where the relatively pacific Nagas and Dravidians people lived. There the Aryans defeated the local kings and settled down, gradually replacing war and plunder with herding, tilling, and commerce.

This admixture of Aryan and indigenous bloodlines was responsible for one of history's great civilizations. This people developed a perspective on the great issues Gilgamesh had grappled with but arrived at very different conclusions, ones that indelibly shaped all of Asia and are interacting with Western values and perspectives today.

The gods and goddesses of the oldest known religion of India, the Vedic tradition, were animistic and totemic, arising out of the religion of the Great Mother—as did all of civilization—and were characterized by the same differentiations described in the previous chapters. The earliest gods personified the forces and elements of nature—the sun, moon, earth, wind, water, sexuality, and so forth.

The most important of the Vedic gods was Agni, the god of fire, who lifted the sacred sacrifice from the altar to heaven. He was also the lightning that pierced the sky, while the great goddess Indra wielded the thunder and the storms upon the earth. It was Indra who brought the rain. In this earliest stratum Vishnu was the sun who covered the earth with his strides; Krishna was a minor local deity of the Krishna tribe.

The Vedic tradition was among the first that asked the great questions concerning life and the universe. The Vedic creation story, the most modest among all the ancient traditions, acknowledges the limits of the intellect in piercing the unfathomable mystery that surrounds all of human life. Gilgamesh raised his fist to the sky and defied the gods, but the Vedic masters intuited that the only effective posture was to bend the knee. Their great myth

of creation stands as one of the greatest statements ever
written about the limits of human knowing:

> There was neither nonexistence nor existence then,
> There was neither the realm of space nor the sky beyond.
> What moved, under whose protection?
> Was there only water bottomlessly deep?
>
> There was neither death nor immortality then,
> There was no distinction of night or of day.
> That One breathed, windless, under its own impulse.
> Other than the One, there was nothing.
>
> Darkness was hidden within darkness in the beginning.
> All was fluid and formless, with no distinguishing sign.
> The One was covered with emptiness,
> The One arose through the power of heat.
>
> Desire came upon the One in the beginning,
> Desire is the first seed of mind.
> The poets know this.
> Searching their hearts with wisdom,
> They know their bond with existence lies with nonexistence.
> They stretch the cord across:
> Was there below?
> Was there above?
> There were seed placers,
> There were impulses below,
> There was giving forth above.
>
> But who can here proclaim whence is this creation
> And from whence it has arisen?
> The gods themselves, they came after,
> With the creation of the universe.
> Who can here proclaim whence is this creation,

Whether it formed itself or did not form itself?

Only He who looks down upon us from the highest heaven,
Only He knows,
Or perhaps He does not know.[2]

This modesty on the part of the Vedic tradition was born of a growing realization in the East that human life is a mere drop in a vast cosmic ocean. Unlike Gilgamesh who vaunted himself in pride against sexual conventions, against nature, against Ishtar, even against death itself, the seers of India became increasingly reflective about how the unseen permeates the seen, how the macrocosm is reflected in and through the microcosm, and how the single individual life is related to the totality, as a drop of water reflects the entire ocean.

The Vedic tradition reached full flower during the second millennium B.C.E., culminating in the Upanishads, which began to take shape at the turn of the first millennium and were completed circa 800 B.C.E. The Upanishads continue the humility of the Vedas. The underlying theme was the experience of the mystery rather than of the known, the essence rather than the manifestation, the silence rather than the thought. Material existence thus became increasingly irrelevant to this tradition; exploring the realms of consciousness became the highest pursuit.

Someone like Gilgamesh was seen as a victim of *samsara* (the web of illusion), destroying himself because he was unable to see himself as a part of a larger whole. The hero of the Upanishadic tradition was one who had the discipline to work through the veils of ignorance that beset us all, cut-

2. *Vedic Hymns and Myths* (London: Penguin, 1987),154.

ting through the seductions of the flesh and the pride of life to experience the unitive state with Brahman, the All. In the Maitri Upanishad we read of a king who, amid splendor and power, abandoned his kingdom for the forest in order to solve the riddles of the universe. The ultimate challenge was to reach the state of unity with Being itself, not to accumulate wealth, exercise political power, or indulge the enticements of pleasure.

Here the hero becomes the sage, not the warrior, nor the king, nor the merchant. Brahman, or the divine in its transcendent and immanent aspects, is also the spiritual essence in each individual, the Atman. Brahman and Atman are the same presence. The momentous declaration throughout the Upanishads is that God is not something external to us, far away, but is something omnipresent, as intimate as our own heart beat. Thus the sage, when asked about God, remains silent. When pressed, he responds, *Neti neti*, "Not this, not this." When pressed further, he states finally the one phrase that condenses all of Eastern thought, *TAT TVAM ASI*, "Thou art That."

It was into this world-view that Prince Siddhartha was born circa 563 B.C.E. in the foothills of the Himalaya to the king of the Sakya clan. His mother, Queen Maya, died seven days after his birth. Dreams and portents indicated that this child was to be a prodigy, and his father kept him in splendid isolation in three palaces, satisfying his every desire. Siddhartha grew gently to manhood, married, had a son, and lived in wealth, serenity, and with good repute.

Then one day, according to tradition, Siddhartha noticed an elderly man and began to question his own youthfulness. The next day, he saw a sick man and questioned his own mortality. The third day he saw a corpse being taken to the cemetery and questioned the purpose of his own life. These experiences were to Siddhartha what the death of Enkidu was to Gilgamesh. Gilgamesh sought to conquer death, but Siddhartha, realizing death was inevitable, sought to extinguish its power. As he recounted it to his disciples later, he realized that

> . . . being myself subject to birth, I sought out the nature of birth; being subject to old age I sought out the nature of old age, of sickness, of sorrow, of impurity. Then I thought: "What if I, being myself subject to birth, were to seek out the nature of birth...and having seen the wretchedness of the nature of birth, were to seek out the unborn, the supreme peace of Nirvana?"[3]

With this awareness, Siddhartha decided to leave the palace and pursue the life of a sage. During the night, he stole furtively from the palace, leaving his wife and son asleep, rode his horse to the edge of the forest, and, abandoning his mount and his clothes, began his search for ultimate truth.

For six years Siddhartha engaged in the mortification of the flesh, depriving himself of even the simplest of pleasures. He lived on seeds and grasses, even on dung, until he existed on single grain of rice a day. He slept among the corpses left to be eaten by the wild beasts and birds, and let the dust and dirt accumulate on his body until he was hardly recognizable as human. He recalled later:

> I thought, what if now I set my teeth, press my tongue to my palate, and restrain, crush and burn out my mind with my mind. I did so. And sweat flowed from my armpits.... Then I thought, what if I now practice trance without breathing. So I restrained breathing in and out from mouth and nose. And as I did, there was a violent sound of winds issuing from my ears.... Just as if a strong man were to crush one's head with the point of a sword, even so did violent winds disturb my head.... My

3. Will Durant, *Our Oriental Heritage* (New York: Simon and Schuster, 1954),425.

body became extremely lean. The mark of my seat was like camel's footprint through the little food. The bones of my spine, when bent and straightened, were like a row of spindles through the little food. When I thought I would touch the skin of my stomach I actually took hold of my spine.... When I thought I would ease myself I thereupon fell prone through the little food. To relieve my body I stroked my limbs with my hand, and as I did so the decayed hairs fell from my body through the little food (426).

One day, spent and nearly dead from his efforts, Siddhartha came to see that any piety he might develop through asceticism would be distorted by the pride he felt in his accomplishments. He decided to renounce the ascetic life and journey onward. Just then, a young maiden tending some cows came by and offered him some milk. This he drank, and empowered by the milk and by the decision to reach wisdom by other means, he sat down in front of a Bodhi tree, resolving not to leave until a deeper truth had revealed itself. For forty days and forty nights Siddhartha sat under the Bodhi tree.

Thus with mind concentrated, purified, cleansed...I directed my mind to the passing away and rebirth of beings. With divine, purified, superhuman vision I saw beings passing away and being reborn, low and high of good and bad color, in happy or miserable existences, according to their karma (427).

Reflecting thus, Siddhartha had a vision of the Four Noble Truths: Life is suffering; Suffering is caused by craving; There is a way to stop suffering; and This way is the Eight-Fold Path, the middle way between extremes.

More broadly and fundamentally, Siddhartha saw that there is no separate existence, no separate ego, no separate individual self: All life is interconnected in a complex web of ever-changing relationships and interactions. We suffer because we seek permanence in an impermanent world. We think we are separate, somehow special, when in actuality we are temporary confluences of mass and energy that have arisen only momentarily and will soon pass away. He was later to offer the image of one candle lighting another candle, lighting the next candle, *ad infinitum*. The light is a constant; the individual candles, only incidental and ephemeral, with no real separate existence in and of themselves. This is the insight of *anatta* (the non-self).

Embracing these truths at a level most would be hard-pressed even to imagine, Siddhartha gained enlightenment. He arose from his seat the Buddha, the "enlightened one."

After washing and resting, the Buddha walked to the holy city of Varanasi and for the next forty years taught throughout northern India an understanding of such profundity that he established the great religion of the East, which two thousand five hundred years later is being embraced throughout the West. The singular insight that he carried and preached until he died was that there is no separate existence: Everything, including every individual ego, is part of a constantly changing, ever permeable flux. Nothing is separate, nothing is distinct, nothing is unique unto itself. Everything is form, everything is emptiness; everything is neither form nor emptiness. In one of his sermons he said: "It is not asserted that things are not born in a superficial sense, but that in a deep sense they are not born of themselves. All that can be said is this, that relatively speaking, there is a constant stream of becoming, a momentary and uninterrupted change from one state of appearance to another."[4]

In this sense the Buddha stated,

> My teaching transcends the whole conception of being and non-being; it has nothing to do with birth, abiding and destruction; nor with existence and non-existence. I teach that the multitudinousness of objects have no reality in themselves but are only seen of the mind and therefore are of the nature of illusion and a dream. I teach the non-existence of things because they carry no signs of any inherent self-nature. It is true that in one sense they are seen and discriminated by the senses as individualized objects; but in another sense, because of the absence of any characteristic marks of self-nature, they are not seen but are only imagined. In one sense they are graspable, but in another sense, they are not graspable (297).

The profundity of this doctrine of *anatta*, the non-self, compelled no less a historian than Arnold Toynbee to state that "the coming of Buddhism to the West may well prove to be the most important event of the twentieth century."[5] Toynbee stated this as he reflected upon the unimaginable destructiveness caused by the two world wars and the systemic divisiveness spawned by Judeo-Christianity out of their sense of chosenness. Only a metaphysic of unity and interdependence will save us, Toynbee believed, and the Buddha is the teacher who developed this notion with the most sophistication and sublimity. We will return to this great sage toward the end of our story, for if there is anything the world needs now it is a philosophy founded upon our internal relatedness with one another and with nature.

4. Dwight Goddard, ed., *A Buddhist Bible* (London: Dutton, 1966), 295.

5. Lama Surya Dass, *The Buddha Within* (New York: Random House, 1997), cover page.

CHAPTER 4

EVE,
MOTHER OF ALL
LIVING

We had the experience but missed the meaning,

And approach to the meaning restores the experience

In a different form, beyond any meaning

We can assign to happiness. I have said before

That the past experience revived in the meaning

Is not the experience of one life only

but of many generations—not forgetting

Something that is probably quite ineffable:

The backward look behind the assurance

Of recorded history, the backward half-look

Over the shoulder, towards the primitive terror.[1]

T HE BUDDHA'S WAS NOT THE ONLY ANSWER to the crisis of human existence and the challenges of civilization. Against the backdrop of Gilgamesh and within the larger context of the Neolithic revolution came the Jews, who through their witness of a God who had called them and had drawn them into an eternal covenant, made their awesome and historical transformational contribution to

1. Eliot, *Collected Poems*, 208.

the evolution of human consciousness.

What was unique to the Jews was the perspective they brought to the already ancient motifs of creation, alienation, sacrifice, atonement, and renewal and how they reframed these great mysteries within the framework of a radical monotheism rooted in the historical event of the Exodus. While the Buddha reflected upon the water, the Jews dug many wells and thereby developed the notions of linear time, history, and the movement of existence toward fulfillment.

The Jews at that time were a small, migratory, sheep-herding Semitic tribe from Mesopotamia, surviving in that war-torn and savage land by wandering at the edges of the city-states they encountered, negotiating temporary allegiance with various warlords but never offering absolute allegiance to anyone. Their founding patriarch Abraham settled finally in Canaan, and his son, Isaac, and grandson, Jacob, continued the presence of the Hebrews there.

Jacob journeyed into Egypt sometime during the seventeenth century B.C.E. to escape famine in the land of Canaan, and his descendants stayed there for over four centuries, ending up enslaved by the Pharaohs to build several cities. Most scholars believe that Moses liberated the Israelites circa 1290 B.C.E. and led them in their exodus from Egypt into the Sinai Peninsula where they wandered for the next forty years. Then Joshua led them back into the "Promised Land" of Canaan where they did what all conquerors have done: fought and displaced the local population and took the land. In Canaan, some three thousand years ago, Jewish seers gave final version to their creation story.

In the polytheistic world of Mesopotamia, myriad gods and goddesses intermingled with each other, with nature, and with humanity to mold and be shaped by events and other divinities. Human existence was very much a part of the drama of these interactive forces. The Jews contradicted this cacophony of voices and forces with the assertion that there was only one God, the One who had redeemed them from slavery in Egypt. This Redeemer was the one Creator of the universe, the one Lord over the whole of humanity, the one God in the face of all other gods. What the others attributed to hundreds of divinities, the Jews attributed to one Divinity. Monotheism was their initial insight and was central to their enduring legacy.

The monotheism of the Jews was quite specific. Israel began with God as Redeemer. The earliest strata of Biblical expressions of faith speak of God as the one who delivered them from the bondage of Egypt. Only later was it proclaimed that the God who delivered them from Egypt was also the Creator of the entire universe and Lord of all peoples. Their first experience of God was an experience of historical deliverance; only later did they recognize God as a cosmic universality.

Thus the Ten Commandments begin by declaring, "I am the Lord your God, who brought you out of the land of Egypt, out of the house of bondage. You shall have no other gods before me."[2] It was only later, in the eighth century B.C.E., that the prophet Amos declared:

> The Lord, God of hosts,
> he who touches the earth and it melts,
> and all who dwell in it mourn,

2. *Revised Standard Version of the Old and New Testament* (New York: Thomas Nelson and Son, 1952), Ex. 20:2,3.

and all of it rises like the Nile,

and sinks again, like the Nile of Egypt;

who builds his upper chambers in the heavens,

and founds his vault upon the earth;

who calls for the waters of the sea,

and pours them out upon the surface of the earth—

the Lord is his name (Am. 9:6).

Linking their historical experience of the Exodus with the Creator of the universe was a unique connection. All other religious world-views of the time began with the creation of the universe and the creation of the gods and goddesses independent of any historical considerations. Human life was viewed as part of an endless cycle of life, death, and rebirth. The Greeks, for example, began with creation and the order they witnessed in the universe; therefore they saw the handiwork of fate as an absolute in history and in individual lives.

The Jews began with political liberation; therefore they saw the handiwork of redeeming grace in history and in their relationship with their Creator. They knew God as Lord of History before they knew God as Lord of the Universe. Thus they developed a dynamic notion of linear time with a purpose that broke through the cyclic patterns structuring that history. The patriarch Abraham was "called forth" out of Mesopotamia. This calling forth allowed him to break out of the cyclic notion of nature and establish the concept of history and with it the concepts of individuality, freedom, and responsibility, notions commonplace today but absolutely radical three millennia ago.

The result of this shift was profound. Rather than multiplicity in the heavens and upon the earth, there was Unity above and a single focus on the covenant with that

Unity here below. Rather than philosophical speculations concerning cosmic universalities and the regimen of fate, there was a response of faith in God because of a historical event: deliverance from bondage. And rather than the absoluteness of nature or fate, there was emphasis on the sovereignty of God above and human choice below. Their redemption was the context of their appreciation of universal divine creativity and human responsibility.

The practical effect of radical monotheism was the radical secularization of the natural world. By placing God above and beyond creation, the Jews made creation mundane and totally dependent upon God. This gave centrality to humanity and therefore to redemptive history rather than to nature and to universalities. The other religions, including those of the mother goddesses, held nature to be sacred in its own right, but the Jews held that the only sacred point was God above the earth; on earth, humanity was given pre-eminence. The earth was part of creation and was affected by divine will and human behavior but had no significance in its own right.

Radical monotheism left only two actors in the world: God and humanity. The Jews understood that to live simply in nature, as the religions of the mother goddesses espoused, is to live and die by the laws of biology. To live in redemptive history is to live with purpose, direction, and fulfillment by the grace of God. It is to become the subject of history rather than merely its object.

In contradistinction to the Buddha who taught that all was one, the Jews articulated the opposite, that the universe was eternally split. There was a higher and a lower; a separateness to God, a separateness to humanity; and within humanity, there was a great divide between the

Jews, the "Chosen People," and the rest of humanity. This metaphysic empowered them—and later the Christians— to heights of power and self-certainty; it also poisoned human relations with a malignancy that culminated in the Holocaust and in the unleashing of nuclear weapons.

Radical monotheism was expressed most precisely and eloquently through the notion of covenant, that God and humanity were bound together with commitments and responsibilities on each side. The covenant obligated God to be loyal to Israel as God's Chosen People; to dispense justice within the context of a mercy that forever tempered that justice; and to love Israel steadfastly, never forsaking her. On Israel's part, the covenant obligated them to acknowledge no God but Yahweh and to obey no law but the Torah. Their thankfulness for their deliverance from Egypt was to be expressed in obedience to the covenant.

This was a remarkable achievement. In all the creation accounts of the ancient world, everything around humanity was sacred and connected with specific deities. All the various aspects of civilization were given to humans by various gods or goddesses. In the Gilgamesh epic, for example, the three elements of civilization of which Enkidu had to partake before he could go into the city— beer, food, and clothing—were under the domain of three different goddesses.

The Genesis account has God decreeing creation by the divine word. But God does not give the elements of culture to humanity; in the Genesis account, humanity develops the accouterments of civilization with the power given within the boundaries decreed by God. When Yahweh commands Adam and Eve to be fruitful and multiply and to have dominion over the earth, He commands them to take control over something created originally by God that is not numinous in its own right. Adam and Eve are told to till and to keep the Garden of Eden.

When the primal pair are expelled after eating of the tree of the knowledge of good and evil, they turn to horticulture. Their first son Cain developed farming; their second son Abel, herding. Civilization in the Biblical account is considered a natural human process beset by corruption. The issue is not which divinity is responsible for which aspect of civilization but the constant danger of Titanism on the part of humanity as it develops civilization.

The only exception to this rule is the giving of the Law. Exodus is clear that the one divine aspect of civilization is the demand for obedience to God's laws as expressed in the Torah. One Creator of the universe implies a single moral law governing that universe, as revealed by Yahweh to Moses on Mount Sinai. Obedience to the Torah is the response Israel is called upon to make, in thankful obedience, to the mystery and miracle of redemption from Egypt.

It should be noted that in the Biblical tradition, the people who developed civilization were not great demigods but ordinary mortals, heirs to the failures and frailties that afflict us all. Adam and Eve rebelled against God in the Garden of Eden. Cain murdered Abel. Their descendants conspired to attain equality with God by building the Tower of Babel, an act of hubris God punished severely.

Humanity is made in the image of God but is created out of the dust of the earth. We are commanded to be obedient to the will of God, but since the disobedience of Adam and Eve, our heart has been infected with pride and deceit. We are called upon to obey the covenant in humility, but we are obsessed with gathering more knowledge to exercise more power, a violation of the very covenant given to us to ensure harmony.

Rebellion as well as obedience shapes human motivations and thus human history. Humanity is not submissive and pliant at the hands of an awesomely powerful Creator. We are not puppets. God decreed certain limits, but, very early in the game, humanity violated these limits and used its knowledge and its technological developments to defy God. Humanity was a junior partner in creation, seeking in questionable and pain-driven ways to be master of the world even as God is master of the universe.

This is the source of our Titanism. We seek to be like God, even though, as humans, we are created to be instruments and channels of divine purpose. The paradox of grace is that in and through our Titanism grace abounds. Indeed, the Bible records that throughout their history, Israel's rebellion continually served the divine purpose at work in history. Redemption for the Jews is forever within the context of history and creation.

With no other operative forces in the universe, the drama of the Bible is that of divine power and grace on the one hand and human responsibilities and willful disobedience on the other. God creates the world and reveals the limits of creatures within the world. In Adam and Eve, in the mysterious dispensation of God, humanity seeks to attain divine power by breaking the limits imposed by God. Yet the redemptive power of God is revealed precisely at the point when humanity can only disobey.

The text of the Garden of Eden story comes from the Torah, which Biblical scholars believe may consist of several sources that were woven together by a later editor. The oldest sources are known as the "Yahwist" and "Elohist." They are distinguished by their distinctive use of the name of God in the early stages of Israel's history. There is widespread but by no means unanimous agreement that the Yahwist source was shaped in a form we can discern circa 950 B.C.E. and the Elohist, circa 850–750 B.C.E.

Other sources for the Torah include the Deuteronomic traditions, which comprise the book of Deuteronomy and are reflected in parts of Exodus, and the Priestly source, perhaps finalized in the post-exilic period, roughly 538–450 B.C.E. All these sources drew on material that was considered ancient even at that time.

It is the Yahwist source in Genesis with which we are concerned. Whoever shaped this source was a creative genius. Some scholars consider its artistic mastery as among the greatest literary achievements of the human mind, to say nothing of its spiritual profundity. The scenes are presented with stark clarity and succeed in encompassing the whole of human life. With utter simplicity, the Yahwist presents the agony and ecstasy of human existence, as well as the paradoxes and conflicts of the human heart. The German Old Testament scholar Gerhard Von Rad said that, among all the Biblical writers, the Yahwist was the "great psychologist."

This tradition concerns itself not only with humanity as it exists in creation but also with God who wills creation. The underlying theme is humankind being addressed by a living God. The stories depict God's revelation to human beings that become the objects of divine action, divine judgment, and divine salvation. In the primeval history of the priestly and Yahwist traditions, of which the story of Adam and Eve is a part, all the great human problems are dealt with in the light of revelation. Human origins are considered within the framework of radical monotheism.

Above all, the Yahwist is concerned with God's actions at the beginning of history and with the call of Israel, in terms of God's overt actions as well as the hidden workings of the divine Spirit in and through human frailty and sin. Yahweh is the God of the world, the divine presence working the divine purpose everywhere. We see Yahweh walking in the garden of Eden; addressing men and women directly; closing the ark after Noah was in safely; looking down, inspecting the town of Babel; selecting Abraham, Isaac, and Jacob as the "Chosen People"; guiding Joseph through his imprisonment and the vicissitudes he suffered in Egypt; and leading Israel to the "Promised Land."

The Yahwist sees God's handiwork in the contingencies of history, in the great public events of a people as well as in the secret recesses of the human heart, discerning divine presence in religious institutions as well as in the secular world. All things and all places, even the depths of the human heart, are legitimate areas of divine initiative and action. The Yahwist depicts these truths by recounting the great sagas that were the origins of the people of Israel.

The unique characteristic of Biblical sagas that separates them from other sagas is their honesty of perspective. In literature there is a tendency to idealize great characters, to transfigure them into ideal images. The sagas of Arthurian England, for instance, express the popular ideals of courage and loyalty through tales of noble kings and warriors who ride out to vanquish evil and save the maiden in distress.

Likewise, all the sagas of ancient Rome, Greece, Egypt, and Mesopotamia idealize their heroes and heroines, whether human or divine, by making them larger than life. The Gilgamesh epic is a classic example of this. Gilgamesh may have been a historical king, but in the epic he is depicted as a demigod.

Compared with these, the Biblical sagas are quite striking. Any tendency to transfigure or to idealize is missing completely. The Patriarchs, for instance, are portrayed in an almost mundane manner. Although their strengths and their wisdom are not ignored, their weaknesses, their sins, and their failures are presented in graphic detail. The reason is important to note.

Biblical sagas are concerned first with God and only then with human beings in the context of God's purpose and action. God is the principal narrative subject of events in human life, even though God is always beyond human life. Humans are significant only as knowing or unknowing participants in divine activity. The sagas reveal divine commands and the consequences of their affirmation or denial by human beings.

In ancient Israel the formative power in the creation and narration of sagas was faith born of revelation, received and interpreted through grace. The sagas of Israel recite the history of salvation as revealed to the faithful. In contrast with myths, legends, and fairy tales, which seek primarily to teach while entertaining, biblical sagas are to be *believed*. Their focus is the theocentric significance of history. Biblical saga is a narrative of faith. It recounts history from the vantage of Spirit. By recounting the history of faith, these sagas challenge us to understand that at one level history is the story of humanity, but the real drama in history is God's actions for our redemption.

One of the striking features of the Yahwist's description

of the original Paradise is that, in contradistinction to the creation myths of many other ancient peoples, there is nothing about opulent fertility and sensual enjoyment. Work seems to have been humanity's lot from the very beginning. The Yahwist recounts that the first human beings were placed in the Garden of Eden "to till it and keep it" (Gn. 2:15). Humans were called to serve and prove themselves in a place not of their possession.

God's first directive was that "you may freely eat of every tree of the garden; but of the tree of the knowledge of good and evil you shall not eat, for in the day that you eat of it you shall die" (Gn. 2:16–17). God offers abundance and restriction. Adam and Eve can move about completely unrestrained except for one tree singled out from the plethora of created things. This prohibition, although not oppressive, presented the primal pair with the serious question of limits.

Nothing in the text indicates that God wished to teach Adam and Eve anything by this restriction. The Yahwist makes the point at the beginning that human beings are subject to God's commands unequivocally and that historical existence means existence within limits. No reason is given for this; it is simply the way it is. We are finite beings. Human life everywhere is lived within limits. Our relation to limits provides the essential context for ethics. The meaning of life in Paradise is obedience within the limits ordained by God.

The Yahwist tells us that humans are not the first to question the prohibition against eating of the tree; the first is the serpent. It is important to note that nowhere is the serpent described as an embodiment of demonic power; the serpent is clearly not Satan. He is part of creation, with the one qualification that he is "more subtle than any other creature that the Lord God had made" (Gn. 3:1). Although the meaning of this qualification is unclear, it could indicate that, even though humans think they are the "be all and end all" of creation, other more ancient life-forms may know much more about life's mysteries than we do.

It is Eve, not Adam, who engages with the serpent, and it is Eve, not Adam, who first plucks the fruit from the tree. Adam shows up only after the drama is essentially over and is dismissed with two words: "He ate" (Gn. 3:6).

The serpent opens the dialogue with a beguiling question: "Did God say, 'You shall not eat of any tree of the garden'?" (Gn. 3:1). The subtlest of all creatures begins by a slight distortion that makes Yahweh appear more demanding than He really is. God had welcomed Adam and Eve to eat of all the trees save one. This distortion draws Eve into the conversation by allowing her to defend the truth. "We may eat of the fruit of the trees of the garden," she tells the serpent, "but God said, 'You shall not eat of the fruit of the tree which is in the midst of the garden, neither shall you touch it, lest you die'" (Gn. 3:2,3).

In defending the truth, however, Eve also engages in a distortion. God did forbid them to *eat* of the tree, but God never forbade anyone to *touch* it. This overstatement betrays a weakness in Eve's position. The serpent had clearly touched a sore point that existed already. It is almost as if Eve were seeking to set further limits on herself by exaggerating. Perhaps she had been eyeing the tree for some time and had been agonizing about the single prohibition that confronted her. Perhaps her desires for the fruit had been kindled and only by forbidding herself from even touching the tree could she keep away. Was she frightened by her own instinct for knowledge? Why is it that whenever we are confronted by limits, we instinctively feel compelled to violate them?

The serpent now drops any pretence of inquiry into God's ordinances. He says simply, "You will not die. For God knows that when you eat of it your eyes will be opened, and you will be like God, knowing good and evil" (Gn. 3:4,5). This statement shifts Eve from simple obedience to the illusion of being able to judge God from a neutral position. The serpent suggests that God put the prohibition there because God was insecure about the extent of human potential. Was God reluctant about the divine gift of freedom to humanity? What would be the power of humanity without limits?

This is the genesis of Titanism, or hubris. In judging God one is no longer subject to the commands of God; now God stands subject to the questioner. The serpent knew that to get Eve to question would be to get her to trespass the limits of creation *with her mind*. What she then did with her hands would logically follow.

The subtlety of the serpent is to question the limits God has imposed and to induce us to think we are wise in doing so. The questioning of limits is the key to the serpent's deceit. It seduces us into justifying what we want by questioning the rules against having it. It allows us the illusion that we, the created, can stand in judgement of God, the Creator. But the pot at the end of the rainbow is tempting: One would be "like God" since one would know good and evil.

For the Yahwist, to know "good and evil" does not mean to know right from wrong. It is not moral knowledge that is implied here. The term was an idiomatic way the Hebrews had of conveying what we mean by "everything." The temptation here concerned omniscience. The fascination of the statement is in its lack of restriction. Moreover, here the Hebrew word "to know" means more than mere intellectual knowing. It signifies the much wider sense of "experiencing," a "becoming acquainted with." In the ancient world an ability "to know" implied always "to be able." Knowledge then, as it does today, meant power.

The serpent is insinuating to the woman the possibility of extending the exercise of human choice beyond the limits ordained by God at creation in order to "know everything." This would give humanity power equal to God's. Since the Hebrews linked knowledge with power, to *know* everything implied the ability to be able to *do* everything. Omniscience meant omnipotence. That the Yahwist understands our Fall as such, rather than as a plunge into moral evil, is utterly profound. The story of the Garden of Eden is not a morality play; it is about humanity's relationship with limits and our quest for power.

The greatest tension for humanity is that obedience is meaningless without choice, yet we cannot live without limits. There is a built-in tension between our need for order, because of our finiteness, and our exercise of choice, because of our quest for power. The divine gift of choice, the divine decree of limits, and the exercise of choice within the context of our obsession with knowledge and power comprise the great *complexio oppositorum* within which human life must be lived.

In and through Eve we exercise choice with an over-powering urge for absolute power through complete knowledge. We all would be "as God, knowing both good and evil." The imposition of limits triggers an overwhelming desire to violate them. We seek to know what is on the other side in order to gain power over the imposer of the limits. Perhaps being made in the image of God instills within us the urge to be like God.

The serpent neither lies nor tells the truth. He speaks no summons; he suggests simply that Eve use her choice to gain omniscience and omnipotence. The serpent personifies the shadow-side of choice and activates the ambivalence of choice. The subtlety of the human condition is that our limits are never very clear. The paradox of limits is that one does not know where limits really are until they have been violated.

Eve is offered knowledge but she must transgress limits in order to obtain it. Since the Garden, the certainty of the violation of limits has been inherent in every exercise of choice. The violation of limits is inescapably present as we exercise choice to overcome limits in search of more knowledge and power. Put theologically, this is "sin" and constitutes the shadow-side of freedom.

The sin of hubris is the root of Gilgamesh's misfortunes; it characterizes the essence of Greek tragedy; Mephistopheles uses it to beguile Faust. Hubris is a lust for knowledge in order to increase power, as opposed to a search for wisdom in order to understand more deeply and to serve more gratefully the will of God. Sin is a transgression of limits in search of power. The paradox is that sin is not possible without the divine gift of freedom, and, since the Garden, human choice has not been exercised without sin. Every human thought, every human act, every human endeavor is within the context of divine judgement upon humanity's obsession with the violation of limits.

Paradoxically, this is the work of grace, for it is within our obsession with knowledge and power—indeed, *because* of this obsession—that redemption is necessary and is achieved. Redemption precedes our seduction by the Serpent, even as Israel's experience of God as Redeemer preceded their experience of God as Creator. Humanity's "fall" in the Garden is a transhistorical event, which, like redemption, has its origin in God. Present in the Creator, it is embedded in creation.

It would be simplistic to place these events in chronological sequence: First there is creation; then the forbidden fruit is eaten; then God reacts, saying, "What am I going to do now? I think I will send Moses, then the prophets, and, finally, Jesus to die for everyone." God is thereby understood as being reactive, as playing catch-up to human initiatives.

The more profound interpretation considers that the original violation of limits, like redemption, takes place in God before creation. The cruciform nature of reality, manifested uniquely in the Exodus and the Cross, is profoundly true in history because it exists before history. History is thus the manifestation of the cruciform nature of reality inherent in the depths of the Godhead.

Pride is at the root of our incessant violation of limits because it is this overweening view of ourselves that leads us to transgress, even if unconsciously, the limits imposed in creation. To question God is to assume equality to God. To sin is to attempt equality with God by exercising the freedom God has given to violate the limits God has ordained. Eve's exercise of freedom, therefore, is distorted by the subtlety of her pride.

"So when the woman saw that the tree was good for

food, and that it was a delight to the eyes, and that the tree was to be desired to make one wise, she took of its fruit and ate; and she gave some to her husband, and he ate" (Gn. 3:6). This great violation of divine limits by Eve opened for us the horizons of knowing and the possibilities of power. Her exercise of freedom was the birth of human consciousness, the ability to differentiate, to "know good and evil." But because her motivation was pride, the result was not more wisdom but the first self-deception, not more power but the first experience of guilt. Consciousness was born, but freedom was further circumscribed.

The great paradox is that in eating of the tree Eve and Adam obtained neither total knowledge nor absolute power. Eve and Adam did not gain omniscience or attain omnipotence; they merely became aware of their vulnerability and their nakedness. By questioning God we do not gain the equality we seek; we only become more deeply aware of our insignificance. Violation of limits produces only awareness of vulnerability.

In exercising their freedom by seeking omniscience Adam and Eve realized for the first time the insecurity and the contingency of existence. This fear touched at the most inward and intimate level of their being: their "private parts," the symbolic channels of human creativity. "Then the eyes of both were opened, and they knew that they were naked; and they sewed fig leaves together and made themselves aprons" (Gn. 3:7). Rather than becoming all-knowing, they experienced shame.

Their illusory quest for absolute freedom and knowledge was cut off by the imposition of new limits. To the serpent God says, "Cursed are you above all cattle, and above all wild animals; upon your belly you shall go, and dust you shall eat all the days of your life" (Gn. 3:14).

To Eve, God says, "I will greatly multiply your pain in childbearing; in pain you shall bring forth children, yet your desire shall be for your husband, and he shall rule over you" (Gn. 3:16). To take up the theme of gender again, it is clear from this that the subordination of woman under man is understood by the Yahwist to be an unnatural state of affairs, not something ordained from creation. To have men rule over women was somehow a curse that women had to endure in an unbalanced world.

In the Garden Adam and Eve lived in natural equilibrium, just as humankind had during the countless millennia of the Paleolithic period. But with the Neolithic revolution, with the rise of urbanization and civilization, something unnatural occurred. When humanity upset its balance with nature, humanity upset also an ancient equilibrium between the sexes, which gave rise to the patriarchal subordination of women described by the Yahwist.

To Adam, God says, "Cursed is the ground because of you, in toil you shall eat of it all the days of your life; thorns and thistles it shall bring forth to you; and you shall eat the plants of the field. In the sweat of your face you shall eat bread till you return to the ground, for out of it you were taken; you are dust, and to dust you shall return" (Gn. 3:17–19).

Man is taken from earth and so is directed toward it. Earth is the material basis of his existence. This violation of limits created an imbalance not only between man and woman but also between man and earth. This imbalance will express itself in a silent, dogged struggle between the plow and the land, almost as if a spell were cast to deny the symbiotic relationship between man and the Mother Earth.

Here, again, the Yahwist discerns the implications of humanity's emergence from the natural equilibrium of our Paleolithic past. In the Garden nature prevailed, and women's mysteries enveloped the male. There were no questions raised when Eve, rather than Adam, took the initiative with the serpent. It was simply assumed that she understood these things more deeply than he did. In this sense Eve, which in the Hebrew means "mother of all living," personified the Great Mother Goddess. But at the very height of her power, she created qualitative changes in consciousness that broke forever humanity's relationship with nature and men's relationship with women. Even as women were now subordinate to men, nature was henceforth an enemy to man.

Punishment for transgression is balanced with the promise of redemption. God says to the serpent, "I will put enmity between you and the woman, and between your seed and her seed; he shall bruise your head, and you shall bruise his heel" (Gn. 3:15). With the imposition of new limits, God promises future redemption from limits: In time, another woman will engage with the ordering principle of creation, only her action will be to obey rather than disobey. Her son will lead humanity to life, but because of our obsession with knowledge and power for their own sake, only through his death. Through him, humanity will experience triumph, but only through crucifixion; will regain freedom, but only through the deepest awareness of and complete obedience to limits.

While in the Garden, the first man and woman lived in abundance without being conscious of freedom and knowledge. They became conscious of freedom only as they lost it by transgressing the one limit imposed on them. After transgressing the first limit, they discovered not equality with God but the bondage of further limits. They were driven out on the perilous journey of life in a fallen world, held continually—though unbeknownst to them—in the redemptive judgment and grace of God.

The human tragedy is that we have been violating limits ever since. Our choices have invariably been exercised in the spirit of pride and therefore in the context of an unending obsession with more knowledge and greater power. The knowledge we have sought has served only to increase our power, whatever the justification. This has been the pathos at the source of the fearful violence and destructiveness wrought by humanity since the Garden. The rebellion of Eve and Adam and the curses leveled against them are as real today as the snakes slithering through the grass.

Equally real is the discernment that the context for punishment is redemption. The awareness of their shame at being naked was the genesis of the human quest for restitution. Living within limits, Adam and Eve had been innocent and psychologically unconscious. Transgressing limits, their innocence was shattered by guilt, and their unconscious was replaced by the ambiguous gift of consciousness. Their shame motivated them to mutual blame, and, clothed by the loving kindness of God, they could only pray, "Come, Messiah, come."

The great insight of the Yahwist in his story of the Garden of Eden is this: that which merits the greatest judgement evokes the deepest grace. There is no judgment without grace, no grace without judgment. In Adam and Eve we experience our first contact with grace as piercing judgment, and our final experience of judgment, as overwhelming grace.

These insights of the Jews shaped the moral trajectory of Western civilization fundamentally. Combined with the later abstraction of Greek metaphysics and modifications by the Christians, they constitute the bedrock of belief, culture, and values for the West, even for the most secular amongst us. In order to understand civilization at the turn of this new millennium we must immerse ourselves in these deep roots at the heart of our collective past. They constitute our deepest identity.

CHAPTER 5

APOCALYPSE

One is no longer disposed to say it. And so each venture

Is a new beginning, a raid on the inarticulate

With shabby equipment always deteriorating

In the general mess of imprecision of feeling,

 undisciplined squads of emotion.

And what there is to conquer by strength and

 submission, has already been discovered

Once or twice, or several times, by men whom one cannot hope

To emulate—but there is no competition—

 there is only the fight to recover what has been lost

And found and lost again and again: and now,

 under conditions

That seem unpropitious. But perhaps neither gain

 nor loss.

For us, there is only the trying. The rest

 is not our business.[1]

1. Eliot, *Collected Poems*, 203.

A CENTURY AFTER THE FINAL DRAFTING OF the story of the Garden of Eden, Israel was no more. Northern Israel was taken over and absorbed by the Assiyrians in 722 B.C.E. A century later the Babylonians sacked Jerusalem and destroyed Judea. In 587 B.C.E. King Zedekiah, the last descendant of David to rule his people, was blinded and taken in chains to Babylon along with most of the Jewish ruling elite.

While in Babylon, the great prophet Isaiah prophesied that they would return to Canaan in a new Exodus reminiscent of when Moses had led them out of Egypt to Canaan seven centuries earlier. He told them that their sins had been forgiven and that Yahweh was going to restore them to glory beyond what they had known at the times of David and of Solomon. But after King Cyrus of Persia captured Babylon and the Jews were allowed to return to Jerusalem to rebuild the Temple in 538 B.C.E., they discovered that the new Exodus described in such glowing spiritual terms by Isaiah was leading to anything but the political glories of Davidic Israel.

Their return was not a release from captivity but merely a mitigation of it, for they were still part of the newly established Persian Empire. Indigenous peoples who resented and actively opposed their attempts at re settlement also confronted them. The Jews returned from exile deprived of their rights to have a king and to be a nation. Their "new Exodus" delivered them from Babylonian captivity into Persian colonialism.

With the spectacular victories of Alexander the Great in the fourth century B.C.E., the Persian Empire crumbled, and the Jews were again swept up in the wider context of world history. Alexander inaugurated an age of great cultural change destined to last through the conquests of Rome and Byzantium, until the time of the Ottoman Empire, some eighteen centuries later. Alexander's military conquests from 334 B.C.E., when he first entered Asia across the Hellespont, to 326 B.C.E., when he reached the Indus River, were motivated by the dream of "one world" united by Greek culture. Indeed, he considered it his divine mission to extend Greek scholarship, art, philosophy, and decorum throughout known civilization. Legend has it that Alexander was overcome with weeping when, standing on the banks of the Indus, he realized there were no more lands to conquer. He died shortly thereafter, age thirty-two.

Will Durant and Arnold Toynbee, perhaps the greatest historians of the twentieth century, concluded that as civilized as we think we may be, we have not yet realized the heights achieved by Greek civilization. After a lifetime of research and reflection, they considered the Greeks living twenty-five centuries ago, not the Americans and West Europeans of today, to have attained the highest reach of the human spirit.

With the conquests of Alexander, Greek became the language of educated persons throughout the Mediterranean world, and the Greek style of education, which emphasized logic, science, and mathematics, gained prominence. The essence of Greek philosophy, religion, art, and architecture—Man the Measure—became the watchword of late antiquity. And Greek politics, which produced the first experiment in real democracy, radicalized the entire notion of governance and began a process in the history of Western civilization that is evident even today.

Since one became a Hellene by education rather than by birth, an international community was forged out of disparate peoples who thought and acted in this new spirit. This put pressure on groups like the Jews to divide their allegiance and self-identities between who they were as descendants of Abraham, Isaac, and Jacob and who the Greeks challenged them to become as freethinking members of the world community.

Hellenization drew its appeal from the compelling and dynamic philosophies of Socrates, Plato, and Alexander's teacher, Aristotle. Moreover, the Hellenistic period inaugurated by Alexander's military conquests coincided with the introduction of two new schools of philosophic thought—Epicureanism and Stoicism, as well as developments in Platonism and Pythagoreanism. All of these contributed to the enthronement of reason as the hallmark of this era, posing a direct challenge to the religion of Judaism, which was based on the supremacy of faith. The wisdom of the Greeks and the meaning of faith for the Hebrews are subjects to which we shall return.

Although Persia had demonstrated benign neglect towards the Jews who returned from Babylon, the generals who succeeded Alexander in governing the eastern Mediterranean, Seleucis in Asia Minor and Ptolemy in Egypt, ruled with the arrogance of those who believed Greek culture was the wave of the future. Palestine fell initially under the sphere of Ptolemy I (323–285 B.C.E.) who ruled the Jews from his capitol of Alexandria in Egypt.

It was during the reign of Ptolemy II (285–246 B.C.E.) that Aramaic was superseded by koine Greek, and Jewish scholars began the task of translating various documents into the new *lingua franca*. It was during this period that the Old Testament was translated into Greek, called the Septuagint. Generally, the rule of the Ptolomys was tolerant and no coercion was used to compel the Jews to Hellenize. It is said of Ptolemy III (246–222 B.C.E.) that on a visit to Jerusalem he deferred to Jewish custom and made a thank offering in the Temple.

Things changed dramatically in 223 B.C.E. when Antiochus III, known as Antiochus the Great, came to power in Antioch, Syria, the capitol of the Seleucid Empire. After fighting with the Ptolemys for two decades over Palestine, he finally defeated Ptolemy V in 197 B.C.E. at Paneas, near the source of the Jordan River, and brought Palestine into the orbit of the Seleucids.

The Seleucids were vigorous in insisting that their subjects embrace Hellenism. Antiochus IV, known as Antiochus Epiphanes, was particularly fanatical about this policy. As a political descendant of Alexander the Great, he also claimed to be divine, in fact the manifestation of the god Zeus. His profile and the name *theos epiphanes* (manifestation of God) was stamped on all the coins of the realm. He proclaimed that worship of Zeus and, by extension, his own holy self, was the criterion of political loyalty.

To show his disregard for Judaism, Antiochus Epiphanes auctioned off the office of the High Priest and then issued orders abolishing Judaism itself: All copies of the Torah were to be burned, and observing the Sabbath, performing the rite of circumcision, and possessing the Torah became capital offenses. When the Jews defied these orders, he marched on Jerusalem in 168 B.C.E., desecrated the Temple by erecting an altar to Zeus in the Jewish holy of holies and sacrificing a pig, the animal most unclean to the Jews. He then proclaimed that all Jews must worship Zeus and eat pork.

Some months later, in the small town of Modein, northeast of Jerusalem, a Syrian general proclaimed the new edict. The village priest, a man named Mattathias, became outraged and killed the Syrian, as well as a fellow Jew who had been willing to bow down before Zeus. Mattathias then fled with his five sons into the mountains where they gathered a band of guerrillas. Their battle cry was the shout of Mattathias after killing the Syrian and the apostate, "Let everyone who is zealous for the Law and stands for the covenant come out after me."

On his deathbed in 166 B.C.E., Mattathias selected his eldest son Judas to carry on the struggle. Judas proved himself brilliantly and became know as Judas Maccabaeus (the hammer). Despite overwhelming odds, Judas defeated several Seleucid generals and regained Jerusalem from where he successfully negotiated a peace treaty, recognizing him as the ruler of the Jews. In December 165 B.C.E. he tore down the "abomination of desolation" to Zeus in the Temple's holy of holies, rebuilt the altar, and restored Jewish rites of worship, thereby inaugurating the feast of Hanukkah (Rededication).

In 162 B.C.E. Jewish religious liberties were recognized by treaty, and to many it seemed as if the political glories they yearned for were at last at hand. But again Jewish hopes were deprived of historical fulfillment. The successors to Judas Maccabaeus became compromised and degenerate until, under the reign of Alexander Jannaeus, domestic discontent grew to open revolt, and the reigning Maccabean king was drawn into a war with his own people.

In 64 B.C.E. the Romans marched in to "restore order" and in doing so ended up adding a Roman yoke to the forces of Hellenization. Again the Jews came under foreign domination until C.E. 70, when after sporadic outbursts, the entire nation rebelled. In retaliation the Romans destroyed not just the altar but the entire Temple. In C.E. 135 after yet another uprising, Jerusalem itself was destroyed, rebuilt, and renamed Aelia Capitolina, in which no Jew was allowed entry.

It is within this milieu that Jewish apocalypticism grew up. Beset by social upheaval and political alienation, by the loss of ancient institutions, by an utter lack of faith in and hope for any deliverance from their oppressors, and by a moral framework within which even their own religion ceased to make sense, many Jewish seers began having visions and premonitions about the end of the world.

After the original Exodus, Moses had promised Israel that if they obeyed the commandments and kept the Law, God would bless them. Only if they disobeyed would God punish them. Under the Greeks and Romans, however, the justice of the Mosaic covenant seemed to be turned on its head. Those of them who clung to the Mosaic covenant were not blessed but persecuted and killed, and those who apostatized were materially blessed and given status and honor. The hated Greeks and Romans administered rewards and punishments. The "God of our Fathers" seemed nowhere in sight. For the faithful, history had entered into the realm of the *eschaton,* the end of time. The outpouring of evil around them was such that only a complete termination of history would suffice to eradicate the injustice they faced and bring them their long-due rewards.

Apocalyptic thinking therefore expressed the agony of a people who were crying out for justice in a world perverted to its very roots with injustice. They were seeking retribution and vengeance upon their enemies but were powerless to do so. They were desperate to be delivered from this plight but saw no deliverer in sight. This was a people who had gone beyond the realm of paradox into the alienation of the absurd.

While the apocalyptists believed that the world was past redemption, they clung nevertheless throughout their despair to the cornerstone of the Jewish faith: Their God was a God who acted in history for their salvation. Amid the most profound alienation, they were persons of faith who could see within history, through history, and beyond history the workings of God's triumphant purpose for persons of every nation who were prepared to follow the way of wisdom and righteousness.

In the face of oppression by their Greek and Roman overlords, the apocalyptists believed in the ultimate victory of God. Amid the despair of seeing apostasy rewarded and orthodoxy persecuted, they asserted the hope that divine justice would finally prevail when God broke the bonds of history and worked the divine will. In essence, they were compelled by their situation to hope that human extremity would be God's opportunity, and that at the nadir of human sinfulness, the apogee of divine justice would save the day. The great denouement of history was close at hand. The cosmic warrior Yahweh would take the initiative as He had done in Egypt.

This ability of the Jews to maintain belief in God under circumstances that compelled ordinary persons to either curse God or be reduced to cynicism and despair is quite extraordinary. What empowered them was their insight that God was not a distant abstraction but an intimate partner in all their affairs. For the early Jews, God was not viewed as simply primal Creator of heaven and earth and the Ordainer of history. God was experienced as actively involved in and intimate with the world, demonstrating different aspects of the divine personality appropriate to their situation.

Thus the book of Exodus records that while still enslaved in Egypt the "people of Israel groaned under their bondage, and cried out for help, and their cry under bondage came up to God. And God heard their groaning, and God remembered his covenant with Abraham, with Isaac, and with Jacob" (Ex. 2:23,24).

God then appeared in the burning bush to Moses, saying, "I have seen the affliction of my people who are in Egypt, and have heard their cry because of their taskmasters; I know their sufferings, and I have come down to deliver them out of the hand of the Egyptians, and to bring them up out of that land to a good and broad land, a land flowing with milk and honey" (Ex. 3: 7,8).

The words of the prophet Hosea provide profound and sensitive depictions of this pathos of God. During Hosea's life in the eighth century B.C.E., Israel was in another period when evil seemed to be triumphant and the God of Abraham, Isaac, and Jacob seemed nowhere to be found. The whole nation of Israel had forsaken Yahweh and had given itself over to apostasy.

God commanded Hosea in a vision to exemplify the wickedness of Israel by taking a prostitute as a wife. This he did despite the bewilderment and ostracism of his friends and family. The woman, Gomar, bore a son. In another vision, God said to Hosea, "Call his name Jezreel; for yet a little while, and I will punish the house of Jehu for the blood of Jezreel, and I will put an end to the kingdom of Israel" (Hos. 1:4–9). Gomer then bore a daughter, and the Lord said, "Call her name Not Pitied, for I will no more have pity on the house of Judah." When Not Pitied had been weaned, Gomer had another son, and the Lord said, "Call his name Not My People, for you are not my people and I am not your God."

Hosea proceeded to prophesy to Israel the tenderness of God toward the Chosen People as well as God's intense anger at their idolatry. The Lord appeals to Hosea,

> Plead with your mother [Israel], plead—
> for she is not my wife,
> and I am not her husband—
> that she put away her harlotry from her face,
> and her adultery from between her breasts;
> lest I strip her naked
> and make her as in the day she was born,
> and make her like a wilderness,
> and set her like a parched land,
> and slay her with thirst....
> She did not know
> that it was I who gave her the grain, the wine, and the oil,
> and who lavished upon her silver and gold which they used for Baal.
> Therefore I will take away my wool and my flax,
> which were to cover her nakedness.
> Now I will uncover her lewdness in the sight of her lovers,
> and no one shall rescue her out of my hand (Hos. 2:2,3,8,9).

And yet, proclaims the Lord to Hosea,

How can I give you up, O Ephraim!
How can I hand you over, O Israel!
My heart recoils within me,
my compassion grows warm and tender.
I will not execute my fierce anger, I will not again destroy
Ephraim;
for I am God and not man,
the Holy One in your midst,
and I will not come to destroy (Hos. 11:8,9).

In the context of this poignant pathos Hosea proclaims that if Israel returns to God and embraces the covenant, God promises "I will make for you a covenant on that day with the beasts of the field, the birds of the air, and the creeping things of the ground; and I will abolish the bow, the sword, and war from the land; and I will make you lie down in safety. And I will betroth you to me for ever; I will betroth you to me in righteousness and in justice, in steadfast love, and in mercy" (Hos. 2:18,19). In that day, says the Lord,

I will answer the heavens
and they shall answer the earth;
and the earth shall answer the grain, the wine, and the oil,
and they shall answer Jezreel;
and I will sow him for myself in the land.
And I will have pity on Not Pitied,
and I will say to Not My People, "You are my people";
and he shall say "Thou art my God" (Hos.2:23).

It is clear from these powerful and beautifully poetic passages that for the Jewish seers God does not stand impassively outside history, beyond the realm of suffering and sorrow. God did not simply create the world and then leave us to our own devices. No, God is intimately involved with creation and genuinely affected by human actions. The pathos of God transcends the gulf between Creator and created; it relates God with humanity. The pathos of God is the link between God and humanity; it connects Eternity with our daily life, providing God a way of involvement and humanity a context for meaning.

The notion of the pathos of God is the essential point to be internalized if we are to appreciate fully the cruciform nature of reality and the expression of faith that the hand of God is discernible all things, in the light as well as in the dark dimensions. The pathos of God is the predicate of the inner connection between the Exodus and the Promised Land, the Crucifixion and the Resurrection, and, by extension, between apocalypse and Sophia, the Black Death and the adoration of Mary, and Hiroshima and the liberation of women. Without God's intimacy with humanity, there can be no cohesion between the opposites, no way for the Spirit to integrate all the aspects of existence into a holistic purpose, and no way for us to empower our life with faith.

Thus the pathos of God involves a supreme antinomy: on the one hand, God as loving and kind, hearing our prayers; and on the other, God as destructive and violent, using even nature herself to bring us back into a right relationship with each other and our Creator. Yet these two mutually exclusive experiences of the divine Pleroma must cohere within the deep holiness of Divinity Itself for God to be able to bring all the strands of life, history, and psyche together into a sacred purpose that redeems.

Apocalypse concerns itself with the dark side of this great antinomy, a situation in which the forces of evil hold sway, cutting off human beings from any sense of intimacy with one another, the earth, or their Creator. Paradoxically, this sense of alienation on the part of humanity is compensated for by an increased sense of intimacy, even vulnerability, on the part of Divinity. God hears the cries of the afflicted. Unable to be indifferent because God cares; God, like humanity, suffers in apocalyptic times. God, like humanity, is pained, and like the elect upon the earth, seeks vengeance, retribution, and a renewal of justice. Reacting to the growing evil, God spills forth a holy wrath of divine judgment.

The wrath of God, which the apocalyptists saw pouring out upon humanity, should not be seen as an anthropomorphic transference of lower human emotions to God but as an aspect of the Godhead itself. The wrath of God should not be seen as antithetical to the love of God but as a part of it, as serving it, even as the discipline of parents toward their children comes not from indifference but from love.

The wrath of God must be understood as a manifestation of the grace of God as it pierces rebellious hearts and minds. Wrath is thus integral to God's pathos; it is the way God's grace is known in the darkness of destruction and rebellion, the way we are confounded by the Holy One. The wrath of God, which spills unimaginable destruction upon the earth, must be understood as rooted in the grace that fills and moves out ceaselessly from the divine Pleroma.

There is something in all of us that finds the prospect of an intimate, much less a wrathful, God somehow quaint, almost abstract, particularly in such a secular age as ours when, for all practical purposes, we have dispensed with the "God hypothesis" altogether. Few believe in God in any way that makes a difference in how they live life; and fewer still retain any notion of pathos and intimacy with God.

Though we acknowledge that this was how the Biblical writers understood it, such a notion offends our modern sensibilities and our civilized opinions concerning how the universe should be structured. We want everything to be straightforward. We want God—if we allow God to exist at all—to be distant so we can get on with our life; to be on the good side, clearly wearing the white hat; and to have nothing to do with the darkness we decry publicly but are secretly tantalized by.

We leave the darkness to one side, fascinated by it almost voyeuristically, particularly when we hear of some monstrous crime or news event. Evil is treated as a mysterious phenomenon that disrupts life from time to time but not as a part of life and certainly not as a part of the divine Pleroma. It is within this context that Satan becomes useful, a little dustbin in the corner of an otherwise clean and well-lighted room into which the shadowy elements of the world can be thrown. But for most of us, Satan, like God, has become something of the past and is without much credibility in our modern world.

But when we go to our synagogues and to our churches for spiritual comfort and are confronted by the Exodus and by the Cross, we are compelled to look a little deeper, to consider the power of God in the ten plagues brought against Pharaoh, and to contemplate the love of God in Jesus, hanging lifeless upon a tree. Though we want to find

God only in the Promised Land, only in the Resurrection, we are forced by these great events to contend with the reality that God is present in the places we fear to go, that God is the Creator of the moon as well as the sun, the night as well as the day, the fall and the winter as well as the spring and the summer. We are challenged to recognize that the Eternal is the Eternal because Eternity infuses all things; the Holy is the Holy because Holiness permeates all things; and God is God because God is Master of all things.

Put simply, our religious traditions compel us to accept God's pathos and evil as realities. We must be willing to expand our understanding of the comprehensiveness of God to include the shadow and evil if the antinomial realities of the Exodus and the Promised Land, and of the Cross and the Resurrection are to be held together in a creative tension and be used to understand more deeply events such as the advent of nuclear weapons and the liberation of women. If God is the Lord of the light and the dark dimensions, then evil emerges with a numinosity and a value with which we must contend.

So, what do I mean by "evil"? By calling something evil, I mean some inner or outer act that in some way deeply violates and destroys life. I understand *natural evil* to be the presence of diseases, plagues, floods, earthquakes, and calamities of all sorts, including the tragedy of children born deformed or handicapped in some way. *Moral evil* I understand to be any action that has some connection with a human agent. In this regard, I make a distinction between *darkness* and evil.

Jung used these terms interchangeably sometimes. My view is that the dark dimension, the shadow, is not evil necessarily, although in our fear of the darkness we may sometimes call it evil. Something can be unknown, hidden, obscure, possibly threatening, and not easily accessible to the clear light of reason, but it is not evil on that account.

Darkness and evil operate on all three of the dimensions we have discussed: the commonsensical, the psychological, and the spiritual. The gulf—indeed the chasm—between these three ways of thinking and their ways of judging darkness and evil is enormous, even though they are often fused and confused in a complex pattern that hardens into a conventional "truth" that is often exceedingly difficult to get anyone to question, analyze, or search out in any depth.

On the historical level of life whatever act goes against social convention is often termed evil by those who feel that the act threatens the security of the clear–cut, black and white guidelines they need and believe society needs. We are all extremely susceptible to molding and influence when we are young. Many taboos and expectations are introduced very early, with all the authority of those semi-divine beings of our childhood—father, mother, teacher, rabbi, priest—so that a transgression or failure can awaken appalling feelings of having done evil.

This conditioning drives us relentlessly to do good, to win approval, to please our superiors, and to hide from others and, if possible, from ourselves, thoughts and actions we have been taught are wrong. Thus the eleventh commandment: "Thou shalt not be found out."

These guidelines of behavior are invariably given the sanction of religious tradition, which precludes any questioning of their validity. They are presented to us as the "will of God," even though they express social conventions, which change as society changes. Our notions of good and evil on the common-sense level of existence arise out of a complex socio-religious grid—almost a mold—which shapes and disciplines each generation into collective and fairly docile conformity to social norms. Thus Hamlet's statement to Rosencrantz, "There is nothing good or bad, but thinking makes it so."

Although this may seem to be a rather benign point of view, it is actually a treacherous position concerning good and evil. Such a perspective gives rise to a rootless and relativistic subjectivism by which it is impossible to determine any common morality at all; moreover, its logical extension is that the end justifies the means.

There may be a brief time of release and euphoria when old constraints are overthrown, but one can soon find oneself in bondage to a different master: the shadow-side of one's own personality with all the destructive effect this can have. Thinking one is free of morality but being, in fact, gripped by one's own shadow, one can engage in the most appallingly destructive activities without qualm because one views good and evil as mere social conventions subject to one's personal approval.

Deeper than any social convention is our personal shadow. This consists of all those aspects of our surface personality that do not fit in with the conventional expectations about what is right and wrong. The shadow can include all the anger, vindictiveness, pride, and sexual drives that do not accord with the loving, forgiving, self-effacing, and sexually correct person demanded by social convention. Dealing with the shadow is a complex and difficult problem, precisely because it contains all the elements social morays force us to hide.

For some, the answer is clear: Repress the shadow

firmly; keep it under iron control by sheer will-power strengthened by good habits. This point of view has the sanction of much traditional religious teaching. Indeed, some consider it wrong, even evil, to turn towards these buried drives and engage in any kind of encounter at all, for to encounter the shadow is to be exposed to its power. Danger and disaster lie ahead, we are warned, the first steps down the slippery slopes from which few, if any, emerge unscathed.

Novels such as *Dr. Jekyll and Mr. Hyde* express this point of view. Traditionally trained persons of any age are told that to express their shadow is to court disaster. And yet in anger can be much needed strength and resilience; buried in pride, much needed recognition of ability and worth; and hidden in sexual desire, much needed energy for seeking fulfilling relationships.

The old phrase "Cold as charity" refers to that straight-laced do-gooder whose fear and repression of their shadow robs them of the warmth and humility necessary to give doing good a human face. On the other hand those who delve into their shadow can be consumed by it and engage in awesomely destructive behavior.

Yet within the shadow are buried treasures that are the key to individual growth and fulfillment. Jung states quite clearly that dealing creatively with one's shadow is the first step towards individuation, towards wholeness. To call this evil because it does not fit into conventional patterns and expectations or because it can lead to destructive attitudes and behavior is to be destructive of life and is perhaps another form of evil.

To discern and engage with the creative elements in the dark depths of the shadow calls for a steadily developing consciousness of and an adult responsibility for ourselves as well as a willingness to recognize the possibility that in what can be and often *is* evil there is a creative element that can only be found and integrated if we risk encounter with the shadow. Not to do this exposes us to a danger that some traditional moralists may not recognize. Jung pointed to it in a chilling image when he said that what is repressed in youth may return later in life, knife in hand, demanding the sacrifice of what it was sacrificed for. This whole process of psychological growth in relation to one's shadow has deep spiritual roots that will be explored in the course of this book.

Jung was fond of quoting an incident reputed to have occurred in the ministry of Jesus, although it appears in only one manuscript of the Gospels, the Codex Bezae of Luke's Gospel. Jesus is walking through the fields on the Sabbath and sees a man working. He says to the man, "Blessed art thou if thou knowest what thou doest; but if not, thou art accursed and a transgressor of the law."[2] Being conscious of what one is doing and taking full responsibility for it is what matters in life, even if such actions are a conscious and deliberate disobedience of the law.

The dangers of this position are obvious and may account for its being recorded in only one manuscript, apart from the more basic possibility that it may not be genuine. But at least one ancient authority saw in this incident a fresh and radical approach to the root motivation of human conduct and valued it sufficiently to incorporate it into a major text of the Gospels as a

2. Erick Hutchison, "Evil: A Personal Exploration from Christian and Jungian Perspectives," unpublished, 4.

teaching of Jesus.

The willingness to engage with our shadow can lead to a dangerous shallowness and complacency if we lose touch with the terrifying reality of the deeper levels of intrinsic evil at work in the very fabric of our being. Deep within the shadow are more than just repressed aspects of our personality that social convention does not allow us to express. The shadow contains veritable evil. Indeed, one of the main objectives in any serious attempt to grow in consciousness is the development of the ability to discern clearly the reality of intrinsic evil at work in the darkness of the shadow, an intrinsic evil that no amount of consciousness can transform into a creative aspect of the personality.

The Ten Commandments imply that the drive to murder, adultery, theft, and lying is endemic, lies deeply buried in every human heart, and needs to be met with a firm and unyielding "Thou shalt not." Although we like to think of ourselves as being rational and basically good with a few psychological complexes and glitches here and there that must be worked out, we need to recognize that the reality of evil goes far deeper than that.

As difficult as it may be, we must take seriously Biblical statements such as this found in the book of Genesis: "The Lord saw that the wickedness of man was great in the earth, and that every imagination of the thoughts of man was only evil continually" (Gn. 6:5). Or as the prophet Jeremiah said, writing in the seventh century B.C.E., "The heart of man is deceitful above all things and desperately corrupt. Who can understand it?" (Jer. 27:8). Evil is not only real, it is present and active at the deepest historical, psychological, and spiritual levels of our being. It infects everyone, even as the goodness is there to inspire us all.

Whatever the relativities of social convention on the historical level of life, and whatever the dimensions of our shadow on the psychological level, the great antinomial reality governing evil at the spiritual level is that, stripped of all else, there is no difference—at least before God—between Mother Theresa and Adolf Hitler. However wide apart they may be in the relative good and evil of their life, they, like we, have evil as well as good buried deeply in their being. All of us are therefore called to a constant and full recognition and acceptance of that intrinsic evil at work at the deepest levels in us all, neither more nor less in one than in another. We all are made in the image of God; we all have feet of clay.

Buried as deeply as good and evil within each of us is the reality of grace. As deeply within our soul as the darkness that infects and the light that inspires, the Spirit is forever working. Therefore, even as we recognize the reality of good and evil at the level of Spirit, so it is at the level of Spirit that we experience the grace of God through which we are redeemed and transformed.

The theologian Karl Barth expressed this antinomy very succinctly when he said of the piercing grace of God interacting with intrinsic evil at this level of Spirit, "A Francis of Assisi is condemned by the Truth by which a Caesar Borgia is set free."[3] It is at these deepest levels that good and evil, the Exodus and the Promised Land, the Cross and the Resurrection cohere, separately *and* together, as one antinomial reality within the grace of God. This bottom line, where

3. Karl Barth, *The Epistle to the Romans*, *6th ed.*, trans. Edwyn C. Hoskyns (London: Oxford University Press, 1933), 288.

we *all* meet, is the one and only place of true unity and equality for the human race.

To say this is to allow the full impact of the mystery of evil and the mystery of grace to be united. At the level of Spirit, these opposites comprise an antinomial totality, which, try as we might, we neither understand intellectually nor accept rationally nor escape spiritually. It is only at this level that the problem of evil and suffering can be dealt with genuinely. The immensely deep living symbols associated with the Exodus and the Cross have the power to illuminate the darkest corners of human experience with meaning, to transfigure and to lead us through the evil to the deepest levels of human growth.

In the symbolic structure of Jewish and Christian faith, evil is seen as an inescapable parasite on freedom. Evil cannot be analyzed in isolation, on its own, as a self-evident reality. Evil has a terrible reality and power, but it must always be seen in its parasitic relationship with God's own freedom, with God's gift of freedom to humanity, and, further, with what God is seeking *in us* through the gift of freedom.

The possibility of evil came into existence with the gift of freedom. As we saw in the story of Adam and Eve, evil became actual when the first woman and man exercised their freedom to violate divinely ordained limits. The very nature of the gift of freedom implies that humanity is free to misuse it.

Freedom carries with it the capacity for an unbounded and destructive misuse of will in the service of an insatiable power drive that does not protect a child from being sexually assaulted; does not protect the innocent from being murdered; does not stop the Stalins and the Hitlers of the world in their continuous, unchecked violations of human life; and does not stop our civilization, with its unquenchable ambition to master the world and even life itself, from creating weapons of unimaginable destructiveness or from tampering with the secrets of the genetic process without any real understanding of the long-term impact of these actions.

The gift of freedom is the most terrible gift our Creator has given us, precisely because of the power and scope of the intrinsic evil that our freedom exposes us to. Our freedom is absolutely real, although it forms an antinomial reality of its own with other dimensions of human life. The responsible exercise of human freedom requires adult behavior and demands adult understanding.

Yet freedom is being exercised by countless millions of essentially unconscious, undeveloped personalities—like you and me—who have little or no idea of how to handle this gift. We have not been given a choice whether or not to have choice. We must contend with it as well as grapple with the equally troubling and compelling reality of evil for as long as we live.

Whether we would have accepted freedom if we had had a choice and had known all its horrible results for the entire human race throughout the whole historical process is an open question. We could say that it was a foolish, even cruel gift, and that God ought to have known better, or should have somehow led us to the exercise of freedom more slowly so that we could have employed it with more maturity and for more constructive purposes.

This is the view of the Grand Inquisitor in Fyodor Dostoyevsky's novel, *The Brothers Karamazov*. The Grand Inquisitor tells Jesus, lest he mislead the multitudes again during his brief and unexpected return to earth, that the Church has found it necessary to take the cruel gift of freedom away from believers out of love for those who could not handle it.

The Church tells its members what to do and what not to do, what to believe and what not to believe. Everything is laid down in terms of black and white, the very opposite of the uncertainty and the instability experienced with real freedom. Jesus died in order to give the freedom to humanity that the Church in its love for humanity found necessary to take away.

In the story of the Garden of Eden we can see how unstable the human situation is relative to good and evil and to freedom. In the highly complex symbolic structure that underlies and illuminates this story we come to see that God, in the exercise of divine freedom, creates human beings as limited, finite creatures and gives us commandments to guide us in living out our life within finite limits.

Concurrently, God gives humanity the gift of freedom, which we can use to debate where the limits should be, and the gifts of power and imagination, which we can use to test where the limits actually are, and, if we so choose, to go beyond them. Rather than using our freedom to walk humbly with God, content within the limits of creation, we reach inevitably for the fruit of omniscience, seeking to violate all the limits we encounter. Thus within the context of goodness we exercise freedom to transgress limits and find ourselves confronted by our ambitious inclinations.

As noted in the last chapter, Adam and Eve's misuse of freedom in exceeding the limits set by God results in the birth of consciousness, "Their eyes were opened, and they knew they were naked" (Gn. 3:7). This reveals the ambiguity of freedom and consciousness in the holy purposes of God. Freedom includes the drive, rooted deep within us, to stand in judgment against God. This is "sin."

Sin and its consequent evil are the shadow-side of freedom in this finite world where we are ceaselessly struggling through the reality of evil in ourselves and in others towards an ever-deepening consciousness and sense of responsibility. This is the purpose of the gift of freedom. We need the continuous encounter with sin and evil in the shadow-side of freedom to grow as authentic human beings.

For the Creator to give us the power to do the very thing we have been forbidden to do may seem like a cruel trick. Or it can be seen as a subtle circumstance that has the power to grip us and open our eyes to the paradoxical depths of what it means to be human, precisely because it catches and reflects the deep reality of the human condition.

Indeed, the whole drama of human life in relation to freedom and evil is fraught with ambiguity. The strange fruit borne by transgressing limits was the birth of consciousness. There the human race began its torturous journey out of innocent unconsciousness, through pride and rebellion, through sin and suffering, through good and evil of every conceivable kind, toward a growing and deepening awareness. The journey ended on Golgotha when a fully realized human being took the entirety of freedom and evil into himself consciously and deliberately and transfigured it in and through his own death, bringing redemption, healing, and the possibility of full maturity and wholeness to humankind.

Jesus could do this because of the extent to which his

own forebears had grappled with the same pattern. From the time of Moses, the high priest on the Day of Atonement had placed all the sins of Israel on an unblemished goat and had driven it into the wilderness. And even before the Jews, all the ancient civilizations had offered sacrifices to atone for wrongdoings. Transgressions and their expiation constitute perhaps the deepest awareness of human religious consciousness.

It is in this spirit that the Jesuit theologian Teilhard de Chardin wrote in *The Divine Milieu* that when a believer suffers, he or she can say, "God has touched me."[4] Not everyone can say these words, according to de Chardin, only those who have gone through a deepening of spirit such that they can perceive the hand of God in all things. Only these "touched ones" can pray:

> After I have perceived You as He who is a "greater myself,"
> grant when my hour comes, that I may recognize You under
> the species of each alien or hostile force that seems bent upon
> destroying or uprooting me...above all at that last moment, O
> God, grant that I may understand that it is You (provided only
> my faith is strong enough) who is painfully parting the fibers
> of my being in order to penetrate to the very marrow of my
> substance and bear me away within Yourself. The more deeply
> and incurably the evil is encrusted in my flesh, the more it will
> be You that I am harboring. Teach me to treat
> my death as an act of communion. (69-70)

4. Pierre Teilhard de Chardin, *The Divive Milieu*, trans. Norman Denny (London: Collins, 1960),69.

To be able to say, "God has touched me," is to be able to face the enigma of God's living participation in evil and in the ways we exercise the gift of freedom. God may long for us to use freedom responsibly, but God does not stop us if we do not. Though sometimes—and *only* sometimes—we are awakened by what happens, and we come to ourselves at the last moment before disaster; if not, we begin to suffer the practical consequences of our folly and repent of our ways. Is this the grace of God? Other times nothing seems to stop either the folly of thoughtless evil or the horrific destructive process of deliberate evil. Is this the grace of God?

In much of the Bible, God is seen clearly and unequivocally as the source and author of evil as well as of good, although this is never used as an excuse to exonerate humanity from its responsibility for wrongdoing. The paradox is stated bluntly as the experience of faith, with no attempt to adapt it to the categories of human reason or ameliorate it to the sophistication of human sensitivities. The prophet Isaiah, proclaims:

> I am the Lord and there is no other,
> I form the light and create darkness,
> I make peace and create evil,
> I am the Lord who does all these things (Is.45:7).

In Deuteronomy there is an equally strong statement:

> See now that I, even I, am he,
> and there is no god beside me;
> I kill and I make alive;
> I wound and I heal;
> and there is none that can deliver out of my hand (Dt.32:39).

"Does evil befall a city unless the Lord has done it?" asks the prophet Amos (Am 3:6). And there is Job's reply to his wife after she says to him, "Curse God and die."

"Shall we receive good at the hand of God," answers Job, "and shall we not receive evil?" (Jb. 2:9,10). These passages state clearly that God uses evil as an instrument of divine purpose, that God creates through evil, and that evil is part of the divine Pleroma.

One particularly interesting passage comes from the Book of Jubilees, written in the third century B.C.E. when the Jews were first beginning to interact with the forces of Hellenism. Though this apocryphal book was not included in the final canon, it is considered inspired writing nevertheless and is much read and quoted by Jewish and Christian scholars. In the Book of Jubilees, the evil spirits who rebel against God at creation are ruled by an angel called Mastema whose sole purpose is "to do all manner of wrong and sin, and all manner of transgression, to corrupt and destroy, and to shed blood upon the earth" (Jub. 11:15). After He and his angelic forces lead humanity into sin, God sends the Flood.

As the Flood approaches and the angels of darkness are being imprisoned, Mastema appeals to God to spare one-tenth of his hosts in order that they may be free to roam the earth after the Flood. God grants this request, fully aware that "they will not walk in uprightness, nor strive in righteousness" (Jub. 10:11). God spares evil, knowing that it will infect the creation again. God uses evil to serve the divine will.

Many will accept that, although this may be the God described in the Old Testament, it is *not* the depiction of God in the New Testament, which presents a gentle God of love. This notion is as widespread as it is misguided. The God of the Old Testament *is* the God of the New Testament. The central event around which the entire

New Testament revolves and without which Christianity would not exist, the Crucifixion and the Resurrection confront us with the same antinomial reality that confronted Moses, Hosea, and Isaiah.

In the Upper Room, on the eve of his betrayal and death, Jesus says to his disciples, "The Son of Man goes as it is written of him, but woe to that man by whom the Son of Man is betrayed. It would have been better for that man if he had not been born" (Mk. 14:21). In other words, all that is happening to Jesus, including his suffering and death, is in full accord with the will of God. But Judas, who sets it all in motion, is deeply and ultimately guilty, even though it is through his evil action that the will of God will be fulfilled. This gives us a glimpse, a frightening glimpse, into the harsh and subtle paradox that lies at the heart of the issue of evil and suffering on the spiritual level of existence.

Jesus makes this clear when, on his way to Gethsemene where he is to receive the kiss of Judas, he quotes a passage from the Old Testament prophet Zechariah, "I [God] will strike the shepherd, and the sheep will be scattered" (Mk. 14:27). In other words, from the ultimate spiritual perspective it is God who is going to kill Jesus, even though, from the common sense and psychological perpsectives, it is the deliberate evil of human beings that will be equally responsible.

The presence of the holy purposes of God for the redemption of humanity did not for one instant absolve the complicity of Judas, of the religious leaders, or of Pilate in the death of Jesus. They were completely guilty; yet God was inexorably involved, using the evil acts they committed for a purpose that redeemed them all.

In this profound network of symbolic interpretation of events that led to the Cross, there is no logical connection between the two perspectives. Yet we need to move concurrently on both levels: the historical level on which Judas, the rabbis, and the Romans were entirely responsible for the crucifixion of Jesus; and the spiritual level on which the holy purpose of God for the redemption of humanity was active.

We must remain completely aware of the inescapable and unyielding tension and disjunction between these perspectives. To take both seriously, to live out fully in ourselves the tension and disjunction as well as the redemption and the hope may give us a clue to what de Chardin means by "God has touched me." It is to experience the suspension between these opposites, which Jung described as "crucifixion."

"What shall we say then?" asks Paul in his letter to the Romans, "Is there injustice on God's part?" (Rom. 9:14). "By no means!" he answers, citing something God said to Moses during the wanderings of Israel in the wilderness of Sinai, "I will be gracious to whom I will be gracious, and will show mercy on whom I will show mercy" (Ex. 33:19). Paul also cites a statement to Pharaoh by Moses through whom the Lord declares, "For this purpose have I let you live, to show you my power, so that my name may be declared throughout all the earth" (Ex. 9:16). Paul concludes, "He has mercy upon whomsoever he wills, and he hardens the heart of whomsoever he wills" (Rom. 9:18).

Paul takes note of those who ask that if God is all-powerful, how then can God find fault with individual actions? Paul answers, "Who are you, a man, to answer God? Will what is molded say to its molder, 'Why have you made me thus?' Has the potter no right over the clay, to make out of the same lump one vessel for beauty and another for menial use?" Then calling to mind the example and prophecies of Hosea, Paul asks, "What if God, declaring to show his wrath and to make known his power, has endured with much patience the vessels of wrath made for destruction, in order to make known the riches of his glory for the vessels of mercy, which he has prepared beforehand for glory…" (Rom. 9:19–23).

Therefore when Isaiah speaks of the Lord creating evil as well as peace and when the Deuteronomist declares that God wounds as well as heals, they are emphasizing the point that the divine presence is in all aspects of reality. The statement that must come before and after every confession of faith is "I the Lord do all these things." There is no element in the entire range of human emotion or experience that is unworthy of God or beneath God's dignity to permeate and control. All the possibilities of human emotion, action, and thought are also possibilities for Divinity; indeed, they are only possible in us, the created, because they already exist in God, the Creator. We are made in the image of God.

Recalling my definition of God in the Introduction, even as our awareness permeates every part of our body, every exercise of our mind, so, too, the presence of God permeates every nuance of history, every aspect of human decision.

Equally important and in contradistinction with our intent, God's hand in all dimensions has one purpose and one purpose only: the redemption of creation. Whether it is to harden Pharaoh's heart to prepare the way for the Exodus and the giving of the law, or commanding Hosea to marry a harlot and have the children Jezreel, Not Pitied, and Not My People so that in time God could save Jezreel, have pity on Not Pitied, and receive again Not My People, God's wrath serves God's love always and without exception. "For from him and through him and to him are all things," as Paul puts it (Rom. 11:36).

That God is in every sphere of life is an insight Elie Wiesel presented starkly and forcefully in his classic book *Night*, which describes his experience in Auschwitz. During his internment, the SS hung two Jewish men and a youth in the presence of the whole camp. The two men died quickly, but the death-throes of the youth lasted for half an hour. Wiesel recalls, "'Where is God? Where is he?' someone asked behind me. As the youth still hung in torment in the noose after a long time, I heard the man call again, 'Where is God now?' And I heard a voice in the back answer 'Where is he? He is here. He is hanging there on the gallows....'"[5]

Wiesel's experience takes the pathos of God to an excruciating degree. Can we dare go further and, in the spirit of de Chardin's prayer, ask whether it is possible that this agonized youth could ever conceivably come to say in his heart, in some form or other, "God, you are touching me now. I recognize you in the hostile force that is bent on destroying me. It is you who are painfully parting the fibers of my being in order to penetrate to the very marrow of my substance and bear me away within yourself."[4]

5. Elie Wiesel, *Night* (London: MacGibbon and Kee, 1960), 75–6.

This possibility, in this eternal moment captured by Wiesel, frames the mystery of evil and the mystery of God's grace. It is a shattering experience to contemplate seriously God as hanging on the gallows and as present in the SS; God as executing death through the Nazis and as suffering death with the Jews; God as mysteriously active in provoking the suffering and as pathetically vulnerable to the suffering provoked. Yet through it all, God is working within a divine purpose somehow for our redemption as well as the redemption of the created order.

These possibilities constitute an antinomy of such depth, so antithetical to what conscious, civilized human beings believe about the world, that it is hard to express. At a minimum, such contemplation humbles us and keeps us from any glib platitudes concerning either the reality of evil or the reality of God, except to confess, in faith, that ultimately, in ways past our understanding, everything we can know or experience resides, from before the beginning and after the end, in the holy purpose of God. Yet to say this does not in any way resolve the mystery, diminish our personal responsibility, or do away with thoughts that can only haunt our deep reflections. Contemplating such an antinomy takes us into the very heart of darkness as well as into a light of blinding brightness.

André Schwarz-Bart, who lost his entire family to the Holocaust, wrote the book *The Last of the Just,* which grapples deeply and seriously with the antinomial mystery of evil in the hands of a gracious God. He begins with a story of a small Jewish community in the English city of York in 1185. On March 11 of that year, the Catholic Bishop William of Nordhouse incited his parishioners to attack their Jewish neighbors for killing Christ. In the general confusion, several Jewish families, along with Rabbi Yom Tov Levy, barricaded themselves in an old abandoned tower at the edge of town.

The Christians laid siege to the tower, and every morning at dawn a priest appeared, crucifix in hand, promising life to every Jew who apostatized and embraced the Christian faith. But not one of the Jews came out. On the seventh day of the siege the rabbi gathered the defiant community and, recalling Masada, said to his compatriots, "God gave us life; let us return it to him ourselves, by our own hands."[6] All the men, women, and children then offered their forehead to the rabbi for blessing and their throat to his knife for cutting. Finally, the rabbi took his own life.

There is nothing of any particular significance about this story, says Schwarz-Bart, for the history of the Jews is replete with martyrs such as these. Yet the deed of Rabbi Yom Tov Levy rose above the mere recording of tragedy and became a legend. To understand this legend, one must familiarize oneself with the Jewish tradition of the *Lamed-waf*, the Just Men, which certain Talmudists trace back through the centuries to the prophet Isaiah and his prophecy that a "suffering servant" would bring about the redemption of Israel.

According to this tradition, the fate of the world rests upon thirty-six Just Men, at one level indistinguishable from others, but at the level of Spirit anointed by God to carry the suffering of their fellow Jews, indeed the suffering of whole world. The tradition has it, says Schwartz-Bart, that "if even one of them were lacking, the sufferings of mankind would poison even the souls of the new-born, and humanity would suffocate with a single cry. For the *Lamed-waf* are the hearts of the world multiplied, into which all our griefs are poured, as into one receptacle" (4).

---

6. André Schwartz-Bart, *The Last of the Just*, trans. Stephen Becker (New York: Atheneum Press, 1961),3.

One very old text of the Haggadah records that the most pitiable of the Just Men are those who do not know they are so anointed. For them, existence is an unspeakable hell. During the seventh century C.E. Andalusian Jews venerated a tear-drop-shaped rock, believing it to be the petrified soul of a Just Man who suffered but did not understand his spiritual destiny. According to one Hassidic story, "When an Unknown Just rises to heaven, he is so frozen that God must warm him for a thousand years between His fingers, before his soul can open itself to Paradise. And it is known that some remain forever inconsolable at human woe; so that even God Himself cannot warm them. So from time to time the Creator, Blessed be his Name, sets the clock of the Last Judgment forward by one minute" (5,6).

As did the cries of Israel during their slavery in Egypt, the solitary courage and agony of Rabbi Yom Tov Levy reached the throne of God. God miraculously caused the rabbi's youngest son to be saved, even though he had placed his knife to the little one's throat. As Schwartz-Bart recounts it, Simeon Reubeni of Mantua, an Italian Jew of thirteenth century Italy, commented that this miracle had to do with a very deep stratum of the Jewish tradition:

> At the origin of the people of Israel there is the sacrifice of one man, our father Abraham, who offered his son to God. At the origin of the dynasty of Levy's we find again the sacrifice of one man, the very gentle and luminous Rabbi Yom Tov, who by his own hand slit the throats of two hundred and fifty of the faithful—some say a thousand.
>
> And there is this: the solitary agony of Rabbi Yom Tov was unbearable to God.

And this too: in the charnel-house swarming with flies was reborn his youngest son, Solomon Levy, and the angels Uriel and Gabriel watched over him.

And finally this: when Solomon had reached the age of manhood, the Eternal came to him in a dream and said: "Hear me, Solomon; listen to my words. On the seventeenth day of the month of Sivan, in the year four thousand nine hundred forty five, your father, Rabbi Yom Tov Levy, touched my heart with pity. To all his line therefore, and for all the centuries, there shall be given the grace of one *Lamed-waf* to each generation. You are the first, you are that one, you are holy."

O companions of our ancient exile, as the rivers go to the sea, all our tears flow into the heart of God" (8).

The descendants of Rabbi Yom Tov Levy traversed the centuries, all suffering in a unique and poignant way so that in some mysterious manner known only to the holiness of God, human life could continue and somehow benefit from their suffering. The final descendant was Ernie Levy who in full consciousness of this gave his life at Auschwitz.

This tradition of the Just Man helps us focus on and contemplate the existence of evil, much as the experiences of the Exodus and the Cross, the parabolic actions of the prophet Hosea, the insights of Paul, the prayer of de Chardin, and the horror of Auschwitz have forced poets, prophets, and visionaries ancient and modern to ask if there is a limit to the presence and suffering of God and if there are realms of conduct and conditions of evil that God cannot bear to behold.

The answer given two thousand years ago, as by Wiesel,

de Chardin, and Schwartz-Bart in our time when evil triumphed over the good, when apostasy replaced devotion, and when the elect were hounded, persecuted, and killed, was that nothing, absolutely *nothing*, was outside God's awareness and participation.

It is within this context that we turn to a parable written during this apocalyptic period of the Jews, which crystallizes the agony of their situation through the experiences of a single individual. This is the story of Job, arguably the most profound treatment of human suffering ever written. I offer it here to give more dimension to the general discussion about the complexities of good and evil as well as to delve more deeply into the suffering of the innocent, which lies at the core of the mystery surrounding the Just Man.

CHAPTER 6

THE TRIALS OF JOB

There is . . .

At best, only a limited value

In the knowledge derived from experience.

The knowledge imposes a pattern, and falsifies,

For the pattern is new in every moment

And every moment is a new and shocking

Valuation of all we have been.[1]

JOB IS THE ONLY PERSON IN THE BIBLE other than Jesus who is described as "perfect" (Jb. 1:1). He was one that "feared God and eschewed evil." He had seven sons and three daughters, was enormously wealthy, and was one of the elders of his city. He was "upright" before God and eminently blessed by God.

One day, "the sons of God came to present themselves before the Lord, and Satan came also among them" (Jb. 1:6). The divine counsel is convened and God asks Satan where he has been. Satan replies that he has just come from "going to and fro" upon the earth. God then asks if Satan has considered His servant Job who is perfect and upright above all others. Satan retorts that Job is perfect merely because God protects and blesses him. But if God would put forth his hand

1. Eliot, *Collected Poems*, 199.

and "touch all that is his," Job would "curse you to your face" (Jb. 1:11).

God takes up Satan's challenge, telling Satan he could do anything he wanted to do to Job except to touch his body. Satan leaves the presence of the Lord and proceeds to devastate Job: His flocks of oxen and asses are stolen by marauding Sabeans; his sheep, along with the shepherds, are burnt up by fire from heaven; the Chaldeans steal all his camels; and finally, all his children are killed at a feast by a great wind from the wilderness.

In the face of this devastation, Job rends his clothes, shaves his head, and falls down and worships God, saying, "Naked I came from my mother's womb, and naked shall I return; the Lord gave, and the Lord has taken away; blessed be the name of the Lord" (Jb. 1:21). And "in all this, Job did not sin or charge God foolishly" (Jb. 1:22).

Satan returns to the divine counsel, and God taunts him by pointing out that Job "holds fast his integrity, although you moved against him, to destroy him without cause." Yes, answers Satan, but "all that a man has he will give for his life." He challenges God to go one step further: "Put forth your hand now, and touch his bone and his flesh, and he will curse thee to thy face." Again God agrees, saying to Satan, "Behold, he is in your hand, but save his life" (Jb. 2:3–6).

Satan descends once again from the divine counsel and smites Job with boils from the soles of his feet to the crown of his head. Job sits in ashes, scraping his boils with a potsherd. His wife asks, "Do you still retain your integrity? Curse God and die." "What," answers Job, "shall we receive good at the hand of God, and shall we not receive evil?" (Jb. 2:9).

At this point Job's three friends come to him and are so moved by his grief that they sit with him for seven days and seven nights without saying a word. There ensues a magnificent dialogue about Job's predicament. It is clear that Job and his friends are convinced that the suffering inflicted upon him comes from God. It is on the basis of this agreement that their dialogues are held. Job describes his horrendous condition:

> I was at ease, and he broke me asunder;
>
> he seized me by the neck and dashed me to pieces;
>
> he set me up as his target, his archers surround me.
>
> He slashes open my kidneys, and does not spare me;
>
> he pours out my gall on the ground.
>
> He breaks me with breach upon breach;
>
> he runs upon me like a warrior.
>
> I have sewed sackcloth upon my skin,
>
> and have laid my strength in the dust.
>
> My face is red with weeping, and on my eyelids is deep darkness;
>
> although there is no violence in my hands,
>
> and my prayer is pure (Jb. 16:12–17).

Job's friends are very sympathetic to his plight but cannot agree that he is pure. The basis of their response is that no one is pure before God, not even the angels. Job's suffering must somehow be due to God's judgement for Job's sins. They exhort Job to submit to this divine correction and to admit that he is a sinner and that God is just.

Job, too, is convinced that his suffering is from God; indeed, Job's foul ulcers were considered one of the divine scourges. Job, however, refuses to admit he is in the wrong and proclaims his righteousness before God. He insists that God deal with his case directly. "I wish to speak with the Almighty, and I desire to argue my case with God" (Jb. 13:3). If only God would let Job speak to Him, Job argues, then he would ask without fear, "Let me know why you contend to move against me" (Jb. 10:2). After all, was not God his creator and the helper of all who suffer?

The novelty of this demand by Job is that he appeals to God against God. Though he rails against God's injustice to him, he is also certain that it is from God that he will receive justice. "Even now, behold, my witness is in heaven, and he that vouches for me is on high" (Jb. 16:9).

Despite this hope, the more consistent theme in Job's discourses is the lament that it is hopeless and impossible to expect only justice. God is clearly free of human morality; God establishes justice by different criteria: "It is all one; therefore I say, he destroys both the blameless and the wicked. When disaster brings sudden death, he mocks at the calamity of the innocent" (Jb. 9:22,23). The philosopher Martin Buber remarks that Job concurs with the prophet Isaiah here in believing in a "God that hides Himself . . . . This hiding, the eclipse of the divine light," says Buber, "is the source of his abysmal despair."[2]

It galls Job that there is no arbitrator other than God to whom he can take his case. God is the only arbitrator, and yet God is free and arbitrary. "Lo, he passes by me, and I see him not; he moves on, but I do not perceive him. Behold, he snatches away; who can hinder him? Who can say to him 'What doest thou?'" (Jb. 9:11,12).

God finally accepts Job's challenge to answer him and appears to Job as a whirlwind. In this tempest of divine almightiness, God demands to know "Who is this that darkens counsel by words without knowledge?" (Jb. 38:2). God appears content to flaunt divine power before Job. "Where were you when I laid the foundation of the earth? ...Have you

2. Martin Buber, "A God Who Hides his Face," in *Dialogues of Job: A Study and Selected Writings*, ed. Nathan N. Glazer (New York: St. Martins Press, 1964), 223.

commanded the morning since your days began, and caused the dawn to know its place?... Declare, if you know all this" (Jb. 38:4,12,18).

This appearance of God must surely have confused Job, for he was never in doubt concerning God's might; rather, he had believed that God's might was always an instrument of God's right. But God in the whirlwind breaks out of this narrow human conception. Job is offered no reason for the actions of God; he is only given a glimpse of Divinity Itself.

Still sitting in ashes, scraping his boils with potsherds, Job answers the Lord: "I know that you can do all things, and that no purpose of yours can be thwarted.... I had heard of you by hearing of the ear, but now my eye sees you; therefore I despise myself, and repent in dust and ashes" (Jb. 42:2,5,6).

Job fell to his knees in worship for the first time. He "despised" himself, for he realized that while he had been demanding that God be called into account because God had violated his sense of morality, he had, in fact, been an individual human focus for the intense conflicts and tensions that characterize the process of antimony at the heart of humanity's full experience of the Godhead. Completely marginalized and dwarfed, Job could do nothing else than repent in dust and ashes. Submitting to the extraordinary will of God in his sufferings, he thereby experienced true spiritual freedom.

Again, Aeschylus:

Drop by drop
Pain that cannot forget
Falls upon the heart
Until in our despair
Against our will
Comes wisdom
By the awful grace of God.

CHAPTER 7

SOPHIA

And what you thought you came for

Is only a shell, a husk of meaning

From which the purpose breaks only when it

   is fulfilled

If at all. Either you had no purpose

Or the purpose is beyond the end you figured

And is altered in fulfillment.[1]

A LL THAT FILLED THE VISIONS OF THE apocalyptists—the evil forces impinging upon the world, the evil inclination of the human heart, the outpouring of the holiness of God—must be seen as being deeply rooted in a purpose ordained by God to be worked out in history, leading inexorably to the creation of a new world-order.

The Jewish visionaries understood that the goodness, bliss, and beauty of a new age are brought forth only from the womb of the conflicted times of the old age. There must be death before there can be a new life; there must be the travails of the Exodus and of the wilderness of Sinai before the delights of the Promised Land; there must be crucifixion before resurrection. God is clearly Lord in each, creating the

1. Eliot, *Collected Poems*, 215.

evil, making the light, bringing the war, ensuring the peace, being eternally present in every moment, working in and through every human intention, whether for good or ill, to weave *all* the strands together for a greater good and higher purpose that serves the redemption of humankind.

Apocalypse is thus a supreme demonstration of the cruciform nature of reality: the opposites in nature, in the human psyche, in human history, and in the human experience of the divine Pleroma, all crashing together with a power that destroys, all serving a purpose that redeems.

The supreme paradox in all these things is that while the apocalyptists looked continually toward heaven for God's action, expecting fire to rain down from the skies and chariots to appear in the clouds, God was, in fact, working divine wrath and divine grace in much more subtle ways. God never appeared in the sky. Earthquakes, floods, famine, wars, and pestilence came to decimate humanity, but they arose within the natural order of things and afflicted believers and infidels alike.

What occurred was a great awakening of the human spirit, a renewed awareness of the coming of a great realignment of humanity and the world. But again, this did not appear out of the heavens; it came from within. The Jewish seers personified this awareness as *hochmah*; the Greeks called it *Sophia*.

The notion of a feminine aspect of creation and of the discernment of wisdom had been a concern of the Jews since the inception of Judaism. But it was the apocalyptists who prayed the most desperately for the wrath of God to pour down upon their enemies who spoke the most eloquently about Sophia. Although their *conscious* wish was for God to wipe the world away in a demonstration of political power, they recognized *unconsciously* that a new ordering of the world was at work and was being articulated by a feminine impulse arising from within themselves. The God they knew as power dispensed wisdom through the subtle and the sensitive.

The dilemma of the Jews during their apocalyptic period is similar to our dilemma today. We tend to pray for God to change an external situation, but when the Spirit comes, the transformation takes place within our soul. Though they yearned for vengeance, the prophets were seeking insight. Though they wanted their enemies destroyed, they were actually searching for the wisdom to understand.

The Jews never considered Sophia as a goddess; rather, she was considered to be a disposition of creation present in their history continuously, which surfaced with particular poignancy and force during times of deepest troubles. She was the handmaid of the Creator within creation, not a goddess in her own right. Sophia speaks of herself in the book of Proverbs:

> The Lord created me at the beginning of his work,
> the first of his acts of old.
> Ages ago I was set up,
> at the first, before the beginning of the earth.
> When there were no depths I was brought forth,
> when there were no springs abounding with water.
> Before the mountains had been shaped,
> before the hills, I was brought forth;
> before he had made the earth with its fields,
> or the first of the dust of the world.
> When he established the heavens, I was there,

when he drew a circle on the face of the deep,

when he made firm the skies above,

when he established the fountains of the deep,

when he assigned to the sea its limit,

so that the waters might not transgress his command,

when he marked out the foundations of the earth,

then I was beside him, like a master workman;

and I was daily his delight, rejoicing before him always,

rejoicing in his inhabited world

and delighting in the sons of men (Prv. 8:22–31).

Brought into being in "the first of his acts of old," Sophia belongs to the created order even though she is distinct from creation, almost a creature above all creatures. She was with God at creation, and she provides in and through creation the *ordering principle* that affects and corrects humankind. As Proverbs puts it: "God has founded the earth in wisdom and established heaven in understanding. By his knowledge the deep bursts forth, and the clouds drip with dew" (Prv. 3:19).

Another non-canonical but important book of Jewish antiquity, the Book of Sirach, speaks of how God "poured wisdom out upon all his works" (Sir. 1:9). This is not mere poetic expression but a description of a cosmological process, a bestowal of something unique upon creation that inhabits it mysteriously and orders it according to divine purpose.

This insight that nature itself is alive, vibrant, and responsive to humanity and to the will of God is utterly profound. The earth is not simply the dirt beneath our feet but a living organism with a separate will and a separate existence. Although contemporary society has essentially forgotten or ignored this insight, the prophets and seers of early Judaism assumed it in all their writings. They understood humanity to be part of creation, and because a single Creator created all, humanity is interconnected with everything.

The prophet Hosea drew attention to this some twenty-seven centuries ago when he warned the people of Israel that their violence to each other was affecting the earth: "By swearing and lying and killing and stealing and committing adultery, they break out and blood touches blood. Therefore shall the land mourn, and everyone that dwells therein shall languish, with the beasts of the field, and with the birds of heaven, yea, the fishes of the sea also shall be taken away" (Hos. 4:2,3).

A Chinese story as ancient as Hosea's prophesy puts a different emphasis on this theme. It concerns a village desperate for rain. The crops were withering and each farmer had turned against his neighbor. Finally, the villagers turned to a wise man who lived in the hills nearby. He promised rain but said it would take several days. He went back into his hut and began to meditate. After three days the rains came. The villagers were incredulous and asked the wise man his secret. "No secret," he replied. "I simply attained harmony within myself and nature responded."

One might assume from this that human beings have ultimate judgment on whether the world is in order or not. On the contrary, we can affect nature creatively and negatively, but we cannot rule her. Nature was here long before we arrived; she surrounds us completely during our brief sojourn upon our small planet; she will be here long after we are gone. She has a complex ecological awareness peculiar to herself, even as each individual has. Call it "Gaia" if you will but know that the earth has her own consciousness. Thousands of species have arisen within nature, held sway for awhile, then disappeared when they were no longer in harmony with nature's ways. Humankind does not have the final say. Ask the dinosaurs.

The ancient seers of Israel believed that nature could be used by the mysterious hand of God to address humankind at the level of Spirit. Thus the prophet Amos, a contemporary of Hosea, witnessing the wickedness of Israel and the natural calamities visited upon Israel during the reign of King Jeroboam II (786–746 B.C.E.), saw in the calamities the redemptive purposes of God. The prophet was given to see that through the pain and suffering caused by the calamities, the God of Israel was trying to reach the hearts of a hardened people:

> I gave you cleanness of teeth in all your cities [famine],
> and lack of bread in all your places,
> yet you did not return to me, says the Lord.
> And I also withheld the rain from you
> when there were yet three months to the harvest;
> I would send rain upon one city,
> and send no rain upon another city;
> one field would be rained upon,
> and the field on which it did not rain withered;
> so two or three cities wandered to one city to drink water,
> and were not satisfied;
> yet you did not return to me, says the Lord....
> I overthrew some of you, as when God overthrew Sodom
> and Gomorrah,
> and you were as a brand plucked out of the burning;
> yet you did not return to me, says the Lord.
> Therefore thus I will do to you, O Israel;
> because I will do this to you,

prepare to meet your God, O Israel.

For lo, he who forms the mountains, and creates the wind,

and declares the morning darkness,

and treads on the heights of the earth—

the Lord, the God of hosts, is his name (Am. 4:6–13).

Paul develops this theme even further in the New Testament, stating in his letter to the Romans that,

> The creation waits with eager longing for the revealing of the sons of God, for the creation was subjected to futility, not of its own will but by the will of him who subjected it in hope; because the creation itself will be set free from its bondage to decay and obtain the glorious liberty of the children of God. We know that the whole creation has been groaning in travail together until now; and not only the creation, but we ourselves…groan inwardly as we wait for adoption as sons, the redemption of our bodies. For this hope we were saved (Rom. 8:20–24).

Here we see the insight that the created order is subjected to bear the impact of humanity's ceaseless relationship to and transformation of power. Not by her own will but by the will of the Creator, nature is subjected to "futility" as humanity's obsession with power devastates her. Yet she endures this "in hope" because the Creator is working through our exercise of untransformed power to bring about power transformed. Thus, humanity and the earth alike have been "groaning in travail together until now" as humanity awaits the "redemption of our bodies." It is "in this hope that we are saved," writes Paul.

In these passages we see the profound and infinitely complex relationship between Creator and created, between one human being and another, and between humanity and the earth. On the one hand humanity is part of nature and yet has dominion, but not ultimate power, over nature. On the other hand nature, compelled to bear part of the consequences of our exercise and misuse of power, is used by the Creator to affect the transformation of human power. Herein lies the sacred bond between humankind and the earth, this blood-stained partnership, as both await their redemption.

Sophia, embedded in creation, is ever-active in the affairs of humankind. She calls to us individually, wooing us towards her, encouraging us by direct address. Sophia is objectified not as an attribute of God but as an attribute of the world, specifically that *ordering principle in creation* that engages us so that she may bring order to our life. Again Proverbs:

> Does not wisdom call,
> does not understanding raise her voice?
> On the heights beside the way,
> in the paths she takes her stand;
> beside the gates at the entrance to the town,
> at the entrance of the portals she cries aloud;
> "To you, O men, I call,
> and my cry is to the sons of men.
> O simple ones, learn prudence;
> O foolish men, become sensible at heart.
> Hear, for I will speak noble things,
> the opening of my lips is righteousness;
> for my mouth will utter truth;
> wickedness is an abomination to my lips" (Prv. 8:1–7).

Sophia is not hidden in creation. She calls out to humanity to hearken to her voice. She is accessible not to just the initiates of the esoteric mysteries, as it was in the mystery religions that pervaded the Mediterranean world at that time. Sophia shouts from the city gates so that we all can hear her:

> Take my instruction instead of silver,
> and knowledge rather than choice gold;
> for wisdom is better than pearls,
> and no jewel can compare with her.
> I, wisdom, am neighbor to prudence,
> and I have knowledge and discretion at my disposal
> (Prv. 8:10–12).

Sophia promises:

> He who finds me has found life
> and obtains God's favor.
> He who listens to me dwells secure
> and is safe from the terror of disaster (Prv. 1:33).

The sages of Israel taught that we are all addressed from creation by an ordering principle from which we cannot escape. And we are addressed *personally*:

> Then you will understand righteousness and justice
> and equity, every good path;
> for wisdom will come into your heart,
> and knowledge will be pleasant to your soul;
> discretion will watch over you,
> understanding will guard you,
> to save you from the way of evil,
> from the man of perverted speech...
> so that you might walk in the way of goodness
> and keep to the paths of the righteous (Prv. 2:9–12,20).

Sophia's call also affects the life of nations:

By me kings reign,

and rulers decree what is just.

By me princes and nobles rule,

and all righteous judges (Prv. 8:15–16).

Indeed, the power and the force of Sophia pervade the earth, uniting every aspect of creation, including the human community, into a single "possession." In the book of Sirach, Sophia proclaims:

I came forth from the mouth of the Most High

and covered the earth like a mist.

I pitched my tent on the heights,

and my throne was on a pillar of cloud.

Alone, I wandered round the circle of heaven

and entered into the depths of the abyss.

In the waves of the sea, in the whole earth,

among every people and nation I have acquired a posses-

sion (Sir. 24:3–6).

In the ancient Near East, the expression "to walk around a place" had a definite legal symbolism. It signified the completion of a legal action, either actual or spoken. Sophia is assuming her proprietary rights, which encompass heaven and earth, the heights and the abyss, the waves of the sea, and the human heart. She rules the whole world by right of possession. Having come forth from the "mouth of the Most High," she covers the earth "like a mist."

Sophia is regal; she is omnipresent; she addresses each aspect of creation with penetrating truth. She loves creation, particularly the meek of heart and the vulnerable.

As Proverbs puts it, Sophia says to us:

> Whoever is inexperienced, let him turn in here;
> whoever has little understanding....
> Come, eat my food
> and drink the wine which I have mixed (Prv. 9:1–5).

Sophia's work is cruciform. Something happens to us when we embark on the quest for knowledge. Reason soon encounters its opposite; it is addressed by the voice of the divine primeval order. Indeed, this "wisdom" addresses us specifically from the place where reason wants to go but cannot reach.

The mystery of the world comes to us, almost as if it were inside us and yet beyond what we could ever reach. Therefore, the sages of Israel teach us to "Love her, and she will guard you" (Prv. 4:6); "Approach her with your whole heart" (Sir. 6:26); "She will honor you if you embrace her" (Prv. 4:8). Sophia, in return, says, "I love those who love me, and those who seek me will find me" (Prv. 8:17), even going so far as to say, "Whoever pays heed to me will lie down in my innermost rooms" (Sir. 4:15).

We are called upon to open our heart with delight to a meaning that comes towards us from creation itself. We are urged to search for and to uncover a mystery that has already found us and offered us her "innermost rooms." The wise ones of Israel taught that to find wisdom one must live in a relationship of obedience to the mysterious order of creation itself. To use Jung's terminology in relation to the psyche, wisdom is the fruit of the ego's opening in genuine humility to being lead by the Self. Wisdom comes at the point where we say, "Not my will but thine be done," where we, having submitted our will to the divine will, our life broken and shattered, experience freedom.

In the end, Sophia's message to humankind is a warning against seeking autonomy from God. In gaining entry
to her "innermost rooms" one is given the recognition that
all of life, the good as well as the evil, can only be understood and creatively dealt with "in God" and according to
the structures inherent in creation. Sophia serves as God's
ordering principle in creation and thus teaches the wisdom
of limits inherent in creation. Only by adhering to these
limits can power be transformed from the obsession to
know in order to control into an understanding that the
beginning and end of knowledge is faith and that the goal
of power is service.

The teachings of Israel's traditional wisdom surpass
what we moderns might consider "objective material
knowledge." They deal with perceptions that have been
developed about a truth already decided on. Faith
becomes the basis of knowledge. Faith *shapes* knowledge.
Thus truth has more to do with *character* than with intellect. One is considered to be "wise" only when one allows
one's whole way of life to be modeled on the interface of
faith and knowledge, a way of life that puts the premium
on *values* rather than on the acquisition of facts. This
distinction has profound consequences for how we understand and exercise power.

Sophia contrasts the "wise one" with the "fool." A fool
is not one who has an intellectual defect; a fool is one who
is unwilling to accommodate himself or herself to the
ordering principle of creation. The fool is undisciplined
and out of control of his or her passions. Folly is a lack of
order in one's innermost being, a lack that often defies all
instruction and engenders the illusion that the fool is in

control. The wise listen to Sophia, adhere to her counsel, and align their personal life with the ordering principle. The fool ignores Sophia, living reactively to events and inner impulses, and is therefore out of alignment with the ordering principle of creation.

Recognition of and submission to the inescapable reality of God and the cruciform structures of creation are the deepest issues with which the traditional wisdom of Israel deals. When truth is offered, obedience is demanded. Whoever refuses to accept truth exposes himself or herself to moral judgment, for what is being misjudged is not humanity, not even the world, but God. As Proverbs says, the fool "rages" against God (Prv. 19:3); and "the fool says in his heart, 'there is no God'" (Prv. 14:1).

For the Jews, wisdom begins with the "fear of the Lord," an expression with many connotations. The simplest statement comes in Job, "The fear of the Lord, that is wisdom, and to depart from of evil is understanding" (Jb. 28:28). Proverbs puts it slightly differently, "The fear of the Lord is training for wisdom, and before honor comes humility" (Prv. 15:33).

The word "fear" in this context focuses attention on ultimate awe; to "fear" God is to recognize the ultimate *centrality* of God. The "fear of the Lord" is the recognition that we are not the center of the world; God is. It involves the willingness to live life in accordance with this recognition. Only in the humility of the "fear of the Lord" can we pray, "Not my will but thine be done."

The assertion that all human knowledge revolves around the question of commitment to God summarizes not only Israel's wisdom tradition but also the entire Hebrew theory of knowledge. Knowing that the "fear of the Lord" is the beginning of wisdom was one of Israel's most precious possessions.

Israel offered the world the conviction that it is only genuine knowledge of God that puts us in a proper relationship with the objects of our perception. Faith in God enables us to know with more acuity and wholeness the world in which we live. Faith does not hinder knowledge. Faith *liberates* knowledge. Faith enables us to realize the true ground of our being; it offers us the context for authentic living and for relating to others and to the earth; and it protects us from the pride of thinking that our mind and intellect are the final authority.

This belief by the ancient Israelites is utterly profound. It demonstrates their awareness that what we think we know is shaped by what we believe, and that our philosophical attitudes about life determine how we arrange the facts, the raw data of life. There is no neutral knowledge, no matter how much we would like there to be. The "scientific" world-view insists that we operate on "just the facts, ma'am, nothing but the facts." But there is no such thing. As Kant and Jung remind us constantly, everything is filtered through our a priori categories of cognition. And as Heisenberg discovered, the observer, through the simple act of observing, alters what is being observed. Belief shapes knowledge. The objective world is discovered, defined, and altered by subjectivity.

The ancient Israelites, intuiting what scientists are only beginning to rediscover today, knew that there are only two choices about the faith that shapes all knowledge: secular faith in one's self, a finite being in a complex universe: the path of the fool; or spiritual faith in God, the Redeemer and Creator of the universe: the path of the wise. To begin and end with ourselves leads inevitably to pride and, eventually, to destruction. This is folly. To begin and end with God leads inevitably to humble obedience and, paradoxically, to freedom. This is wisdom.

Belief shapes knowledge and can, of course, distort both. Conflict can arise when authentic insights become dogma and when experience ceases to liberate what is known and is forced into a grid of hardened so-called "truth." Then pseudo-knowledge and pseudo-truth conflict with reality. This is true in the development of scientific theories; it is certainly true of religious belief. We must continually guard against confusing living "in God" with any particular religious or sectarian dogma. Living in the "fear of the Lord" requires an attitude of awe at and openness to the mysteries of life. Any system of belief is, in the end, an intellectual attempt to quantify the Unquantifiable, to control the Uncontrollable, and to know the Unknowable.

The interface between faith and knowledge must remain dynamic and dialectic, always challenging us to either modify or to leave the old and to embrace the new. There can be no "orthodox" belief in either science or faith, and we ought not to let something pass uncritically just because it presents itself to us as orthodoxy.

Orthodoxy seeks to define in order to control; wisdom presents humanity with an awareness of our fragility and contingency. Sophia makes us aware time and again that we are not the center of the universe and that because of this, we are subject to being buffeted and victimized by forces and events outside our control. Everything about our life is contingent. We may be one of only two players in the cosmic drama of covenant, but in the face of the reality of God, we are mere specks, specks that have a place in the eternal purpose of God, but specks nevertheless.

Proverbs says, "All the ways of man are pure in his own eyes, but it is Yahweh who tests the spirits" (Prv. 16:2); and, "The arrangements of the mind belong to man, but the answer of the tongue comes from Yahweh" (Prv. 16:1). To human beings belong the "arrangements of the mind"—the framing of plans, the exercise of intellect and will in history. This is what I have called pragmatic choice. But all our schemes and manipulations of reality accomplish little. God is the incalculable element who decides the fate of our "arrangements." Thus, "A man's mind thinks out his own way, but Yahweh directs his step" (Prv. 16:9); and, "Many plans are in a man's mind, but Yahweh's decree endures" (Prv. 19:4).

We are not dealing here with something the human mind could know if it tried; it is something it can *never know*, as Faust discovered after selling his soul for unlimited knowledge. As Jeremiah says, "I know, O Lord, that a man does not have his way in his own power; no one who walks succeeds in directing his own steps" (Jer. 10:23). Rather than despairing at this, the sages of old saw God's beneficence in this: God can protect us even from ourselves. As Proverbs puts it, "There is no wisdom, no understanding, no counsel against God. The horse is made ready for the day of battle, but it is God who gives the victory" (Prv. 21:30).

The gift of Sophia is not to discourage us from preparing for battle because God is going to take care of everything. No, her aim is to put a stop to the erroneous notion that success can be guaranteed by human effort alone. In every human vision, in every human action, God is the chief agent and final arbiter. All human activity must remain open to the mystery of divine activity, for between the putting into practice of the most carefully thought out scheme and its outcome lies the unfathomable Unknown.

It is our neat categories, our logical belief structures, and our dogmatic orthodoxies that Sophia assaults with the cruciform principles of reality. Her final "No" to all of our carefully constructed edifices takes place in the Exodus and on the Cross. Self-importance cannot be combined with trust in God, nor can Sophia herself become the object of trust. The locus of trust and faith must ultimately and always rest in God. Thus the prophet Jeremiah advises:

> Let not the wise man glory in his wisdom,
> let not the mighty man glory in his might,
> let not the rich man glory in his riches.
> But let him who glories glory in this,
> that he has understanding and knows me,
> that I am the Lord who practices kindness,
> justice and righteousness on earth;
> for in these things do I delight (Jer. 9:23,24).

In their darkest hour, the Jews intuited a most profound truth: The chaos afflicting them was destroying them as a nation and yet was simultaneously yielding a new ordering principle, which was beckoning them to a higher sense of truth, to a deeper commitment of faith, to a firmer belief that, before the beginning and after the end, God reigns supreme. It is almost as if they intuited something akin to a moral chaos theory.

At the point when their world seemed the most random and pointless, an order emerged out of their disorder. In fact, inherent in and emerging from their disorder was the new order for which they were praying. They were looking for it to come from outside, from God above history, to replace their disorder within history. But it came from within history, a new ordering of the already created, not a command from the Creator for a new creation; and it was experienced in feminine, not masculine, terms. The darkness without had activated the feminine within.

Sophia, the ordering principle of creation itself, arose out of their darkness, emanating from the depths of their soul and from the earth herself, speaking to them about the moral bedrock of life and about the redemption that comes when a suffering people learn anew the wisdom of limits. Sophia promulgated her cruciform wisdom, not exclusively for the elite but for everyone to hear: Their deliverance was to be not at the level of mundane politics but at the level of psyche and spirit.

It was at this point of strongest tension, deepest suffering, and most profound insight that historic circumstance and inner transformation collided for the Jewish people. Their world was indeed ending, as the apocalyptists prophesied. The Mosaic promise of blessings for obedience, curses for disobedience became interwoven with the politics of colonialism, as first the Greeks and then the Romans conquered their land, subjugated them to servitude, and mocked and inverted their Mosaic covenant.

Their visions of the end of time and the beckoning of Sophia took place as the Romans were destroying them as a nation. They rebelled, of course, but in the end Jerusalem was destroyed and placed off limits to any Jew. Masada came a few years later. The Diaspora had begun. Their end became their beginning.

Paradoxically, this denouement came just as they

produced their last and greatest prophet, Jesus of Nazareth. He was destined to fill the old wineskins of Judaism with new wine and generate a new religious consciousness. Though the Jews rejected it, this new consciousness was destined to become a universal religion. Just at the point when they thought their world was ending, the Jews ushered in a new world-order. And they did so with someone who spoke with all the power and subtlety of Sophia, who was, in fact, to be called the Sophia of God.

CHAPTER 8

MARY

I said to my soul, be still, and let the dark come upon you

Which shall be the darkness of God....

I said to my soul, be still, and wait without hope

For hope would be hope for the wrong thing; wait

　without love

For love would be love of the wrong thing; there is

　yet faith

But the faith and the love and the hope are all in

　the waiting.

Wait without thought, for you are not ready for thought:

So the darkness shall be the light, and the stillness

　the dancing.[1]

THE GRANDEUR OF JESUS WAS POSSIBLE ONLY because of the obedience of his mother. Mary, a woman exquisitely attuned to the wisdom of Sophia, emerges as the great counterpoint to Eve. ————— As it was Eve who led humanity to transgress limits by her *disobedience*, so it is Mary's

1. Eliot, *Collected Poems*, 200.

obedience that made possible the birth of the one for whom humanity had waited since the original transgression. Both women either broke or accepted limits, in disobedience or in obedience, to make possible the subsequent actions of their male counterparts. Thus Mary, linked with Christ, plays an important part in Church theology. She is seen as a *mediatrix of graces*, interceding on our behalf before the throne of God.

What is known about Mary historically is highly ambiguous and limited to accounts in the Gospels and in the book of Acts. Matthew offers the most puzzling characterization of Mary. Like Luke, Matthew traces the genealogy of Jesus through Joseph, but unlike Luke, he traces Jesus back to Abraham; Luke traces Jesus back to Adam. Matthew's genealogy is interesting because he not only traces Jesus' ancestry by a different family tree than Luke does, he also makes no effort to cover up the irregularity of Jesus' birth.

This was an audacious way to start a book for a Jewish readership about "the Christ." The Torah makes it clear that "no descendant of an irregular union, even down to the tenth generation, shall become a member of the Assembly of the Lord" (Dt. 32:2). Yet Matthew seems to emphasize that irregularities were notable in Jesus' lineage, as if to argue by implication that human frailty can be as much an instrument of God's grace as the most legitimate of human actions.

No women are included in Luke's genealogy, but Matthew points to four women in Jesus' lineage who gave birth to one of Jesus' ancestors through dubious sexual relations. The first is Tamar, the mother of Perez and Zarah, who lived in the seventeenth century B.C.E. She became pregnant with these forebears of "the Christ" by disguising herself as a prostitute and having incestuous sex with her father-in-law, Judah, son of Jacob and one of the twelve patriarchs of Israel. The second woman is Rahab, from the thirteenth century B.C.E., a common harlot and not even a Jew, who lived in Jericho and protected the spies Joshua sent. She eventually married Salmon, a descendent of Judah's.

The third woman is Ruth of the eleventh century B.C.E., a Moabitess, meaning that she was the fruit of incest between Lot and his eldest daughter after the fall of Sodom and Gomorrah. Ruth gained entry into the Messianic line by the fairly shameless sexual exploitation of her kinsman Boaz, a descendent of Salmon. In fact, Boas likens her to Tamar. Their son, Obed, was the grandfather of King David.

David, who reigned from 1,000 to 961 B.C.E., brings the fourth irregularity into the Messianic line through his liaison with Bathsheba. David had an adulterous relation with Bathsheba before he had her husband, Uriah, killed in battle. The offspring of their adultery was King Solomon. Matthew refers to Bathsheba in his genealogy as "the wife of Uriah." (In contrast to this, Luke traces Jesus' lineage through Nathan, another one of David's sons, born before David met Bathsheba.)

Finally, there is Mary who is introduced by the same formula as the other women. What are we to conclude from this except the obvious?

This does not imply moral condemnation in the least. Tamar was commended in Jewish tradition, which stressed not the immorality of her act but Tamar's desire—blessed by God—to share in the royal line from which she had unjustly been excluded. Rahab, too, was called blessed. Because she was a harlot, she could hide the spies sent by Joshua to spy on Jericho, thereby ensuring victory for the Israelites. The book of Ruth records that her mother Naomi's significant words, "May you do great things in Ephrathath and keep a name alive in Bethlehem" (Ru. 4:1), sanctions Ruth's stratagem with Boaz. Bathsheba, for her part, gave birth to Solomon, the wisest king of Israel; and Mary, of course, gave birth to "the Christ."

What is essential to understand here is that for Jesus to be a son of David and of the lineage of the tribe of Judah, he would have had to be born of the seed of Joseph, for Joseph, not Mary, was of the Davidic line. What was scandalous was Mary's conceiving out of wedlock, an act punishable by stoning under Mosaic Law. Yet God used this scandal to work redemption.

It is worth reflecting that Jesus' irregular birth followed closely the pattern set forth by the prophet Hosea, noted earlier, who was specifically commanded by the Lord to marry "a woman loved by another man, an adulteress" (Hos. 3:1). The Lord chose this method deliberately in order to raise children of promise who were to be called "Sons of the living God." The examples of Hosea's and Matthew's genealogies show that what seems to be a scandal in the realm of legal righteousness is sometimes the hidden work of divine grace.

The theme of God's blessing what the world considers weak, foolish, or scandalous in order to accomplish God's high purpose is a consistent one throughout the biblical tradition. Indeed, it is invariably out of the quagmire of human frailty that the divine alchemy is worked. Mary's premarital sex with Joseph is consistent with the biblical assertion that humanity's importunity is God's opportunity and exemplifies judgement and grace as bound inseparably in a redemptive *complexio oppositorum*. Her situation conforms also to the alchemical principle that lead must exist before it can be transformed into gold. Thus the powerful of the world are brought to their knees by the "foolishness of God," and the strictures of orthodoxy are shattered by the truths of heresy.

Matthew's genealogy is not meant to contradict the stories about the Virgin birth. The writer was affirming Jesus' descent from David *and* his heavenly conception by Spirit. As Paul states in his letter to the Romans, Jesus "descended from David according to the flesh and designated Son of God in power according to the Spirit of holiness" (Rom. 1:4). A scandal on the historical plane was the vehicle for the creative power of the Word, operating on the spiritual plane.

The Gospel of John affirms this point of view in its Prologue, which states that believers become "children of God" and are born "not of blood nor of the will of the flesh nor of the will of man, but of God" (Jn. 1:13). This is not to deny that believers have earthly existence and are born of flesh and blood; rather, it is to say that God works in and through our earthly life, which is full of magnificent attempts to be pure and strong but is nonetheless replete with deceit and shame.

As Jesus himself says to Nicodemus, one must be "born anew" to enter the Kingdom of God. "That which is born of the flesh is flesh and that which is born of Spirit is Spirit." Because the power of the flesh and the power of the Spirit came together dramatically at Jesus' conception, he had two distinct but interrelated identities: the one after the flesh, Jesus of Nazareth, born of Mary and Joseph; and the other after the Spirit, "the Christ." Hence the epithet "Jesus Christ."

The New Testament is not a bit embarrassed by this. "Is not this the carpenter, the son of Mary, the brother of James and Joseph and Judas and Simon? And are not his sisters here with us?" asks the writer of the Gospel of Mark (Mk. 6:3). Although Paul makes no reference in any of his letters to the Nativity stories, he joins Mark in this affirmation of Jesus' earthly family, asserting that Jesus had a sister-in-law through Jesus' brother James and that he (Paul) had personally met James, "the Lord's brother" (Gal. 1:19). Paul is quite clear in saying that Jesus was "made of a woman, made under the law" (Gal. 4:4). The Gospel of John refers to Jesus twice as the "son of Joseph" (Jn. 1:45; 6:42). The Gospel of Matthew states that Joseph had sexual relations with Mary after Jesus was born (Mt. 1:25). The Gospel of Luke calls Jesus Mary's *prototokos* (first born son) (Lk. 2:7), not her *monogenes* (only born son), a word used nowhere in the New Testament to describe Jesus.

Mary as blemished virgin and Mary as Virgin Mother is an antinomy in the deepest meaning of the term: two truths, mutually exclusive, yet deeply interrelated with and completely inseparable from one another; one pertaining to the flesh, the other pertaining to the Spirit. Both statements rest within the power of *bara*, the Hebrew word used only to refer to God's capacity to create something out of nothing that God in his absolute freedom chooses to create. The Word of God is sharper than any two-edged sword, piercing to the division of bone and marrow.

We know from scattered references and allusions in

the Gospels that Mary seemed to live an ordinary life. She seemed to endure the commonplace and the obscure, to be anxious in the face of the unknown, unsure of her son's destiny. The Gospel of Luke records that when Jesus was twelve and stayed behind in the Temple, she reproached him, saying, "Son, why hast thou done so to us? Behold, thy father and I have sought thee, sorrowing." Jesus replies coolly, "I must be about my father's business" (Lk. 2:48,49). Luke records two other occasions during Jesus' youth when Mary did not seem to understand the implications Jesus' identity (Lk. 2:33,50).

The Gospel of John recounts that when Jesus performed his first miracle at Cana, he rebuked his mother when she attempted to speed up things, saying, "O woman, what have you to do with me? My hour has not yet come" (Jn. 2:4). The Gospel of Mark states that Mary sought to contact him after he had begun his ministry and was forced to hear Jesus say, "Who is my mother and my brethren?...Whosoever shall do the will of God, he is my brother and my sister and my mother" (Mk. 3:33–35). Mary, clearly an integral part of the original Christian community, stood near the cross at the Crucifixion, but her presence is ordinary and unexceptional, and she is mentioned only as being among the relatives of Jesus and the other women present. It was only several centuries later in Church history that her role became magnified.

Whatever we say about Mary, therefore, must begin with her full humanity. It was in and through humanity that Mary became *theotokos* (the Bearer of God). As a humble maiden, she became the "new Eve"; as a scandal, she served the purpose of divine grace.

Luke describes the fragility of Mary's humanness by

saying she was "greatly troubled" (Lk. 1:2) when the angel Gabriel announced himself to her. She "considered in her mind what sort of greeting this might be," clearly having no idea what was to come from it. The angel here must be seen in deep contrast to the serpent in the Garden of Eden. Serpent and angel informed the women of the issue at hand and challenged them to either obey or disobey the limits set by God. The serpent seduced Eve into violating the divine limits; Gabriel challenged Mary to obey the divine limits.

After announcing himself and sensing Mary's trepidation, Gabriel says, "Do not be afraid, Mary, for you have found favour with God. And behold, you will conceive in your womb and bear a son, and you shall call his name Jesus. He will be great and will be called the Son of the Most High; and the Lord God will give to him the throne of his father David, and he will reign over the house of Jacob forever; and of his kingdom there will be no end" (Lk. 1:31–33).

Mary, like Eve, is bewildered and confused by this dramatic entrance of a superior being. She tries to clarify, even correct the angel, saying, "How can this be, since I have no husband?" (Lk. 1:34). Gabriel replies, "The Holy Spirit will come upon you, and the power of the Most High will overshadow you; therefore the child to be born will be called holy, the Son of God. And behold, your kinswoman Elizabeth in her old age has also conceived a son; and this is the sixth month with her who was called barren. For with God nothing will be impossible" (Lk. 1:35–37). Mary's reply to this decree is simple and unreserved, "Behold, I am the handmaid of the Lord: let it be to me according to thy word" (Lk. 1:38).

The Virgin Birth is not about Joseph's not being the father of Jesus. It is about Mary's obedience concerning the angel's announcement that her conception, despite the scandal surrounding it on the physical side, would be used by Spirit to accomplish a great work. Mary's capacity to acknowledge and accept this great mystery, particularly when Joseph considered putting her away, was an act of true obedience.

Mary, by her consent of faith, became the one through whom "the Christ" appeared among us. Her motherhood involves her at once in the great historical drama being acted out between the creative will of God and human choice. Mary's motherhood was not just a physical event. In the power of the Spirit, it was a graced, personal act of obedience and faith within the context of sacred history. Through her, the "Word was made flesh" (Jn. 1:14) and the serpent was bruised on the head. Because of Eve's disobedience, Eve was cursed with pain in childbirth. Because of Mary's obedience, Mary was blessed with "the Christ" in childbirth.

According to Matthew and Luke, it appears that Mary had disobeyed Mosaic Law by becoming pregnant out of wedlock; yet she had obeyed the divine summons, which was operating according to the hidden purposes of God. Somehow, in some mysterious way, through the most insignificant of actions and scandalous of choices, God's grace broke through and revealed to Mary and the early believers deeper truths concerning the mystery of redemption. I suspect that neither Mary nor Joseph ever considered that their premarital sex would transform human history. Yet God's grace, working in and through Mary's obedience, accomplished just that.

God's decision to work through Mary created her ability to say yes and to dissolve the wrath of condemnation of the illegitimate nature of her pregnancy. Again, the Codex of Luke: "Blessed art thou if thou knowest what thou doest. If not, thou art acursed and a transgressor of the law." It is not obedience to civil law or social morays that matters but obedience to the will of God. This higher law is sometimes in sharp contradiction to societal norms. But we are commanded to obey it, nevertheless, "if thou knowest what thou doest."

Mary became conscious that divine grace was using the very transgression for which the legalisms of her day would have stoned her to death. Obeying the higher law of grace and knowing of what she was doing, she carried the fruit of her scandal and the redemption of the world in her womb *simultaneously*. Concurrent within her were the wages of sin *and* the deliverance from sin. Obeying the higher law, she submitted to the contradiction willingly, living out in her own way the cruciform nature of reality "the Christ" within her would exemplify when he was crucified.

Eve, living in purity in Paradise, seduced by the serpent to believe she was equal with God, disobeyed the divinely imposed limits placed in creation; thereby humanity experienced the Fall. Mary, living in fallen creation, engaged in premarital sex, obeyed the summons of the angel, and believed in God's power to use her scandalous situation as an instrument of God's grace; thereby humanity was offered redemption.

As was Mary, we are called upon to trust and believe that God will always use our opprobrium for a higher purpose. In the Spirit, we can come to know that God will meet us with consuming judgement and immeasurable mercy concurrently. Judgement is our first experience of grace. Divine mercy uses what God condemns as a vehicle of grace. At the very point where we experience divine judgement we experience divine affirmation. The Great Alchemist uses scandal, corruption, and wickedness as the essential ingredients to be transformed into gold.

CHAPTER 9

THE JUST MAN

The dove descending breaks the air

With flame of incandescent terror

Of which the tongues declare

The only discharge from sin and error.

The only hope, or else despair

Lies in the choice of pyre or pyre—

To be redeemed from fire by fire.

Who then devised the torment? Love.

Love is the unfamiliar Name

Behind the hands that wove

The intolerable shirt of flame

Which human power cannot remove.

We only live, only suspire

consumed by either fire or fire.[1]

1. Eliot, *Collected Poems,* 221.

THE GOSPELS CARRY FORWARD THE JEWISH epistemology that faith shapes knowledge, and knowledge directs itself toward faith. They narrate what happened *before* the Cross in the light of what they came to believe *after* the Cross. It is impossible today to separate fact from faith in the Gospels. The Gospel writers, as witnesses for the believing community, offer accounts about Jesus that were selected, ordered, shaped, and linked in light of their experiences of the Crucifixion and the risen Christ.

The central issue at the core of the New Testament is the antinomy of God, as experienced by Jesus of Nazareth. When Jesus hung in agony upon the Cross, ridiculed by humanity and forsaken by God, the man who many proclaimed as "the Christ" chose to drink from the same cup from which Job had been forced to drink. Like Job, Jesus experienced the anomie of being made "to be sin who knew no sin." God did to Jesus what He had done to Job. Job was stripped of family, possessions, friends, and health until he lay in ashes, scraping his boils with pot- sherds; Jesus at Gethsemene was "greatly distressed and troubled," and on Golgotha died with "loud cries and tears." His last words, according to Matthew and Mark, were "My God, my God, why hast thou forsaken me?" In the end, Job was blessed with his family, possessions, and land restored ten-fold; Jesus was raised from the dead.

The Gospel of Mark deals with the antinomies and the cruciform nature of reality, as expressed in the life and death of Jesus, with particular clarity. The paradox with which Mark grapples is that though Jesus is "the Christ,"

Jesus must suffer death by the will of God. It was this central and fundamental antinomy that the disciples began to accept slowly and incredulously in the aftermath of the Resurrection.

As most Jews of their time, the disciples of Jesus believed that to be "the Christ" meant to share in and reflect decisively the victorious power of God over the forces of darkness. This meant for them that the Messiah would deliver Israel from the Greek and Roman oppressors, just as Moses had delivered the children of Israel from the bondage of Egypt. They believed that the Messiah would come in greatness and exercise cosmic strength through political liberation.

Jesus taught his disciples that he must suffer, not conquer; that he must die, not reign for a thousand years. And yet he was also "the Christ." His power was transformed power. He came not as a conquering hero to vanquish the Romans but as a suffering servant to bear the sins of the world. If the Fall awakened in all of us the craving for knowledge and power, the question is, What does God do with power? The answer Jesus gave was that God suffers willingly under untransformed power in order to transform it by embracing it in the spirit of forgiveness, even unto death.

The Gospel of Mark explores this paradox of the transformation of power. In the first half of his Gospel, Mark depicts the immense power at work in Jesus and explores its meaning in relation to Jesus' being "the Christ." In the second half, he explores the transformation of that power and Jesus' becoming "the Christ," not by fulfilling expectations of a Messiah who would bring political liberation but by accepting death upon the Cross as the will of God. As the book of Hebrews puts it, Jesus was made "perfect through sufferings" (Heb. 2:10). He was a Just Man, a *Lamed-waf.*

At the center of Mark's Gospel is a story that distills the essence of this paradox of power in relation to Jesus' being a Just Man. The opening of the eyes of the blind man at Bethsaida parallels the confession of Peter at Caesarea Philippi. Both occurred in two stages. At first, when Jesus spit in the blind man's eyes, the man said he could see "men as trees, walking" (Mk. 8:24). When Jesus placed his hands upon his eyes, the man saw clearly. Jesus told him to tell no one.

When Jesus asks the disciples, "Who do men say that I am?" they are initially as vague as the blind man, venturing that Jesus is said to be John the Baptist or Elias or one of the prophets. Only when Jesus asks a second time, "Who do *you* say that I am?" does Peter confess clearly, "You are the Christ" (Mk. 8:29). As with the blind man, Jesus tells them not to tell anyone. This concealment of Jesus' purpose and identity is known as the "messianic secret" of the Gospel of Mark.

Mark links the confession that Jesus is the Christ with Jesus' teaching to his disciples that he was to suffer many things, be crucified, and rise on the third day. But given what they thought the Messiah was supposed to be and to do, they found the paradox unbearable. Peter rebukes Jesus. Jesus replies, "Get thee behind me, Satan, for you savor not the things of God but of men" (Mk. 8:33).

Mark thus draws a parallel between the healing of the blind man with the confession of Peter. Both involve the giving of sight, one at the physical level, the other at the spiritual level. In both cases, seeing comes gradually. Paradoxically, though the Spirit opens Peter's eyes to see that Jesus is "the Christ," he cannot see that Christ's glory would be the Cross.

After healing the blind man and hearing Peter's confession, and after teaching about the way of the Cross, Jesus takes Peter, James, and John to a high mountain and is transfigured before them there. Again, a two-stage "seeing" process takes place. First, they see the transfigured Jesus accompanied by Moses and Elijah who symbolize the Law and the prophets respectively. Second, they see a cloud, symbolizing the glory of God, overshadow them. Out of this cloud a voice speaks, "This is my beloved Son: hear him" (Mk. 9:7).

As they descend the mountain Jesus charges them again to tell no one until "the Son of Man was risen from the dead" (Mk. 9:9). Still, Peter, James, and John do not understand; instead, they question one another about the meaning of "rising from the dead." They ask about the prophecy that Elias would come before the Christ. Jesus affirms this, stating he had already come, an obvious reference to John the Baptist.

In fact, Mark begins his Gospel with John the Baptist, for the prophets had said, "Behold, I send my messenger before thy face, which shall prepare thy way for thee" (Mk. 1:2). Jesus comes to John to be baptized, and the Spirit descends upon him as a dove. A voice from heaven declares, "You are my beloved Son, in whom I am well pleased" (Mk. 1:11).

After being affirmed by the Spirit at his baptism, Jesus is driven by the Spirit into the wilderness. After fasting for forty days and forty nights, he is tempted by Satan. Although Mark is silent about these temptations, Matthew describes three, which test Jesus' attitude towards power. The crux of these temptations is, How is Jesus going to use the immense power that was given to him?

The first temptation is the use of power for material benefits: "Command these stones to become loaves of bread" (Mt. 4:3). The second temptation is the use power for wonder-working: "Throw yourself down from the pinnacle of the temple and he will give his angels charge over you" (Mt. 4:6). The third concerns political power, with Satan showing Jesus all the kingdoms of the world: "All these I will give you, if you bow down before me" (Mt. 4:9).

In rejecting these temptations, Jesus refuses to offer any visible proof of worldly power, for this would give no clue to his true power. Piercing the veil covering him who hangs despised, tortured, and dying on the tree is the only way to see the true power of Jesus as "the Christ." Only the Cross offers the full measure and expression of transformed power, not a man riding at the head of a vast army intent on the political liberation of his people.

Mark depicts Jesus clearly as a man of power. Empowered by the Spirit, he moves with speed and deliberateness to the Sea of Galilee where he gathers his disciples and begins a whirlwind of preaching, healing, and performing miracles. Mark records that the public is "astonished" at his doctrine, for though he is not a trained religious leader, Jesus teaches with authority.

In a synagogue in the town of Capernaum Jesus meets a man possessed by an unclean spirit. The spirit cries out in recognition, "I know who you are, the Holy One of God" (Mk. 1:24). Jesus rebukes the spirit and commands it to leave the man and to hold its peace. This first recognition of Jesus' true identity comes not from the disciples or townspeople but from the dark spirit world. The public is amazed, and his fame spreads throughout the region.

There is much to be amazed at. After leaving the synagogue, Jesus heals Simon's mother-in-law and "all that were diseased, and them that were possessed with devils, such that all the city was gathered together at the door" (Mk. 1:33).

After demonstrating his power to heal, Jesus demonstrates his power to forgive sins. Again in Capernaum, a man sick with palsy is brought to Jesus by four men (Mk. 2:5–11). Jesus, seeing their faith, says, "Son, your sins are forgiven." There are scribes present who are offended by this. "Why does this man speak blasphemies?" they ask. "Who can forgive sins but God only?" Jesus responds by revealing the antinomy inherent in the situation, "What is easier," he asks, "to say to the sick of the palsy, 'Your sins are forgiven;' or to say, 'Arise, take up your bed and walk?'" From the pragmatic point of view, here are two mutually exclusive realities. What does the forgiveness of sins have to do with healing palsy? Surely there is no connection, yet Jesus insists that there is. Turning to the sick one, Jesus says, "But that you may know that the Son of Man has power on earth to forgive sins, I say unto you, Arise, take up your bed and go your way into your house." And immediately the sick man rises up, takes his bed, and departs, leaving the scribes and onlookers "astonished."

Jesus expands his demonstration of power further by healing on the Sabbath. In a synagogue—once again and in front of Pharisees—he commands a man with a withered hand to stand forth. Then turning to the Pharisees, he asks, "Is it lawful to do good on the Sabbath days, or to do evil? To save life, or to kill?" (Mk. 3:4). The Pharisees say nothing. Jesus looks upon them "with anger, being grieved at the hardness of their hearts," and says to the man, "Stretch forth your hand." He does so, and it is restored whole. And "straightway," records Mark, the Pharisees take council with the Herodians how they might destroy Jesus.

Jesus withdraws to the Sea of Galilee, healing all that come. Again, though all are amazed at his power, it is the cast-out unclean spirits that recognize him for who he really is. "You are the Son of God," they proclaim (Mk. 3:11). Immediately Jesus charges them not to make his identity known.

Jesus demonstrates even more power when, after teaching the multitudes, he and his disciples cross the Sea of Galilee in a boat. Jesus falls asleep in the stern and remains asleep, even when a storm rises and waves begin to wash into the boat. Finally his disciples wake him up, saying, "Master, do you not care that we perish?" (Mk. 4:38). Jesus rises up, rebukes the wind, and says to the sea, "Peace, be still." The wind ceases, and there is a great calm. At the beginning of Mark, the public says, "Who is this?" when Jesus casts out demons. Now the question is repeated by the disciples, "What manner of man is this, that even the wind and sea obey him?" (Mk. 4:41).

Crossing over into the country of the Gadarenes north of Galilee, Jesus is met by a man possessed so powerfully by a group of demons that no one could bind him, even with chains. He lived among the tombs, crying incessantly and cutting himself with stones. When he sees Jesus, he runs to him and worships. He cries out with a loud voice as his demons proclaim Jesus' identity as "son of the most high God." Jesus casts them out of the man but allows them to enter a large herd of swine. So powerful are the demons that they cause approximately two thousand pigs to run violently down a steep slope into the sea where they drown. The Gadarenes are unnerved by this demonstration of power, and they beg Jesus to leave their shores.

Jesus makes his way to Decapolis and performs an ultimate act of power by raising the daughter of Jairus from the dead. On his way to the house a woman who has had an issue of blood for twelve years touches his garments, believing that even to touch them would be enough for healing. She is healed instantly, and Jesus, though thronged by a crowd, knows immediately that "virtue had gone out of him" (Mk. 5:30). He stops and asks, "Who touched me?" After he locates the woman and blesses her, he continues on his way and raises the daughter of Jairus from the dead, saying simply "Arise." Witnesses "were astonished with a great astonishment" (Mk. 5:42).

As if this were not enough, Jesus feeds a multitude of five thousand with five loaves of bread and two fishes, walks on water, using the divine epithet "I AM" to still the wind, cures all manner of diseases, and feeds another multitude of four thousand with seven loaves. Still his disciples do not understand, "for they considered not the miracle of the loaves: for their heart was hardened." The Pharisees, for their part, kept asking him for a "sign from heaven." Jesus "sighed deeply in his spirit" and said to them, "Why does this generation seek after a sign? Verily I say unto you, there shall be no sign given unto this generation" (Mk. 8:12). Jesus then upbraids his own disciples, asking, "Having eyes, do you not see? And having ears, do you not hear? And do you not remember?" (Mk. 8:18). The point is very difficult to grasp: The resurrectional power at work in the ministry of Jesus remains opaque except to those empowered by grace to "see."

The disciples are blind to what Jesus is attempting to demonstrate, because the entire expanse and content of the life of Jesus was one antinomy after another. Because antinomies are internally consistent but mutually exclusive truths, in ordinary consciousness we can grasp only one truth to the exclusion of the other. As were the scribes and the Pharisees witnessing the healing of the man with palsy, we cannot perceive the inner connections, which seem completely disconnected on the common-sense level of experience. Jesus' extraordinary power came from his ability to discern the deep inner connections between the polarities and to live authentically with their contradiction as well as their integration.

Paradoxically, this same ability left his disciples dazed, confused, and unbelieving, and the religious leaders, defensive, alienated, and vengeful. Not one person grasped the entirety of who or what Jesus was during his lifetime. The spirit world and a few of those healed recognized his numinosity. The rest were "astonished" and unnerved by the antinomial realities he manifested and drew to their attention, particularly that the destiny of Jesus as "the Christ" was not to lead Israel to political liberation from Rome but to die on a Roman Cross. So great was the disjunction between what the public expected of "the Christ" and what Jesus actually did in relation to those expectations that it was one of his own disciples who betrayed him. When he was on trial not a single person, not even his mother, came to his aid or spoke on his behalf.

It is after Jesus is identified clearly as "the Christ" by demonstrating absolute power over the spirit world, over diseases, over nature, over the Torah, even over death, that he begins to teach his disciples that the "Son of Man must suffer many things, and be rejected of the elders, and of the chief priests, and scribes, and be killed, and after three days rise again" (Mk. 8:31).

Peter, having witnessed all the amazing feats and miracles and having just understood that Jesus is "the Christ," nevertheless continues to assume, as most Jews did, that Jesus will now use his power to overthrow the Romans and to lead Israel to political greatness. He rebukes Jesus for saying that it was now time for the Son of Man to die, for he is unable to "see" that the Cross is to be Jesus' way and destiny. Although he can call him "the Christ," Peter does not truly understand the one so named. In the end, Peter is destined to deny "the Christ" three times.

Jesus teaches Peter and the disciples patiently the antinomial truth: "Whosoever will come after me, let him deny himself, and take up his cross, and follow me. For whosoever will save his life shall lose it; but whosoever shall lose his life for my sake and the gospel's the same shall save it. For what shall it profit a man, if he shall gain the whole world, and lose his own soul?" (Mk. 8:34–36).

The key to the transformation of power is the crucifixion of power. We are called upon to give up the unbridled pursuit of knowledge and of power for their own sakes. We are challenged to take up our cross at any and every point when ego power is at work and to follow the path that Moses took into the desert and that Jesus took to the Cross.

This is the hero's journey. Our impulse to gain knowledge and power for their own sake, embedded within us since the Garden, must be sent out into the desert and be crucified. Our strength must be broken in weakness; our assertiveness must become receptive through obedience; our will to power must be transformed into the will to serve. In doing this, we answer Sophia's call. Thus Moses could return to Egypt after his forty years in the desert in *real* power and liberate his people; and thus Christ could lay down his life and be resurrected the third day. This is true freedom.

This paradox is impossible to embrace except through grace. When a rich young man comes to Jesus and says, "Good master, what shall I do that I might inherit eternal life?" Jesus replies, "Why do you call me good? There is none good but God." After ascertaining that the young man has kept all the commandments, Jesus says, "One thing you lack: go your way, sell whatsoever you have and give it to the poor...and come, follow me." The young man went away grieved. Jesus turns to his disciples and says, "Children, how hard is it for them that trust in riches to enter the kingdom of God" (Mk. 10:17, 21,24). The strength of the world is the weakness of God. To be weak before God is to be truly strong.

The disciples listen to Jesus but do not hear him. Having realized that he is "the Christ," they are far more interested in partaking in his glory than in his suffering. Immediately after Jesus tells them again that as Christ he is to suffer and die, his disciples James and John come to him privately and ask to sit on his left and right hand "in thy glory." Jesus replies that they do not know what they ask.

When the other disciples hear about James and John's request, they begin to quarrel. Jesus intervenes with another antinomy:

> You know that they who are accounted to rule over the
> Gentiles exercise lordship over them; and their great ones
> exercise authority upon them. But so shall it not be among

you: but whosoever will be great among you shall be your minister; and whosoever of you will be the chief shall be the servant of all. For even the Son of Man came not to be ministered unto but to minister, and to give his life a ransom for many (Mk.10:42–45).

Peter and the other disciples want a share in heavenly imperial power; Jesus tells them that they must serve in order to lead. They are not destined to understand this truth until long after the crucifixion.

On the way to Jerusalem where he is to be crucified, Jesus opens the eyes of another blind man, Bartimaeus, who, when he hears that Jesus is near, cries out, "Jesus, thou Son of David, have mercy on me" (Mk. 10:47). Whereas the disciples sought power, Jesus, in opening the eyes of the blind, wants them to "see" that recognition of his Messiahship involves taking up the cross and following him. The rich man was told this and went away grieved, unable to become weak in the eyes of the world. The disciples are to betray Jesus for the same reason. A simple blind beggar is the only one who can really "see" Jesus for who he is as he goes to be crucified.

Jesus now enters Jerusalem. The man who has demonstrated immense power over every adversary now accepts with meekness his destiny to suffer the ultimate indignity at the hands of untransformed power. His renunciation of the worldly uses of power is of his own free will. According to the Gospel of John, he says to his disciples, "I lay down my life. No one takes it from me, but I lay it down of my own accord. I have power to lay it down, and I have power to take it again. This charge I have received of my Father" (Mk. 10:17,18).

The man who demonstrates authoritative power in worldly terms becomes obedient to the higher power of Spirit as worldly power prepares his death. He is receptive to the woman anointing him; receptive to his disciples sleeping while he prays; and receptive to the ultimate antinomy: It is his father in heaven, not just the Pharisees, who is demanding his death. In his agony, Jesus turns to a passage from Zechariah, a prophet who had lived eight hundred years earlier:

> And if one asks him
> What are these wounds on your back?
> He will say, "The wounds I received in the house of my
> friends."
> Awake, O sword, against my shepherd,
> against the man who stands next to me,
> says the Lord of hosts.
> Strike the shepherd, that the sheep may be scattered;
> I will turn my hand against the little ones.
> In the whole land, says the Lord,
> two thirds shall be cut off and perish,
> and one third shall be left alive.
> And I will put this third into the fire,
> and refine them as one refines silver,
> and test them as gold is tested.
> They will call on my name,
> and I will answer them.
> I will say, "They are my people";
> and they will say, "The Lord is my God" (Zec. 13:6–9).

Realizing the full impact of this prophecy, Jesus, sweating drops of blood, offers up his great prayer, "Father, all things are possible to thee; remove this cup from me;

yet not what I will, but what thou wilt" (Mk. 14:36). In this spirit, he is receptive to being kissed by Judas, to being led away by the Romans, to enduring the crown of thorns, to being reviled. He is silent before the High Priest when witnesses accuse him falsely, answering only the High Priest's question, "Are you the Christ...?" He replies, "I am..." (Mk. 14:61,62).

Jesus' choice of words is deliberate and profound, recalling the interaction between Moses and God in the burning bush some twelve centuries before. The book of Exodus records that God commanded Moses to return to Egypt after his forty years in the desert and to deliver his people from the scourge of Pharaoh. Moses, unwilling at first, finally consented and then asked, "If I come to the people of Israel and say to them, 'The God of your fathers has sent me to you,' and they ask me, 'What is his name?' What shall I say to them?" God said to Moses, "I AM THAT I AM. Say this to the people of Israel, I AM has sent me to you" (Ex. 3:14).

Jesus' reply echoes also the prophecies of the prophet Isaiah to the children of Israel seven centuries before:

> Who has performed and done this,
> calling the generations from the beginning?
> I, the Lord, the first, and with the last; I AM HE (Is.41:4).

> I am God and also henceforth I AM HE;
> there is none who can deliver from my hand;
> I work and who can hinder it (Is.43:13)?

The implication of Jesus' words is not lost on the High Priest, who tears his clothes and says, "Why do we still need witnesses? You have heard his blasphemy. What is your decision?"(Mk. 15:63). With one accord, the combined body of priests, elders, and scribes condemns Jesus to die for the crime of blasphemy.

Under Roman law, the Jews were authorized to stone blasphemers, something they did later to Stephen, considered traditionally to be the first Christian martyr. Strangely, they did not carry out this punishment on Jesus. Instead, they brought him to the Roman governor Pilate, charging him not with blasphemy but with sedition. Jesus was taken to Pilate not as the Son of God but as the King of the Jews.

In the profoundest of ironies, the man who rejected the temptation of political power, healed in the name of God, and claimed finally to be the great "I AM," was not stoned under religious law for a spiritual sin but turned over to the foreign authorities for a political offense. The man who eschewed political power for spiritual strength was charged with sedition against Caesar. The man trying desperately to teach his disciples the mysteries of the transformation of power was taken to trial before the representative of ultimate untransformed power. Jesus, standing before Pilate, as Moses had stood before the throne of Pharaoh, is the supreme personification of absolute transformed power meeting absolute untransformed power.

Even as he had remained silent to all the accusations of his religious accusers and had answered only the one question about him being "the Christ," so Jesus remains silent to all these accusations and answers the one question of Pilate's, "Are you the king of the Jews?" "Thou sayest it," he answers simply, confirming that he is as much the son of David and therefore King of the Jews, Pilate's concern, as he is Son of God and therefore "the Christ," the religious leaders' concern.

Pilate, marveling at the man before him, offers the Jews a choice between Jesus and Barabbas, another prisoner being held by the Romans. Tradition has it that Barabbas was a Zealot, a member of a political group that sought to liberate Israel from the Roman yoke by force of arms. Ironically, he was engaged in the very political activities that the disciples believed Jesus, as "the Christ," should have engaged in. Barabbas had been captured and charged with murder and robbery but was a popular hero among the Jews.

The parallel between Jesus and Barabbas is striking. Barabbas means "son of the Father." In the Gospel of Matthew, Barabbas is referred to as "Jesus Barabbas." Jesus is being tried for claiming to be the King of the Jews and the Son of God, whom he referred openly to as "Abba," meaning "father." Jesus, too, is the "son of the father." In the profoundest of ironies, Barabbas and Jesus are both "Jesus, the son of the father," one a symbol of political Titanism, the other of spiritual obedience. Mark is asking, "Do you want Jesus Barabbas or Jesus Barabbas?" "Do you want untransformed power or transformed power?"

When the final choice is made, the crowd, the religious leaders, the Romans, the disciples, and the world want Barabbas. Jesus Barabbas is released; Jesus Barabbas is condemned. In the face of this triumph of untransformed power, "the Christ" still remains silent, even when he is scourged and tormented by the soldiers. Without protest, he carries his cross until a passing Cyrenian relieves him. He is taken to Golgotha, the place of the skull, where in Jewish tradition, Adam was buried. Jesus in death finally answers Adam in death. The seed of Eve bruises the head of the serpent. Redemption answers the Fall.

Jesus is receptive to his own crucifixion, his only words, according to Mark, being, "My God, my God, why have you forsaken me?" (Mk. 15:34). The crowd watches, still looking for a "sign." They think he may come down. His power is still with him, absorbing the entire event— the human sin, the divine will, the Cross, the nails. Transformed power was in the grip of untransformed power. What would it do now?

To Jesus' right and left are two thieves, being crucified also. As the Gospel of Luke recounts it, one thief, echoing the sentiments of the crowd, demands of Jesus, "Save yourself and us" (Lk. 23:39). The other thief is given to "see" that Jesus is "the Christ" and begs, "Lord, remember me when you come into your kingdom" (Lk. 23:42). James and John had come to him, asking to be on his right and left hand in glory. On the Cross Jesus was in his glory; yet on either side were not his disciples but two thieves. Jesus, in his glory, gives his sign not by coming down but by staying up. Then with a loud voice he cries out, breathes his last breath, and dies.

CHAPTER 10

THE PARADOX OF POWER

Human kind

Cannot bear very much reality.[1]

I T TOOK THE DISCIPLES YEARS OF PONDERING before they began to understand what they had witnessed in the man Jesus and why they believed him to be "the Christ." Ironically, the disciples were never very clear about what had happened. It was left to Saul of Tarsus to describe for posterity the profundity of what had occurred.

Saul, the son of a Pharisee and educated in Jerusalem, was an orthodox Jew as well as a Roman citizen. Like his compatriots, he was unable to perceive the deep interconnections in the antinomies embraced and lived by Jesus. Indeed, he felt sufficiently offended that the man who had been crucified was being proclaimed as "the Christ" by a growing number of Jews, that he spent his time debating and persecuting the early believers. According to tradition, Saul was present at the stoning of Stephen, when the Jewish authorities did to him what they were authorized but chose not to do to Jesus.

On the way to Damascus to persecute other believers, Saul had a vision in which Jesus appeared to him and asked, "Why are you persecuting me?" (Acts 9:4). Upon hearing the voice, Saul was struck blind, a condition that lasted for three days and nights, until a Christian in Damascus placed

1. Eliot, *Collected Works,* 190.

his hands on Saul's eyes and his sight was restored. Saul was physically blinded in order to gain the spiritual capacity to "see" that Jesus was "the Christ." As a sign of his conversion, he changed his name to Paul and spent the rest of his life travelling throughout the Mediterranean world, preaching the new faith. According to tradition, Paul was finally martyred in Rome, beheaded by the emperor Nero in C.E. 64.

Paul intuited the antinomy at the heart of the Crucifixion and provides us with a clue for understanding the mystery of transformed power. In his second letter to the church at Corinth, Paul speaks of his "thorn in the flesh" that he asked the Lord three times to take away. Paul recounts that God said to him, "My grace is sufficient for you, for my strength is made perfect in weakness." "Most gladly therefore," says Paul, "will I rather glory in my infirmities, that the power of Christ may rest upon me. Therefore I take pleasure in infirmities, in reproaches, in necessities, in persecutions, in distresses for Christ's sake: for when I am weak, then I am strong" (2 Cor. 12:8–10).

Paul is not calling for masochism or for asceticism. Rather, he is addressing the central cruciform reality lying at the heart of faith: Our weakness is the base element Divinity transforms into gold; our sin is where grace abounds. We are not called upon to be strong by being assertive and combative. We are called upon to be strong by being receptive vessels through which the Spirit can work. Our life, our ego must be offered up upon the altar of the Great Alchemist. Like Mary and Jesus, we must say, "Not my will but thine be done." The goal is not a relentless pursuit for more knowledge in order to exercise more power but a willingness to become a conduit for the transforming power of the divine.

Paul proclaims this message because it is the way of Jesus himself and the central paradox of the Cross, "For though he was crucified through weakness, yet he lives by the power of God. For we also are weak in him, but we shall live with him by the power of God toward you" (2 Cor. 13:11). Jesus became increasingly receptive and obedient to the divine will that he be crucified, revealing the power and glory of the Cross. Out of his obedience unto death came affirmation: the Resurrection. Through Jesus' weakness, God's strength became manifest in the world.

"The preaching of the Cross is to them that perish foolishness," says Paul, "but unto us which are saved it is the power of God" (1 Cor. 1:18). To the world, the Cross was Jesus' final humiliation and defeat. The Pharisees and Sadducees congratulated themselves that this upstart had come at last to his just reward after claiming to be the great "I AM." Pilate and Herod were relieved to be rid of one who would be king of the Jews. Religious power and worldly power had prevailed.

But "I will destroy the wisdom of the wise," says the Lord, "and will bring to nothing the understanding of the prudent. Where is the wise? Where is the scribe? Where is the disputer of this world? Hath not God made foolish the wisdom of the world?" (1 Cor. 1:19,20).

The wisdom of human civilization knows not God. By its strength, the world seeks to do violence to the will of God. The Jews demand a sign in order to believe; the Greeks demand wisdom in order to understand. The world is obsessed with power and knowledge. If it cannot control, if it cannot understand rationally, it rejects, and does so aggressively out of fear. In the world, the ego with its lust for power reigns supreme, but in the realm of spirit, the ego must be sacrificed.

The Cross is where the ego, when it is crucified *with* Christ, receives the power of redemption and is transformed. Thus, Paul preached Christ crucified, knowing that to the Jews, demanding signs of power, it would be a stumbling-block; and to the Greeks, obsessed with reason, it would be considered foolishness.

But, says Paul, "it pleased God by the foolishness of preaching to save them that believe.... Because the foolishness of God is wiser than men; and the weakness of God is stronger than men" (1 Cor. 1:21,25). Because of this, God deliberately "has chosen the foolish things of the world to confound the wise...and the weak things of the world to confound the things which are mighty" (1 Cor. 1:27).

It is this supreme paradox of the transformation of power that forces all human endeavor, all of human history, not toward itself, that we might boast, but toward the grace of God, that we might be redeemed. "God has chosen the despised and base things of the world through which to work that no flesh should glory in his presence" (1 Cor. 1:29).

In this way, power and wisdom are transformed. The wisdom of the world defines power as the ability to compete and to overcome. In the world, to be weak is to fail. The wisdom of God is foolishness to the world, for weakness under God means being able to contain one's power without using it aggressively; it means absorbing aggression and transforming it through forgiveness. Strength becomes the ability to attune one's will with the will of God. This is the cost and the fruit of being crucified with Christ. This is at the heart of the cruciform nature of reality.

This antinomy is not unique to the Pauline interpretation of Jesus or limited to the Gospel of Mark. It is replete throughout the Bible and is central to that other great event, the Exodus.

Israel came to be in Egypt through Joseph, son of Jacob and great-grandson of Abraham. The book of Genesis records that Joseph was his father's favorite son of twelve, which was not lost on his ten elder brothers "who hated him and could not speak peaceably to him" (Gn. 37:4). To show his love, Jacob gave to Joseph a long robe with sleeves, something that infuriated his brothers even more. To make matters worse, Joseph had dreams, which he interpreted for his entire family, indicating clearly that he would reign over his brothers.

On one occasion Joseph was sent by Jacob to locate his brothers who had taken the family flocks out to pasture. When they saw him coming, they plotted to get rid of him. They threw him into a deep pit and then sold him as a slave to some passing Ishmaelites headed for Egypt. They saved his coat, which they dipped in lamb's blood, and took it back to their father, telling him they had found it along their way.

Joseph was sold to an officer of Pharaoh's named Potiphar and was eventually imprisoned because of the jealousy of Potiphar's wife. There he interpreted the dreams of several fellow prisoners, including one by Pharaoh's butler who was told that he would be released from prison and returned to his former post. After this came to pass, Pharaoh himself had dreams that seemed important, but neither he nor his wise men could interpret them. The butler told Pharaoh of his experience with Joseph, and Pharaoh had Joseph brought before him.

Joseph interpreted the dreams of Pharaoh as a presage that seven years of plenty would be followed by seven years of drought. Pharaoh was astonished at the clarity of this interpretation, and he made Joseph responsible for all the preparations during the bountiful years so that Egypt would have plenty of grain during the lean years. The man betrayed by his brothers and sold into slavery was now second only to Pharaoh in Egypt. Weakness had been made strength. The wisdom of Joseph's brothers had been brought to naught. The untransformed power of Pharaoh now was serving power transformed.

The drought extended to Canaan where Jacob and the eleven brothers were living. Jacob, hearing that there was corn in Egypt, sent his ten oldest sons into Egypt to buy grain, keeping Benjamin, his youngest son, at home. Joseph, by now shaven and dressed as an Egyptian aristocrat, sat in the storeroom dispensing the grain. He recognized his brothers when they came in to purchase grain, but they did not recognize him. After a number of such encounters, Joseph finally revealed himself and invited Jacob and the entire family to join him in Egypt. Jacob, ecstatic at learning his favorite child was really alive, packed up everything he owned and journeyed to Egypt. Pharaoh showered gifts and enormous wealth upon Jacob and his family as a reward for Joseph's services.

After the death of Jacob some years later, the brothers feared that Joseph would take the opportunity to exact vengeance. Instead, he offered one of the great utterances of the entire Bible, "You meant evil against me; but God meant it for good, to bring it about that many people should be kept alive, as they are today" (Gn. 50:20).

Joseph is a precursor to Jesus. Both were forced to pay

a heavy price for their innocence. Yet no matter what they were forced to endure, they sustained their faith in God and returned good for evil. Out of this humility, divine grace was able to bring about a great redemption, using the evil intended to destroy the suffering servant to bring about the redemption of many. In the end, transformed power conquered untransformed power, not with violence but through forgiveness.

The Israelites continued to live a privileged and peaceful existence in Egypt for the next four centuries. Then a Pharaoh arose who did not remember Joseph, and, seeing the number and power of the Israelites, sought to subdue them. From the pinnacle of power, they were reduced to despair when, ironically, the Pharaoh ordered them to build his great cites of Pitahm and Ramses, designed especially to store excess grain. He gave them a quota of bricks to make each day, but the more he oppressed them, the stronger and greater in number they became.

The Pharaoh then doubled their quota and cut by half the straw they could use to build the bricks. They exerted themselves further and endured, still multiplying. Then Pharaoh ordered the Hebrews to kill their sons and only spare the daughters. Most went along with the regimen and submitted to this raw exercise of untransformed power.

All except one, a lowly woman of the tribe of Levi who refused to kill her son. In "foolishness," she hid the infant for three months. When she could hide him no longer, she did something even more "foolish": She fashioned a basket of bulrushes with pitch on the bottom, placed the baby and basket among the reeds along the banks of the Nile River, and had the baby's older sister watch from a distance.

None other than Pharaoh's daughter found him when she came to bathe.

Seeing this happen, the sister appeared and offered to find someone to nurse the baby. None other than the baby's own mother was chosen to do so. After he was weaned, the Pharaoh's daughter took the toddler into the palace and adopted him as her own son, calling him Moses, which means "Because I drew him out of the water." Moses ended up living in the palace as the son of the Pharaoh who was trying to decimate the Jewish people.

Here we see the real profundity of the Judeo-Christian notion of God working in history. God does not need us in our strength; God needs us in our weakness. Only then can God work the divine will through us. Like Joseph before and Jesus long afterward, Moses is victimized in innocence but in and through the evil befalling him grace abounds and deliverance is provided. But deliverance is not accomplished through anything Moses does out of his own strength; deliverance is only accomplished as Moses obeys the will of God.

The powerful, relying on their strength alone, blinded by their own arrogance, believe they have everything under control. Pharaoh never even noticed Moses in his own house; and Moses, according to the tradition, stayed there forty years. During the fortieth year, he tried to liberate his people and killed an Egyptian. He tried to fight untransformed power with untransformed power. He tried to be strong like Pharaoh. He failed, was exiled, and spent forty years in the desert. The result was further oppression of the Jews and forty years of sheep herding for Moses, until he was pliable enough, "weak" enough, to be used as a vessel of God for the redemption of Israel.

Finally, God confronts Moses in the burning bush, fills him with the Spirit of "I AM," and sends him back to the palace of Pharaoh with such power that all of Egypt is soon decimated by the Ten Plagues: The Nile turns to blood; frogs cover the land; gnats arise out of the dust; flies swarm in such numbers to cover the sun; pestilence kills off the livestock; boils inflict the Egyptians; hail rains from the sky; locusts eat all the crops; darkness settles over the land for three days; and finally, all the first-born Egyptian males are slain in a single night.

The same night when all the first-born males of Egypt were killed, the Israelites, who had been spared the plagues, were commanded to hold their first Passover, the eating of a prescribed meal with unleavened bread. As the cries of grief rose throughout all Egypt the Israelites fled, Moses leading them. When they reached the Red Sea, they looked behind them and saw the Egyptian army pursuing them. The Israelites lost heart and complained that Moses should have left them in bondage in Egypt rather than let them die in the wilderness. Moses replied, echoing the words of Joseph, "Fear not, stand firm, and see the salvation of the Lord, which he will work for you this day.... The Lord will fight for you, and you have only to be still" (Ex. 14:13).

Moses then raised his rod and commanded the Red Sea to part its waters. Israel marched across on dry land with walls of water on either side. Pharaoh and his hosts pursued them, but the water, which parted for the man of faith, descended upon this paragon of untransformed power. Pharaoh and all his troops were drowned, and Israel proceeded into the Sinai.

God's strength working through human weakness,

God's wisdom working through what the world calls foolishness, God's transforming power, working through
humanity's untransformed power, is a consistent theme
throughout the biblical narrative. This is a principle reason
why in contradistinction to every other tradition, the Jews
did not present their heroes as great Titans of unblemished splendor. For them, human extremity, not human
strength, was God's opportunity. Human depravity was
the very elixir for the Great Alchemist to refine into spiritual gold.

Jesus followed in this tradition. He was conceived out
of wedlock; hunted by King Herod; chased into Egypt
while still an infant; despised by the religious leadership;
and killed by unanimous consent at age thirty-three,
deserted even by his own family and disciples. Yet every
act recorded of him was an act of goodness. Like Joseph
and Moses, he exemplified a deeper dimension of the
truths concerning the transformation of power embedded
in the Hebrew tradition. Thus when Pilate said to him,
"Do you not know that I have the power to crucify you or
release you?" Jesus replied, "You could have no power over
me except it were given to you from above" (Jn. 19:10,11).

Pilate actually believed he was in control. But in his
"wisdom," he was enslaved; in his exercise of power, he was
obsessed with the desire to dominate, thereby empowering
the very one he sought to vanquish. When Pilate condemned
Jesus to die, he could not know that he was, in fact,
condemning the very empire he represented to overthrow
by the followers of the man he was executing.

CHAPTER 11

THE BLACK DEATH

Time present and time past

Are both perhaps present in time future

And time future contained in time past.

If all time is eternally present

All time is unredeemable.

What might have been is an abstraction

Remaining a perpetual possibility

Only in a world of speculation.

What might have been and what has been

Point to one end, which is always present.

Footfalls echo in the memory

Down the passage which we did not take

Towards the door we never opened

Into the rose garden.[1]

1. Eliot, *Collected Poems*, 189.

W HAT WE CAN SEE THUS FAR IN CIVILIZATION'S great odyssey from the dim reaches of our hominid past to the nurture of the Great Mother, to the defiance of Gilgamesh, to the enlightenment of the Buddha, to the transgression of Adam and Eve, to the agony of apocalypse, to the trials of Job, to the sublimity of Sophia, to the obedience of Mary, and to the transformation of power in Jesus is that human civilization has long grappled with the deepest of issues: the wisdom of limits and the consequences of violating them; the need for redemption in the aftermath of hubris; and the transformation of power for-and-of-itself into power for service unto others. And always before us is the challenge to assimilate into our ordinary categories of cognition the understanding that everything we experience, from the lightest of the light to the darkest of the dark, emanates from a single unitary source. It is this that allows us to discern the highest definition of freedom as a submission to a higher will not our own.

All these issues arising out of our spiritual depth, embedded in the created order itself, confront us repeatedly throughout our history and in our everyday life. To understand the interrelationship between our common-sense decisions and these deep, eternal verities of nature and psyche is, in the end, what the process of civilization is and should be about: wrestling with our own contradictions in order to build a more holistic world.

The great tragedy of the Church was that, like the disciples, it tended to interpret the manifestation of the Spirit in the

Exodus and in Christ crucified within the common-sense categories of time, space, and causality. It sought to express the antinomies that characterized the lives of Joseph, Moses, Job, and Jesus within the limitations and distortions of rational mind and of culture.

Consequently, the Church interpreted transformed power within the context of untransformed power. Under the influence of Greek philosophic thought, the early Christians sought a logical simplicity that dichotomized good and evil, God and humanity. They abandoned the cruciform profundity of the Jewish sages for the simplicities of linear logic and the expediencies of political advantage.

The fate of Sophia was equally tragic. The early church incorporated the attributes of Sophia into an apotheosized Jesus, and she ceased to exist as an independent entity. The Greeks, who viewed women as not only inferior in stitutionally but as inferior ontologically—almost as if they were another species—reinforced her demise. For the Greeks, the distinction between male and female described an essential polarity. Men represented what was rational and civilized, therefore superior, and women represented what was irrational and uncivilized, therefore inferior. Jewish thinkers in late antiquity, such as Philo of Alexandria, adopted this view.

The Greeks also negatively influenced the Judeo-Christian notions concerning the earth. The Jews had taught that, though humanity had been given dominion over the earth in order to subdue it, this dominion entailed enormous responsibilities. One's actions affected the earth for good and for ill. The Greeks viewed the earth as an unruly female, the antithesis of civilization, which, like women, needed to be conquered and tamed.

Ironically, Sophia reached the pinnacle of her influence in late antiquity and received her most powerful expression in Christ crucified. But Christianity utilized the linear wisdom of the Greeks to interpret the cruciform wisdom of Sophia and Christ, which required masculine energies on the political level to conquer the Roman empire and, on the theological level, to stamp out the mystery religions prevalent throughout the ancient world, as well as various heresies within its own ranks.

The Roman Emperor Constantine converted in C.E. 323 and announced that Christianity would henceforth be the State religion. He convened a series of great councils that developed the orthodoxy of the church and put down heresies. By the twelfth and thirteenth centuries C.E., papal power in Europe was predominant, and church dogma was undisputed.

The religion founded with a power independent of Rome now ruled from Rome with more power than Rome had ever exercised. Rome ruled by the sword; the Church ruled with the sword and the Cross, wielding, as Jesus himself had prophesied, the keys to heaven and earth. The Church held sway in Europe for over a thousand years. Preaching transformed power, it ruled with an untransformed power rivaling that of the Caesars.

At the apogee of papal power in the thirteenth century, the tide began to turn. Gradually the secular power of the kings replaced that of the pope; the intellectual acuity of science, that of church dogma. The great denouement came in the fourteenth century. If the several centuries before Christ were a time of great crisis for Israel, so the fourteenth century after Christ was a time of great crisis for Christians. The historian Barbara Tuchman writes in her book *A Distant Mirror* that the fourteenth century was "a violent, tormented, bewildered, suffering and disintegrating age, a time, as many thought, of Satan triumphant...."[2] This may be an understatement, for the fourteenth century experienced the most lethal disaster ever to beset the human race: the Black Death of 1347, which was to infect Europe in various forms for the next 150 years.

Until quite recently historians and theologians alike have tended to ignore this time of troubles because it does not fit with our firmly held belief in humanity's inexorable march of progress. After the destructiveness of the twentieth century, however, we are discovering more of a kinship than perhaps we would like with other ages where institutions and assumptions snapped under the pressure of adverse and violent events.

The fourteenth century started badly, very badly. The Baltic Sea froze twice, in 1303 and 1306. The following years were extraordinarily cold and fraught with bitter storms, which meant nothing less than disaster for the Europeans. The population had already reached the limit of what could be accommodated with normal seasonal farming. The clearing of productive land had also reached its limit, and crop yields could not be raised substantially nor could the already poor and soggy soil be made more productive. The transport of grain was difficult, except when conducted by water; therefore, many inland populations had to live on local resources. When these reserves dwindled, people starved.

The rains in 1315 were so relentless that people recalled the days of Noah. When crops failed all across Europe and

2. Barbara Tuchman, introduction to *A Distant Mirror: The Calamitous Fourteenth Century* (New York: Ballantine Books, 1978), xiii.

famine swept the land, the desperate people recalled also the dark horseman of the Apocalypse. Reports spread of parents eating their children, of the poor in Poland feeding on the bodies of executed criminals. The decade 1310–19 experienced the worst famine in European history. From 1316 to 1322 the European population declined 10 percent to 25 percent, depending on the region.

Social and political upheaval accompanied climactic cataclysm. As with the Jews at the hands of Greece and Rome, morality during this century was turned on its head. Christianity had been the matrix of feudal life in Europe. It governed birth and death, marriage and taxes; it determined the rules for medicine and law; it provided guidance and content for theology and philosophy. To be or not to be in the Church was not an option. It was simply *the* fact of existence.

Above all, the Church had given answers. For a thousand years since Constantine, it had provided the framework for Western culture, articulating meaning and purpose in an otherwise capricious world. It had affirmed that human life on earth was but a passage either to paradise or to perdition. As the fourteenth century Italian poet Francesco Petrarch wrote, life was nothing but "a hard and weary journey toward the eternal home for which we look; or, if we neglect our salvation, an equally pleasureless way to eternal death" (28). The Church offered salvation through rituals it had established and through priests it had ordained. *Extra ecclesiam nulla salus* (No salvation outside the church) was taken for granted as much as the idea that the world was flat.

The Pope was the Vicar of Christ. He held the keys to heaven and earth, subsuming all secular power under his religious command. His ultimate authority lay with his power to excommunicate, to condemn to Hell anyone, from king to beggar, by casting him or her out of the Mother Church. Excommunication was a fate worse than death. It came as something worse than a shock, therefore, when at the beginning of the fourteenth century, the King of France, under threat of excommunication, not only challenged the Pope but also brought him to his knees.

The issue was temporal versus papal authority, arising in the last decade of the thirteenth century when King Philip IV of France insisted that he could levy taxes against the French clergy without the consent of the Roman Pontiff. Pope Boniface VIII responded with the defiant Bull *Clericos Laicos* of 1296, forbidding the clergy to pay any form of tax to any secular ruler. He argued that the growing tendency of the clergy to hesitate between allegiance to king or to Pope posed a direct threat to the Church's claim that the Pope was the universal Vicar of Christ. King Philip refused to give way, so in 1302 Pope Boniface issued a second Bull, proclaiming that it was imperative that every person wanting salvation be subject to the Roman pontiff.

The king acknowledged that salvation might indeed be determined from Rome but that French taxes were to be determined from Paris. He called for a council to judge the Pope on charges of blasphemy, sodomy, simony, heresy, murder, sorcery, and failure to fast on the fast days. The Pope immediately drew up a Bull of excommunication, but before it could be issued, agents of the King, aided by anti-papist Italian armed forces, seized the eighty-three-year-old pontiff at his summer retreat at Anagni near Rome. The citizens of Anagni freed Boniface after three days in bondage, but the trauma of the ordeal was more than he could bear. Within a month, he was dead.

Under the influence of King Philip, a Frenchman was elected Pope Clement V. Clement refused to go to Rome to take up his See because he feared Italian reprisals for the French treatment of Boniface. The Italians said that it was because Clement kept a French mistress, the beautiful Countess of Perigord. In 1309 Clement settled in Avignon in Provence, near the mouth of the Rhone River. It was a strategic choice. Avignon was clearly within the French political sphere, though technically not in France itself, since Provence was a fief of the Kingdom of Naples and Sicily. It was also suitably close to Foix, the home of the beautiful Countess.

Six French popes, under whom Avignon became a great city-state of pomp, great cultural splendor, and unbridled corruption, succeeded Clement V. With its authority diminished by its absence from Rome and by its subservience to the French king, the Avignon papacy sought to gain power through finance.

Besides the regular revenue from tithes and the income from papal fiefs, every office, every nomination, every appointment, every dispensation of rules, every judgment of a claim, every pardon, every indulgence, every absolution—everything the Church possessed or brokered, from the cardinals' robes to the pilgrims' relics—was for sale. Excommunication, formerly the utmost measure a pope could command against infidels, blasphemers, and the disloyal, was now used to extract money from reluctant believers.

Petrarch observed that "the successors of the poor fishermen of Galilee were in Avignon loaded with gold and clad in purple.... I am living in the 'Babylon of the West,' where prelates feast at 'licentious banquets' and ride on snow white horses decked in gold, fed on gold, soon to be shod in gold if the Lord does not check this slavish luxury" (28, 29).

The papacy in Rome was equally corrupt. In one of the tales of *The Decameron*, Boccaccio, a contemporary of Petrach's, describes the journey of a Jew named Abraham to Rome to examine the spirituality of the papacy. What he discovered was that "from the highest to the lowest they all generally and most unworthily indulged in the sin of lechery...without the slightest remorse or shame. And this to such an extent that the power of courtesans and boys was of considerable importance in obtaining any favor.... They were openly gluttons, winebibbers and drunkards, and after lechery were, like brute beasts, more servants of their bellies than of anything else."[3]

Abraham discerned that the Pope and his court "were all avaricious and grasping after money, and that for money they bought and sold human, and even Christian blood, and also every sort of divine thing whether appertaining to the sacraments or to benefices. They did more trade and had more brokers than there were for all the silks and other goods of Paris, and gave the name of 'Procurator' to the most flagrant simony and that of 'Maintenance' to gluttony" (57).

Some sought to bring reform from within. A small sect of Franciscans called *Fraticelli* challenged the sumptuous wealth of its own order. Founded only a century earlier by Saint Francis in the spirit of poverty and humble obedience, it had

3. Giovanni Boccaccio, *The Decameron*, trans. Richard Aldington (New York: Dell Publishing, 1976), 57.

grown into one of the richest orders of the church. The *Fraticelli* insisted that since Christ and Saint Francis had lived without possessions, so should all true Christians.

A whole host of similar poverty movements and mystical sects arose in an effort to sweep away the ecclesiastical obsession with wealth. They sought intimacy with God through cutting their bonds with the material world. The *Fraticelli* insistence on the absolute poverty of Christ and the Apostles was acutely embarrassing for the Avignon papacy, which condemned the *Fraticelli* as a "false and pernicious heresy" in 1315. In 1318, the Inquisition tried twenty-seven of them in Marseilles and burned four at the stake.

In 1320 a mass movement, called the Pastoureaux for the shepherds who started it, broke out. The peasants were starving; the monarchy was brutalizing them; and church corruption was scandalizing them. Inspired by prophecies that the poor would rise up against the rich, overthrow the Church, defy an unspecified monarch, and usher in a new age amidst bloodshed and fire, thousands of rootless peasants and poor began marching south from northern France toward Avignon in an imagined embarkation for a new crusade in the Holy Land. They stormed abbeys and castles, burned town halls and tax records, and launched concentrated assaults against Jews and lepers.

Finally the Pastoureaux menaced Avignon itself, attacking priests, seizing Church lands, and threatening the nobility. Pope John XXII excommunicated the whole lot, forbidding anyone to help them on pain of death. Royal and papal troops then joined forces to crush the inspired but disorganized peasants, and the Pastoureaux revolt ended, as did the *Fraticelli* reform—as corpses hanging from trees.

The growing corruption of the Church invited secular encroachments. In 1307 King Philip the Fair of France turned against the Templar knights, an event that was the sensation of the fourteenth century. No downfall was as spectacular as that of this order of monastic knights. Formed during the Crusades to be the sworn arm of the Church in its defense of the Holy Land against the Moslem armies, the Templars, like the Franciscans, had abandoned their original ideals of asceticism and had evolved into an international brotherhood of immense power, wealth, and influence beyond the power of either Church or State.

Tax-exempt from the beginning, they had amassed vast riches as the bankers of the Vatican and as money-lenders, undercutting the interest rates of the Lombards and Jews. Unlike the Knights of Saint John, they supported neither hospitals nor charity, and, with over two thousand members in France alone, they accumulated the largest treasury in northern Europe and maintained headquarters in "the Temple," a formidable fortress in Paris. They seemed to have no purpose other than the accumulation of wealth, power, and influence.

Having exhausted every other source of money, including taxing the clergy, King Philip turned his attention to the Templars. Without warning, Philip seized their Temple and had every Templar in France arrested. To justify these confiscations and arrests, Philip charged the Templars with the very kinds of corruption the Church was becoming associated with, adding a few colorful ones to appeal to the public's prurient interests. The Templars were charged with bestiality, idolatry, sodomy and intercourse with demons, urinating and trampling on the Cross, even drinking a powder made from the ashes of dead Templars and their own illegitimate children.

Philip demanded that Pope Clement V authorize trials. Since the king had been his principle patron in his election as pope, Clement complied. With this papal authority, Philip subjected the Templars to extraordinary tortures in order to extract confessions. As might be imagined, medieval justice was not particularly scrupulous about holding proper trials and being careful not to condemn without proof of guilt. Confessions, not evidence, were usually the sources of proof, and torture, not due process, was the usual method of obtaining them. The Templars, many of them old men, were thumbscrewed, beaten, starved, racked, and hung with weights until their joints dislocated; their teeth and nails were ripped out; their feet were held over fire; and their bodies dipped in boiling oil. The only pauses in these tortures were for questioning, and they either confessed or died. Needless to say, the Templars were judged guilty, and the king got his money.

It was in the midst of all this turmoil, with assumptions built up over a thousand years being shattered by intellectual, political, and economic ferment in an era of unbridled corruption and obsession with wealth and power, with no respected authority to guide anyone through the uncertainties, the despairs, or the tragedies, that rumors began to reach Europe of a horrible plague spreading from the East. First heard in 1346, the rumors told of a disease that had started in China and had spread through Central Asia to India, to Persia, to Mesopotamia, to Egypt, and to Asia Minor. Travelers from India reported that the country was depopulated and covered with dead bodies. Little alarm accompanied these reports, however, because there was very little contact with these regions and no one knew about contagion.

As recounted by an Italian historian of the time, Gabriele de Mussis, the plague entered the Mediterranean at the Genoese settlement of Caffa in 1347. A street fight between Genoese merchants and local Muslims degenerated into a war, and the Muslims enlisted the aid of a neighboring Tartar warlord named Janibeg who raised a large army. The Genoese fortified Caffa, and Janibeg laid siege. During the siege, infected rodents probably brought the plague, which began to decimate Janibeg's army.

With his own troops dying en masse, Janibeg decided on a devious but successful strategy: He catapulted the corpses of the plague victims over the walls into the Genoese citadel. The rotting bodies infected Caffa, and the city fell in October. A few survivors secreted away in ships, arriving in the harbor of Messina on the eastern coast of Sicily with dead and dying sailors at the oars. Although the sailors were forbidden to leave their ships, no one thought to stop the rats.

As Boccaccio describes it, the plague "began both in men and women with certain swellings in the groin or under the armpit. They grew to the size of a small apple or an egg…. In a short space of time these tumors spread…all over the body. Soon after this the symptoms changed and black or purple spots appeared on the arms or thighs or any other part of the body, sometimes a few large ones, sometimes many little ones. These spots were a certain sign of death" (31).

A number of infected Messinians made their way to Catania, another coastal town approximately fifty-five miles to the south. They were initially treated with kindness, but as soon as the Catanians understood the virulence of the disease, they shunned contact with anyone coming from Messina and refused to extend any further assistance. Their quarantine had no effect; by early November, not only Catania but also all of Sicily was infected.

That same month the plague spread to Constantinople, the capitol of the Byzantine Empire. From there, it spread down to Egypt, across North Africa, and east throughout the Middle East and the Caucasus. By 1349 the plague had ravaged the entire Islamic world.

In December 1347 the plague spread to southern Italy. In January 1348 it penetrated France via Marseilles and North Africa via Tunis. It spread quickly from Marseilles through Languedoc to Spain and northward up the Rhone River to Avignon where it arrived in March. It reached Narbonne, Montpellier, Carcassonne, and Toulouse between February and May and continued spreading east and south into Florence and Rome. Between June and August, the plague decimated Bordeaux, Lyon, and Paris, followed by regions of Burgundy, Normandy, and southern England. During the same summer it crossed the Alps from Italy into Switzerland and eastward into Hungary.

In 1349 the disease raged through the Low Countries and spread from England to Ireland, Scotland, and Norway. From there it decimated Sweden, Denmark, Prussia, Iceland, even Greenland, although Bohemia was curiously untouched. Russia was uninfected until 1351 when it was hit with a vengeance. The disease left most of Europe in mid-1350, only to reappear in sporadic outbreaks from 1361 to 1429. The plague continued to infect different parts of Europe until the end of the fifteenth century.

The mortality rate was erratic, ranging from 20 to 90 percent of the affected populations. The disease accomplished its kill in four to six weeks and then faded away, except in the larger cities where, rooted in crowded quarters, it abated during the winter, only to reappear and rage from springtime till fall.

"So violent was the malignancy of this plague," observed Boccaccio, "that it was communicated, not only from one man to another, but from the garments of a sick or dead man to animals of another species, which caught the disease in that way and very quickly died of it" (32). He himself witnessed two pigs browsing through the ragged clothes of a man who had died in the streets of Florence. After only a short time, the pigs died also.

Venice, the largest and wealthiest city in Europe at the time, with a population of one hundred fifty thousand, lost approximately one hundred thousand in the eighteen months after the plague hit it in December 1347. In Paris people died at the rate of eight hundred a day, until half its population of one hundred twenty thousand lay dead. Boccaccio estimated that Florence lost over one hundred thousand to the plague, roughly three-quarters of its population. Hamburg and Bremen lost two-thirds of their population.

In crowded Avignon, with a population ranging from twenty thousand to fifty thousand, four hundred people died daily at the height of the plague. Half the population, including one-third of all the cardinals and seventy of the lesser prelates were wiped out. A single graveyard received eleven thousand corpses in six weeks. Toward the end, until mass burial pits were dug, bodies were simply thrown into the Rhone River.

Amid the accumulating bodies and mounting terror, people were left to die without last rites and were buried without prayers, a horrible prospect in a culture with a strong belief in the hereafter and with an eroding belief in ecclesiastical credibility. Boccaccio states that "one citizen avoided another, hardly any neighbor troubled about others, relatives never or hardly ever visited each other" (33). There was such terror afoot, he said, that "brother abandoned brother, and the uncle his nephew, and the sister her brother, and very often the wife her husband.... Fathers and mothers refused to see and tend their children, as if they had not been theirs."

Alienation was coupled with sensuality and debauchery. Most of the one hundred tales comprising Boccaccio's *The Decameron* deal with sexuality, pleasure, corruption, and intrigue, and describe the pervasiveness of the Epicurean response to the plague. In the face of shocking unexplainable and unimaginable death, people pursued the gratification of the senses. Boccaccio's tales recall the Greek historian Thucydides's observations concerning the great plague of Athens in 430 B.C.E., in his classic work *The Peloponesian War*, "For seeing how the rich died in a moment and those who had nothing immediately inheriting their property, they reflected that life and riches were alike transitory, and they resolved to enjoy themselves while they could."[4]

4. Thucydides, *The Peloponnesian War*, trans. Rex Warner (London: Penguin Books, 1952), 155.

Ignorance of the plague only increased the fear. Medieval Europe had no awareness of bacterial infection or that rats and fleas were the carriers. Contemporary plague writings do not mention fleas once; and rats, only incidentally, because folklore commonly associated them with pestilence. The legend of the Pied Piper arose from an outbreak of plague in 1284. The plague bacillus, *Pasturella pestis*, was not discovered until the eighteenth century. Living in the stomach of the flea and in the bloodstream of the small, black rat, *Rattus rattus,* as well as in the heavier brown rat, the bacillus was transferred to humans and animals by either flea or rat bites.

Although scientists still do not know what caused the bacillus to change from an innocuous to a virulent form, it is now believed that the plague arose in the Gobi desert and then spread along the caravan routes of the Mongol empire east into China, south into India, and west into Central Asia, the Middle East, and the Mediterranean. Called the Black Death only later, it was known then as the Pestilence or Great Mortality.

The medical faculty of the University of Paris, asked by Philip VI in 1348 to deliver to him the reason for this calamity, ascribed it to a triple conjunction of Mars, Jupiter, and Saturn in the fortieth degree of Aquarius, which occurred on 20 March 1345. The report acknowledged, however, that the Pestilence was a curse "whose cause is hidden from even the most highly trained intellects."[5]

Although this explanation satisfied alchemists and philosophers and, in fact, became the accepted official version, it was widely believed that the plague, like the Flood, had been sent to wipe away corrupted Christendom. Boccaccio believed that the plague started "either through the influence of the heavenly bodies or because God's just anger with our wicked deeds sent it as a punishment to mortal men; and in a few years killed an innu-

5. Tuchman, A *Distant Mirror,* 103.

merable quantity of people."[6] The Italian commentator Villani concluded that the plague was retribution for the sins of greed and usury that oppressed the poor. Such a sweeping devastating scourge, he said, could only be a divine punishment for human sin. Even the Pope issued a Bull in September 1348 speaking of the "pestilence with which God is afflicting the Christian people."[7]

It is profoundly important, given the previous discussion concerning the interrelationship between humanity and the earth and the presence of the Eternal in all the dimensions of life, that in the midst of the most devastating natural catastrophe in human history, which seemed to be wiping away the very foundations of medieval Christian civilization, many could discern, even if unclearly and with many distortions, the mysterious handiwork of God, wiping away the corruption and ushering in something more purified.

The perennial tragedy of human affairs is that however much one senses the reality of the divine in and through one's afflictions, the natural impulse is to blame somebody else. During the Black Death, unable to admit that the proper response was repentance, most Christians blamed the plague on the Jews.

The lynchings began in the spring of 1348, right after the first onslaught of the plague. Charged with poisoning the wells and with intent "to kill and destroy the whole of Christendom and have lordship over all the world," the Jews in Narbonne and Carcassone, France were dragged from their homes and thrown into bonfires.

In the hysteria incited by the plague, it was easy to attack the Jews, particularly since the Church had for decades been issuing one decree after another designed

6. Boccaccio, *Decameron*, 30.

7. Tuchman, *A Distant Mirror*, 105.

to isolate Jews from Christian society, the theory being that any contact brought the Christian faith into disrepute. When Pope Clement VI issued a Bull in 1348 prohibiting the killing, looting, or forcible conversion of Jews without trial, few took him seriously. Although attacks against Jews were halted in Avignon and the Papal States, authorities in most places either succumbed to or incited popular anti-Semitism, with an eye to benefiting from the seizure of Jewish property.

It was during September 1348 in Savoy, Spain that the first formal trials against Jews began. All their property was confiscated as they stood trial on charges of participating in an international Jewish conspiracy emanating from Spain to poison the wells of Europe. The prosecution produced confessions from the Jews—extracted through tortures similar to those used against the Templars—that they carried in small packets a powder used to poison the wells. The accused were duly condemned to death. Eleven were burned alive; the rest were subjected to a tax of 160 florins every month for six years in exchange for permission to remain in Savoy. Their property was never returned.

These trials began a wave of accusations and attacks throughout Europe, especially in Alsace, Switzerland, and in Germany. In Basle on 9 January 1349, an entire community of several hundred Jews was herded into a specially constructed wooden house on an island in the Rhine and burned alive. A decree was passed that barred Jews from Basle for two hundred years. In February 1349, even before the plague had reached the city, the two thousand Jews of Strasbourg were taken to a burial ground and all, save the few who converted, were burnt to death on rows of stakes. As the ashes smoldered, citizens participating in

the massacre sifted through the bones to find valuables
not already taken.

Attacks against the Jews were given religious sanction
by a wave of flagellants, a movement that erupted in a
sudden frenzy and spread across Europe with the same
fiery contagion as the plague. Organized in groups of
several hundred to one thousand, the flagellants, stripped
to the waist, marched from city to city, scourging themselves with leather whips tipped with iron spikes. They
saw themselves as redeemers, who could atone for the
wickedness the plague had been sent to punish by
re-enacting the scourging of Christ, until their blood
flowed. They believed their own suffering, as Christ's
death on the Cross, would atone for the sins of Europe.

Forming first in the German states where they enjoyed
their greatest popularity, the flagellants spread quickly
through the Low Countries and into France. Hundreds
of bands roamed the land singing hymns of woe to the
Virgin Mary, proclaiming that if not for them all
Christendom would meet perdition.

Upon entering the towns and cities, the flagellants
prayed in the churches, often threatening the priests, and
rushed to the Jewish quarters, vowing revenge against the
"poisoners of the wells." In Freiburg, Munich, Nuremberg,
Augsburg, and Koenigsberg, the Jews were liquidated
with frenzy and precision. In Speyer massacred Jewish
bodies were loaded in wine caskets and floated down the
Rhine. In March 1349 in Worms, the Jewish community
of four hundred, recalling Masada, burned themselves to
death inside their houses before the flagellants could
reach them. In July the Jews of Frankfurt-am-Main took
the same recourse.

Not until August, when the flagellants reached Mainz, home of the largest Jewish community in Europe, did the Jews fight back. They killed two hundred of the attackers, inciting the entire city against them. Fighting until overpowered, the Jews retreated to their homes and set them on fire. Some six thousand are said to have perished.

The last pogroms in Western Europe took place in Antwerp and Brussels in December 1349, when the Jewish communities were entirely exterminated. Pogroms then broke out along the Baltic coast and in Eastern Europe where the Black Death was beginning to ravage those populations. By 1351 the flagellants and other anti-Semitic groups had conducted more than three hundred fifty massacres. They succeeded in exterminating sixty major and one hundred fifty minor Jewish communities. It was not until the Final Solution of the Nazis, some seven hundred years later, that the Jews were again to suffer such carnage.

By the time the plague and flagellants had passed, few Jews were left in either Germany or the Low Countries. Most who escaped went to Eastern Europe, accepting the protection of King Casimir of Poland, the single monarch in all of Europe to stand firmly against any persecution of the Jews because of the plague. A fundamental legacy of the Black Death was this eastward migration of the Jews into Poland and Russia, where they were to remain until the Holocaust.

By the end of 1351, the initial onslaught of the Black Death had run its course. The Vatican calculated a death toll of 23,840,000. Before the plague, the population of Europe was approximately seventy-five million, which, if we take the Vatican's figures, would mean a casualty rate of 31 percent. The Islamic world suffered the same fate; roughly, one-third of the populations of northern Africa and the Middle East were wiped out.

The Islamic scholar and historian Ibn Khaldun, whose parents were taken by the plague, provided what is considered perhaps the best contemporary summary of its impact:

> Civilization both in the East and the West was visited by a destructive plague, which devastated nations and caused populations to vanish. It swallowed up many of the good things of civilization and wiped them out. It overtook the dynasties at the time of their senility, when they had reach the limit of their duration. It lessened their power and curtailed their influence. It weakened their authority. Their situation approached the point of annihilation and dissolution. Civilization decreased with the decrease of mankind. Cities and buildings were laid waste, roads and way signs were obliterated, settlements and mansions became empty, and dynasties and tribes grew weak. The entire inhabited world changed. The East, it seems, was similarly visited, though in accordance with and in proportion to civilization. It was as if the voice of existence in the world had called out for oblivion and restriction and the world responded to its call.[8]

In the Islamic world, the religious institutions were much newer, having been established in the eighth and ninth centuries C.E. The inspiration of Mohammed was still fresh, empowering an expanding empire. Social cohesion and political institutions were extremely strong. Although similar numbers died and there was concurrent

8. Robert S. Gottfried, *The Black Death: Natural and Human Disaster in Medieval Europe* (New York: The Free Press, 1983), 41–2.

social and political upheaval, there was no serious or sustained questioning of the authority of Islam.

Christian survivors of the plague, however, were traumatically demoralized and unable to discover purpose or meaning in the pain they had suffered. The Black Death had simply been too terrible and the agony too great to be accepted without question. Tragically, Church corruption was such that it was impossible to go to that institution for credible answers concerning the widespread intuition that somehow, in some mysterious way, the judgment of divine grace was working in and through this devastation. The Black Death, coupled with the inability of the Church to provide moral leadership at a time of great crisis, destroyed the moorings of medieval Europe, fixed for over a thousand years by Catholic dogma. Christians, searching for God, began to look elsewhere for the meaning they knew had to be there.

CHAPTER 12

NOTRE DAME

But to apprehend

The point of intersection of the timeless

With time, is an occupation of a saint—

No occupation either, but something given

And taken, in a lifetime's death in love,

Ardour and selflessness and self-surrender.[1]

PERSONS IN PAIN WANT THEIR MOTHERS. Under normal conditions the first point of sustained nurturing for an infant is its mother's breast. It is the breast, the smiling face of the mother, the warmth of her lap, the affection of her arms encircling her baby that provide the security for the passage from her watery, dark, and all-enveloping womb into the realities of the external world. When the external world becomes dangerous beyond our ability to cope, understand, or transform, we want our mother back. When the existing social structure consumes itself and destruction is all around, we seek naturally and instinctively to return to the maternal well-spring from whence we came.

This is what the Jews had experienced fifteen hundred years before at the hands of the Greeks and the Romans. In the midst of their apocalyptic despair, Sophia had risen with

1. Eliot, *Collected Poems*, 212.

particular force to grace the world and speak to their hearts. Amid the Black Death with its concomitant ecclesiastical corruption, anti-Semitism, brigandage, wars, and economic dislocation, Christians in unprecedented numbers across Europe began to supplicate the Virgin Mary. In fact, the outpouring of adoration for her during the fourteenth century has had no parallel in the entire history of Christendom until the present generation.

Mary was the obvious and, in some ways, the only place for Christians to turn. From the time she had been depicted as the Queen of Heaven in Rome's Church of St. Maria Antiqua in the sixth century C.E., Mary's position and power in the Catholic Church and therefore in Europe had been pre-eminent. The image of Mary as Queen of Heaven had been a principal component of the rise of the Roman papacy as it consolidated power against other Christian centers and against secular seats of power. The image of the Virgin Mary in triumph emphasized the orthodoxy of Church dogma itself, as well as the role of the Church as spiritual and secular leader of Christendom and Europe. The cultivation of her cult was something that the papacy, in particular, and the Catholic Church, in general, tended with care.

During the twelfth century Mary's power was augmented with a new dimension of reverence, which peaked during the Black Death. This was a reverence for the Virgin not only as Queen but also as Mother. As Queen, Mary was a political instrument and an object of religious veneration; as Mother, she touched the suffering of the believers. The beginnings of this personalization came with Saint Bernard, the Cistercian abbot of Clairvaux, who dominated the twelfth century with his magnetism and influence.

From 1135 to 1153 Bernard gave eighty-six sermons on the Song of Songs, which stand today as one of the monuments of Christian mysticism. In these sermons Bernard uses, for the first time in Christian liturgy, explicitly erotic imagery, as sensual and sexual as the Song of Songs itself. His thesis was that carnal desire disfigures the soul and distances the individual from God, but spiritual desire glorifies the soul and reunites the individual with God. The imagery for both is the same, however, and on this paradox, Bernard lived out what it meant to him to be a Christian.

For Bernard the phrase "kisses of his mouth"[2] personifies the gateway to perdition at the physical level and the signal for ecstatic union with Christ at the spiritual level. God is love, Christ is love, and Christ's kiss transfigures the believer in and with love. However, this moment cannot be sustained and only prefigures the future grace that the believer will enjoy in heaven. Only the Virgin Mary, filled with love because she gave birth to love, can mediate the intensity of the mystical experience. As Mother of God and Mother of the Church, Mary alone can bridge the vast distance between the sin-prone and carnal believers on earth and the loving Christ enthroned in heaven.

Paraphrasing the Song of Songs, Bernard exalts that Mary is "as the morning, fair as the moon, clear as the sun," rising into heaven from the earth as "pillars of smoke, perfumed with myrrh and frankincense" (130). Thus he transfigures Mary in European Christian minds into someone personal, someone of flesh and blood, someone approachable. Mary the Queen becomes in Saint Bernard the compassionate,

2. Marina Warner, *Alone of All Her Sex* (New York: Random House, 1983), 136.

sensual Mother.

This personalized love of Mary the Mother swept Europe. The Cistercian order established hundreds of abbeys all over Europe, each with her image over its entrance. The priests and monks wore white in honor of her purity and sang the antiphon *Salve Regina* at vespers:

> To thee we cry, banished children of Eve.
>
> to thee do we sigh, groaning and weeping
>
> In this vale of tears (115).

This adoration was not limited to the Cistercians. Hundreds of cathedrals and thousands of chapels were built in her honor. In cathedrals already built, the practice of erecting a special chapel to Mary began. In France alone, eighty cathedrals were built in Mary's name over the next century.

As the cult of Mary was reaching its zenith there was a revolution in secular literature for which her cult was a cause and an effect. This was the literature of the troubadours with its emphasis on courtly, physical love. After centuries of literature deprecating the flesh and pointing only heavenward for value and meaning, poets and writers began to celebrate human love as good and valuable in its own right. After more than a millennium of denigrating the flesh in favor of the spirit, honoring human love signaled a veritable revolution in consciousness.

The first troubadour was Guillaume, 9th Duc d'Aquitaine (1071–1127). His granddaughter, Eleanor of Aquitaine, emerged as not only one of the most powerful and celebrated individuals of the century but also as the personification of the troubadour tradition, which she brought to the French court upon her marriage to Louis

VII in 1137 and, after he died, to the English court of Henry II in 1152.

Eleanor's daughter, Marie de Champagne, inspired the celebrated French writer Chrétien de Troyes to compose the poem *Lancelot*, which combined the primitive Celtic legend of King Arthur and his knights at Camelot with the principles of courtly love. The poem became immensely popular throughout Europe, scandalizing the Church with its account of the love affair between Lancelot, a knight of King Arthur's Round Table, and Arthur's Queen, the beautiful and amorous Guinevere.

In one scene, de Troyes portrays Lancelot kneeling to pray at a shrine beside Guinevere's bed before joining her upon it. "Love," says de Troyes, "is a certain inborn suffering derived from the sight of and excessive meditation upon the beauty of the opposite sex, which causes one to wish above all things the embraces of the other and by common desire to carry out all love's precepts in the other's embrace" (138,139).

The troubadours celebrated love, but they were still medieval enough, in Bernard's sense of the term, to accept the notion that their lady was worthy of love precisely because she was too pure to consummate it physically. Although de Troyes's endorsement of actual sexual consummation was the logical conclusion of the troubadours, sexuality remained a scandal to medieval society. It was the Italian poet Dante Alighieri in his immortal *Divine Comedy*, finished around 1315, who, by synthesizing the ardor of the troubadours with the mysticism of Saint Bernard, expressed the highest reaches of the medieval mind in its adoration of the feminine and the Virgin Mother Mary.

Dante was a man in mid-life when he saw the nine-year-old Beatrice dei Portini adorned in a crimson dress. He immediately fell deeply, passionately, and completely in love with her, but consummation was not their destiny. His most wretched moment was her refusal to greet him when they passed each other next. Several years later, Beatrice was married to a Florentine merchant, Simone dei Bardi, and never, as far as we know, interacted with Dante beyond a few short conversations. Nevertheless, she inspired *The Divine Comedy*, in which Dante states that Beatrice "inparadises my mind."[3]

Dante's genius was that in *The Divine Comedy* he reconciled the paradox between body and spirit that divided and tortured the medieval soul. The story line is a simple one: Dante, a mortal in search of the infinite mercies of God, is taken in his Godward journey down through the depths of hell and upwards through purgatory to the sublimity of heaven. The inspiration for his heavenward ascent is not a saint or ascetic practice or inner vision. It is the lovely Beatrice, a mere mortal like Dante, who in her corporeality personifies the highest reaches of Spirit.

In Beatrice, Dante discovers that God does not forbid us earthly attachments; God has not set womankind on earth to seduce and to lead mankind astray. In and through Beatrice, Dante is inspired to understand that it is through the physical that the spiritual is realized; that it is actually in and through our materiality that we discover the deep bonding between heaven and earth. As does Saint Bernard, Dante understands that God is love and that love is the fountainhead of the physical universe and the realms of Spirit. It is

3. Dante Alighieri, "The Divine Comedy," in Warner, *Alone of All Her Sex*, 161.

through human love that one experiences the divine love. Through Beatrice, Dante touches Divinity.

It is with this profound understanding that Dante appreciates Mary as Virgin as well as Mother. She is not merely an expression of courtly love par excellence; nor is she a surrogate sweetheart, as some of the troubadours seemed to experience her. She appears to Dante only twice, and only after he has entered paradise. In both instances, she represents for Dante the Queen of Heaven, "the face that most resembles Christ." Nevertheless, standing before even her, Dante cannot take his eyes off Beatrice. Beatrice chides him for this, asking, "Why does my face so enamor thee that thou dost not turn to the fair garden that flowers under the rays of Christ" (169)?

Beatrice describes Mary to Dante as the "rose" in which the Word became flesh and as the sapphire that swathes all of heaven in regal blue. As Dante watches, the archangel Gabriel encircles Mary and sings a hymn to her as the Mother of God and the Lady of Heaven. All the saints of heaven take up the chant as she rises above them to the highest reaches of paradise. All rise with her, as children reaching for their mother's breast.

This image of the community of saints supplicating to Mary the Mother, as babes for nurture at her breast, conveys the deep need European Christians of the late Middle Ages had for the feminine spirit and explains why Mary's presence had by the time of the Black Death inspired a crescendo of cathedrals, chapels, and hymns in her honor. She appeared to believers not only as Queen of Heaven but was experienced as *Notre Dame* (Our Lady), a term first used in the twelfth century.

One can see in the art of the thirteenth and fourteenth

centuries the degree of closeness with which she was held. Earlier depictions of Mary in regal splendor gave way to new depictions of Mary as a meek and gentle maiden, holding the baby Jesus in her arms. In the 1220s, Saint Francis placed a manger with a cow and donkey beside it in the woods near his monastery at Greccio, Italy, thereby inaugurating the now almost universal Christmas custom of depicting the nativity scene, with its emphasis on there being no room in the inn on a cold winter's night for a woman heavy with child.

Saint Bridget of Sweden, a member of the Franciscan Tertiaries and a contemporary of the Black Death, had visions of Mary on her knees giving birth to Jesus and then worshiping him. Reports of her visions swept Europe, inspiring beautiful paintings, frescoes, hymns, and poems, which emphasized the tender, compassionate, and very human qualities of Mary as Mother of Jesus rather than as Mother of God. The believers, experiencing all the turbulence and violence of the fourteenth century, needed Mary to leave her throne and scepter in the starry realms above, to come down to earth and rest in a lowly stable, and to become part of humanity by holding Jesus in her arms and giving suck to the one destined to die.

With the onslaught of the Black Death, the supplication to and depictions of Mary took on increased intensity. The cult of Mary as *Mater Dolorosa* (the Lady of Our Suffering) blossomed with the agony of the plague. During the thirteenth century, artists depicted Mary as holding the baby Jesus. Under the impact of the Black Death, she is depicted mostly as holding his broken, crucified body.

One of the miracles associated with her during this time, popularized by the Cistercian and Dominican monks, concerned a monk dying of a disease that had filled his mouth and nose with putrid ulcers. He supplicated Mary, reminding her that he had performed all his good works in her name. She was pulled to his bedside by his desperation and pain and "with much sweetness and much delight, from her sweet bosom she drew forth her breast, that is so sweet, so soft, so beautiful, and placed it in his mouth, gently touched him all about and sprinkled him with her sweet milk."[4]

In the Italian city of Pisa, struck by the plague in 1348, frescoes were painted in 1350, entitled "Three Living and Three Dead" in which three lords out hunting come upon three dead kings, wrapped to be buried. One of the huntsmen holds his nose as the dead proclaim, "What you are we were, what we are you shall be." Adjacent to this depiction are frescoes of the Virgin Mary kneeling before the throne of Christ, begging his mercy for the citizens of Pisa still living.

In nearby Siena, which lost sixty-five thousand out of a population of eighty thousand to the plague, the chapel of Palazzo Pubblico was erected and dedicated to Mary in 1348. It was decorated with scenes of Mary's death and of her triumphal assumption into heaven. In other Italian towns, statues were made showing Christ's wound on the Cross spurting blood onto Mary's exposed breast. Prayer books displayed depictions of the scythe of death; rosary beads were shaped as skulls; frescoes represented Mary covering the world with her cloak, with Christ at her side as Ecce Homo (Christ crowned with thorns).

At the height of the plague's violence and in the depths of the ensuing human suffering, Christ is appreciated in all his human pain as he offers himself as a blood sacrifice for

4. Tuchman, A
Distant Mirror, 324.

human sin. Mary is experienced as the tenderly loving mother who gives the healing milk of her breast to all those in need. She leaves the sanctity of heaven to give succor to those who are suffering. Jesus lies broken on her lap; she becomes the abiding earth.

A negative aspect paralleled this positive, transformational aspect of the feminine. A belief that there was a dark feminine force behind the plague counterbalanced the devotion to Mary and Mother. Scandinavians believed a Pest Maiden in the form of a blue flame emerged from the mouth of the stricken and then flew to infect her next victim. Lithuanians told stories of a maiden who waved a red scarf at one's window to let the plague in. According to a legend of the time, one brave man waited by his window until the maiden arrived. When she waved her scarf, he drew his sword and chopped off his own hand. He died of his deed, but his village was spared. The scarf was preserved as a relic in their church.

On the walls of the Lamposanto in Pisa, one finds another feminine personification of Death. Painted by Francesco Traini in 1350, "Triumph of Death," as it is called, is part of a series that includes scenes from the Last Judgment and the tortures of hell. Rather than the usual depiction of a skeleton or a demon, there is a black-cloaked old woman with wild eyes and streaming hair, carrying a broad scythe. Her feet have claws in place of toes, and she comes to vanquish the living.

This burst of acknowledgment of the feminine in her nurturing and devouring aspects as Europe was disintegrating under the onslaught of the Black Death parallels the emergence of Sophia amid the alienation and apocalyptic visions of ancient Israel. The confluence of apocalypse and

Sophia was followed by the new ordering of reality initiated by Jesus of Nazareth. The confluence of the Black Death and adoration of Mary was followed by a whole new ordering of reality in Europe, which resulted in the Renaissance, the Reformation, and, eventually, the Enlightenment.

Almost concurrently with the ravages of the Black Death, an intellectual and cultural movement started in Italy, spread throughout Europe, and flourished until the middle of the sixteenth century. Fundamental to this "renaissance," as it was called, was the revival of classical architecture, art, learning, and morals. The sweeping Gothic spires of medieval architecture, designed to lift one's gaze and attention heavenward, were replaced by rounded architecture, calling to mind the ancient glories of Rome and Greece, where the human, not the divine, was the central focus of culture.

In art, painting ceased to focus on the grandeur of Church and God, concentrating instead on "man the measure," as Leonardo de Vinci described it. The power of Michaelangelo's *David*, standing in the nobility of his nakedness, expressed this credo in marble. The *Pieta* portrayed the centrality of the feminine. If Mary were standing, she would be over seven feet tall. Christ, measuring only five feet, eight inches, lies broken across her lap.

Voyages of discovery embarked from Portugal and Spain around the world. The Italian Christopher Columbus, sailing for Queen Isabela of Spain, discovered the New World in 1492. The fleet of the Portuguese explorer Ferdinand Magellan circumnavigated the earth in the years 1521–3.

In England where the effects of the Black Death had

been especially vicious, a powerful expression of the new ordering began that was to culminate in the Reformation. Intellectual foment had been increasing for over a century in conjunction with the growing power of the monarch and with the developing capitalistic economies. As the credibility of the Church eroded, thinkers began to question the centrality of the Church in the expression of faith. Increasingly, Christians began to believe that one ought to have the right to go directly to God on one's own, without the necessity of having the Church act as an intermediary.

A particularly astute and incisive proponent of this new theology was the English Franciscan, William of Ockham, known as the "invincible doctor," whose philosophy of nominalism opened the door to direct intuitive knowledge of the world without recourse to Biblical authority or to ecclesiastical guidance. In 1324, Pope John XXII excommunicated him. Upon receiving news of his excommunication, William promptly charged the pope with seventy errors and seven heresies.

A generation later, during the 1370s, John Wycliffe, a churchman and an Oxford don, began to preach that the corruption and the schism of the papacy were signs that the Avignon and Roman popes were Antichrists and that the papacy was finished as a credible institution. He proclaimed further that, from the moment the Church had begun to charge money for the remission of sin, only evil had been gained.

For Wycliffe, the only solution was to sweep away the entire ecclesiastical superstructure, including the papacy, the hierarchy, the priests, and even the system of sacraments, and to give final authority on earth to the State. God would take care of heaven and things spiritual. Moreover, neither God nor sinner had any need for the Church structure to mediate divine grace. The mediator between Divinity and humanity was Christ, not the Church.

All this was too much, even for his supporters, who still feared papal excommunication and the terrors of hell. In 1381 a council of twelve doctors of Oxford pronounced eight of his theses unorthodox and fourteen, heretical. They prohibited him from lecturing or preaching ever again. Wycliffe continued his work in silence and translated the entire Bible from Latin into English, making the scriptures available directly to the public, thereby bypassing the need for a priest. After the Peasants Revolt of 1381, the Church, outraged at Wycliffe's actions, made possession of a Bible an act of heresy and burned any copies that were found.

Wycliffe died in 1384, and his followers were forced underground. In 1415, when the Czech reformer Jan Hus was burned at the stake for heresy by the Council of Constance for views similar to Wycliffe's, Wycliffe's bones were ordered exhumed and burned also.

Nevertheless, the ideas of Wycliffe and Hus spread. Individuals began to look within for the answers they formerly accepted from the priests. In 1517, Martin Luther nailed his ninety-five theses to the door of the cathedral in Worms. Economic independence blossomed concurrently. Protestantism and capitalism became the new ordering principles of the day.

The Black Death decimated humanity and destroyed the moorings of the Catholic Church. It also ignited a deep, passionate appeal to the feminine, which nourished a new ordering of life. Whereas the Church had for over a thousand years pointed heavenward, denigrating the things of the earth for the things of the spirit, the adoration of Mary from the twelfth through the fifteenth centuries honored the substance and shapes of the earth again and brought the healing power of the spirit into the realm of the human community. Saint Bernard celebrated the sensuality of spirit and flesh, using the same language for both. Dante touched the hem of divinity itself through his love for the maiden Beatrice.

Apocalyptic Judaism ushered in a new age; so, too, did the violence and horror of the Black Death. As Tuchman writes, "Once people envisioned the possibility of change in a fixed order, the end of an age of submission came in sight; the turn to individual conscience lay ahead. To that extent the Black Death may have been the unrecognized beginning of modern man" (339).

CHAPTER 13

OUR GOD COMPLEX

Only a flicker

Over the strained time-ridden faces

Distracted from distraction by distraction

Filled with fancies and empty of meaning

Tumid apathy with no concentration

Men and bits of paper, whirled by the cold wind

That blows before and after time,

Wind in and out of unwholesome lungs

Time before and time after.[1]

I F THE BLACK DEATH WAS THE GENESIS OF modernity, it was the seventeenth century French philosopher René Descartes who gave the most significant expression of our epoch-making resolve to break away from the reassuring security of Church. Descartes liberated science from theology and thereby created the philosophical legitimization for all the advances of the modern world.

This "enlightenment" is one of the greatest achievements in the history of humankind, for it is the source of much we take for granted in our modern world: democratic governance,

1. Eliot, *Collected Poems*, 192,193.

our notions of equality and fairness, free-market economics, and all the technological advances we use on a daily
basis to make our life more comfortable, secure, and safe.
The combination of the Renaissance, the Reformation,
and the Enlightenment opened for humanity virtually
unlimited access to knowledge and power and are, in fact,
the predicate of modernity itself.

We must celebrate these achievements, for they define
what we have come to be. At the same time, we must also
realize that they have come at great cost, for they
unleashed deep psychological complexes of arrogance,
insecurity, and alienation, which constitute the
shadow-side of the very benefits we enjoy. Indeed, the
greater our technological advances, the deeper their shadow
has become until, in our generation, we seem to have
broken all the bounds of knowledge and power and, in the
process, decimated the earth and brought ourselves to the
brink of catastrophe. It is therefore the shadow-side of the
Enlightenment that we must explore in order to understand
more fully the limitations of modernity and the roots of
our contemporary predicament. Both the accomplishments
and shadow side of the Enlightenment are central to
understanding the advent of nuclear weapons and the
liberation of women, which, taken together, I believe to be
the enduring legacy of our time.

In 1619 Descartes had a profound vision in which he
conceived the reconstruction of all of philosophy, modeled
on mathematics and supported by absolute rationalism,
without any recourse to theology or Church dogma. After
this vision Descartes set out to present this new way of
thinking systematically. He published his *Discourse on
Method* in 1637, and it was immediately hailed as a

masterpiece of originality. Asking the question How and what do we know?, Descartes arrived at his famous statement "*Cogito ergo sum*" ("I think, therefore I am").

Whereas philosophy and theology before him had started with the reality of God and then worked out the implications for humanity, Descartes started with the reality of the human mind and then tried to prove the existence of God. Discarding the entire philosophical and theological tradition that preceded him, Descartes attempted to provide a new sense of security based on human reason. He offered a new baby—human reason— and new water—science.

This radical rethinking was necessary for Europe to break the hold of the devouring Mother Church. Descartes offered a philosophical rationale for the societal assertion of primacy over God, replacing the supremacy of faith, which the Church taught, with the supremacy of human reason, which the scientists demanded. With Descartes, rationality superseded belief; the scientist replaced the priest. His genius lay in demonstrating logically that God not only sanctioned this, it was God's idea in the first place.

Descartes devised a logical "proof," arguing that God himself was the source of the idea that all knowledge could be deduced through an individual's own intellectual self-assurance. Because God was good and true, all conceptions of the human mind that exhibited a similar clarity and precision must likewise be good and true. A good God, said Descartes, would not choose to mislead us. Cartesian philosophy replaced obedience to the will of God with obedience to the rationality of the human intellect, asserting that this was God's will.

Synchronistically, this philosophical shift occurred just at the same time that Galileo, despite his humiliation at the hands of the Inquisition, conclusively demonstrated that the sun, not the earth, was the center of the solar system. Our pride in being intellectually liberated from the Church was being fed just as the reality of our insignificance in the universe was being confirmed. This interface between a growing intellectual arrogance on the one hand and a growing realization of insignificance on the other is important to grasp, for it opens up the deep paradox at the heart of modernity.

The psychological root of modern civilization, while impressive on the surface, is, in fact, an unfettered power drive mixed with deep uncontrolled anxieties. Since the end of the Middle Ages, Western civilization has exhibited the symptoms of stress due to the excessive demands we have placed on our own power. Seeking to know everything in order to control everything, we have only become more aware of our contingency. Although we think we have left religion behind, we have in fact re-enacted the drama of Adam and Eve in the Garden. Grasping for equality with God, we have only become more aware of our nakedness. Alone and naked, we fashion fig leaves from the magic of technology.

Indeed, modernity has taken human hubris even further by dispensing with the "God hypothesis" altogether. As children of the Enlightenment, we live as if humanity, not divinity, were the center of history and the world. However, our exaggerated sense of self-importance is and has always been a mirage. Our sense of power, based on technological dominion over nature, represents a denial of the true state of affairs: We are frail, vulnerable beings, far more dependent on the natural world we exploit than we can bear to admit; and we are as deeply in need of a consciously held sacred relationship with our Creator as ever.

Because we have overcompensated for our feelings of helplessness by uncritically overestimating our rational powers, we have become incapable of perceiving and accepting those natural dependencies that limit and define human existence. We careen around in a finite world as if we were infinite, seeing every natural limitation as a challenge to be broken. Our technological progress, although affording material affluence, leads us from catastrophe to catastrophe, seducing us into believing that the material comforts it provides are worth the price it demands.

When we repressed Sophia, we lost the one anchor in creation, the function of which is to remind us of the wisdom of limits. The ordering principle of creation has ceased to be the great feminine presence in the world and in human affairs. Since Descartes, the ordering principle has simply been what we *think* is appropriate at any given moment. Science sanctions what we think and proclaims it objective truth.

It is difficult for us to come to terms with this "impotence-omnipotence complex," as the German psychologist Horst Richter calls it in his book *All Mighty*, because we do not perceive the weakness underlying our grandiose self-image. As Richter points out, whose thinking I follow in this chapter, our intellectual certitude, bolstered by the productivity of our scientific-mathematical method, has ruled out the possibility of self-deception. Because of this, few of us appear capable of reacting authentically to the predictions of the natural scientists that humankind is headed down the path of collective self-destruction unless we stop our expansionist policies of ruthless exploitation of nature and deadly threats against our fellow human beings.

We seem unable to accept the notion that we must re-evaluate our scientific principles and techniques, which have seemed empowering and have enhanced our feeling of being in control of the world. It is a supreme irony that now when scientific technology threatens to destroy us, we find it impossible to question its centrality. We built technology to serve us; now we are forced to interlock with it. The master has become the slave; the tool has become the goal.

Collectively, we are afraid to admit to ourselves that we still occupy the same position of infantile dependency upon God and nature as we always have, a truth we have repressed since the Middle Ages. Our fear of admitting this truth continues to outweigh our fear that we may destroy ourselves with the technology that supports our illusions.

It is a tragedy that virtually the entire philosophical and theological tradition since Descartes has supported rather than questioned this hubris. The modern era has produced material abundance beyond measure; it has also been indelibly stamped with the mark of egocentrism and self-conceit. We have overlooked the early Hebrew's insight that we are made in the image of God. We have come to believe that God—if God exists at all—is made in the image of humanity; we regard ourselves as not only the rulers of creation but as the fountainhead of all virtue. If it is not rational, it is not acceptable; if it is not scientific, it is not true.

In the process, the logic of the Enlightenment has distorted truths that the human collective consciousness has carried since the time of our Paleolithic past. We act as if what we decide on the common-sense-historical plane with scientific calculations and linear logic were the final determinant of reality. We are no longer aware of the cruciform nature of reality, let alone that the Exodus and the Cross stand as profoundly interrelated and central signposts to its truth; or that the Buddha, sitting quietly far to the East, has a deeper metaphysical perception than anything suggested by modern science.

From the dawn of human religious reflection, seers have understood the fundamental interconnections between individuals and society, human beings and nature, the sacred and the profane. The ancients as well as mystics of every tradition have intuited that the inner and the outer are inseparable, that each point of existence is a microcosm of the Totality, and that the Many and the One contain and reflect each other. Such is the relationship of human beings and the Totality. Moreover, there has always been the intuition that consciousness and the material world are inseparably interwoven. Mind and body, spirit and matter are simply different aspects of a single reality.

In the East, the Buddha and all the great Eastern traditions taught variations of the doctrine of anatta (the self has no separate existence), that to consider oneself as distinct from the rest of reality is simply an illusion. There is unanimity that the One and the Many belong together, and that to negate their connection is the most funda-mental mistake one can make. To live as if one were separate from the whole, to separate the polarities of existence and see them as unconnected, is samsara (illusion).

In the West the Judeo-Christian tradition has wrestled with the same problem, albeit differently. Emphasizing that God is everywhere but not everything, this tradition has sought to bring the One and the Many together through *covenant,* an agreement that binds things that are inherently distinct but not separate. For the Jews, the covenant was bound up in the Torah; for the Christians, the covenant was expressed through the Just Man, Christ crucified, suffering for us our inability to fulfill our obligations in our covenantal relationship with God.

The bedrock of human religious intuition, whether in the East or the West, has been the awareness of *connectedness* between humanity and the rest of existence. The philosophical tradition in the West since Descartes has negated this understanding, using the subtleties of logic to make such a negation scientifically credible and morally acceptable. Although medieval and Renaissance natural philosophy established a relationship between God and the world, as mystics such as Jakob Boehme and the Cabalists did, rationalists from Descartes onward have not. The modern world is built on the delusion of separateness.

This delusion is the cornerstone of modern science. Drawing a distinction between spirit and matter, consciousness and nature, scientists since Descartes have presented to society a mechanistic universe devoid of spirit and consciousness, a universe that can be measured, defined, and utilized according to the "laws" of science. Everything is broken down to its component parts; nothing is accepted as valid unless it can be "proven" empirically.

This point of view is as universally accepted as the flat earth was accepted by medieval Europeans on the eve of the Black Death. Whether in the classrooms of Tokyo, Delhi, Nairobi, Ankara, Bogota, or New York, scientific materialism—the universe as machine—is accepted as objective truth.

Thus we build machines to conquer an earth we consider lifeless; we ravage other plant and animal species we consider to be soulless; and we send probes to explore the universe merely to quantify the atmosphere on far-off planets. Having taken the Creator out of creation and the subtleties of Spirit out of the realm of nature, we have built a world of sterile logic in which our passions, lusts, and destructiveness seethe under the surface but through which the Creator and the Spirit remain ever active, though incognito.

Ironically, it was a contemporary of Descartes', the French philosopher Blaise Pascal, who provided the richest alternative to him. The two first had contact when, at age sixteen, Pascal wrote a paper on the mathematics of conical spheres. It was of sufficient brilliance to attract the attention of the already famous Descartes who refused to believe the paper was the product of someone so young. Pascal soon joined Descartes as among the most prominent scientists of the day.

Pascal coined the term *logique du coeur* (logic of the heart). In his book *Pensées* (Thoughts)—unfinished when he died—he writes, "We know the truth not only through our reason but also through our heart."[2] For Pascal, human beings gather data and apply logical analysis to the surrounding world by reason, using the laws of physics and mathematics. This is the basis of science and the scientific method. Equally important, humans intuit first principles and the virtues that support human conduct with the heart. This is the basis of spirituality and religion.

"The heart has its own order," Pascal

2. Blaise Pascal, *Pensées*, trans. A.J. Kraitsheimer (London: Penguin Books, 1966), 110.

reminds us. "The mind also has its order, which resides in principles and proofs. The order of the heart is different. We cannot prove that we ought to be loved simply by expounding the reasons for love..." (235). Moreover, "It is the heart which perceives God and not the reason. That is what faith is: God perceived by the heart, not by reason" (54). Or as he said in another passage, "The heart has its reasons of which reason knows nothing" (54).

Because reason and the heart have their own order, their own methods of perceiving truth, their own ways of communicating, there is often a "civil war" between the two. "If there were only reason without passions," writes Pascal, or "only passions without reason," we would all be much happier. But since we have both, we cannot be free of inner strife and we are perpetually "torn by inner divisions and contradictions" (235).

Descartes put his faith in mathematics and logic alone, but Pascal understood that science and Spirit, logic and intuition form a great antinomy. Separately, they seem internally consistent and mutually exclusive of one another. However, if united in creative tension, Pascal asserted they might inform each other and deepen one's interior life.

Pascal managed to keep a creative tension between these two realms. Brilliant and internationally famous as a mathematician, Pascal had an equally rich interior life. For him, the heart of faith was as real and important as the logic of reason. God was as real to him as his mathematics were. As it turned out, Pascal became famous for his mathematical logic while alive, but he stayed famous for his faith in God.

As a scientist, Pascal was acutely aware that the intellectual momentum of the Enlightenment was moving towards the Cartesian emphasis on the primacy of human reason to the exclusion of the "God hypothesis"; towards the enthronement of the intellect to the exclusion of the heart; and towards a scientific materialism devoid of any room for consciousness or for Spirit. "I cannot forgive Descartes" for this, he writes. "In his whole philosophy he would like to do without God; but he could not help allowing him a flick of the fingers to set the world in motion; after that he had no more use for God" (356). Cartesianism, reflected Pascal, is no more than the antics of Don Quixote tilting at windmills.

Pascal understood the predicament of modernity, that after escaping from total dependency on the Church, Western civilization had become emotionally adrift, relying on human intellect and feelings of omnipotence to protect it from feeling altogether insignificant in an empty and vast universe. The question Pascal put to his contemporaries, and to us today, is, How can we develop human powers and accept human limitations at the same time?

Pascal saw with prophetic clarity that if Western civilization abandoned itself to the intellect alone, believing only in scientific materialism, it would inevitably be led to the presumptuous claim of dominion over the whole world and to maniacal despotism and violence. "There are no limits to things," he writes. "Laws attempt to set limits but the human mind cannot endure this" (90). Giving up the law of God for the dogma of science, we were destined to break all the Ten Commandments and to do so whole-heartedly. In our arrogance, we forget that, although it is possible to break the law, it is not possible to do away with it. The law endures because it is embedded in creation itself. We can only break ourselves against the law; that is why breaking the law leads to destruction.

For Pascal, the essential problem for modernity is the issue of how humankind comes to terms with its finiteness in the face of an infinite universe. "Nature is an infinite sphere whose center is everywhere and circumference nowhere," he asserts. "In short, it is the greatest perceptible mark of God's omnipotence that our imagination should lose itself in that thought" (90).

"After all," asks Pascal, "what is man in nature? A nothing compared to the infinite, a whole compared to the nothing, a middle point between all and nothing, infinitely remote from an understanding of the extremes; the end of things and their principles are unattainably hidden from him in impenetrable secrecy.... Equally incapable of seeing the nothingness from which he emerges and the infinity in which he is engulfed" (90).

Refusing to acknowledge their limitations in the face of the vastness of Infinity, scientists, through intellect, have "rashly undertaken to probe into nature as if there were some proportion between themselves and her.... They wanted to know the principles of things and go on from there to know everything, inspired by a presumption as infinite as their object" (90). Instead of falling to our knees in reverence for the Creator, humankind, deluded by overweening pride, strides forth violently to conquer nature. The humility of the heart is supplanted by the arrogance of the mind; obedience to the will of God, by manipulation of the laws of physics.

Our problem, argues Pascal, is pride. We cannot bear to be the mean between Nothing and Everything. We cannot bear that we know neither the origin of life nor its end. We are bewildered at being "an All in comparison with

Nothing" and at the same time "a Nothing in comparison with the Infinite." Thus, we are plunged into "eternal despair" (90). Humanity is "neither angel nor beast," he says, "and it is unfortunately the case that anyone trying to act the angel acts the beast" (91). In trying to act like God we do not become more human, we simply become more demonic.

Putting the paradox of the human condition another way, Pascal asks, "If man was not made for God, why is he only happy in God? If man was made for God, why is he so opposed to God?" (92). Thus the eternal conflict within the depths of our soul: As created beings, we long for God, even as we deny God; as fallen beings, we defy God, even though we are redeemed by God.

The challenge for humankind as finite beings in an infinite universe lies on two fronts. The first is to recognize that the One and the Many are inseparably interconnected. The infinitely small and the infinitely large depend on each other and lead to each other. They are different aspects of a singularity without beginning and without end. "These extremes touch and join by going in opposite directions," writes Pascal. "They meet in God and God alone" (94). We cannot appreciate this truth through logic, because science creates distinctions in order to measure. Science, by definition, must divide what is naturally united. We can only know the interconnectedness of being through the intuitions of the heart.

The second challenge is to recognize that, although we may have yearnings for the infinite, we are, in fact and in the end, limited. "Let us realize our limitations," writes Pascal. "We are something and we are not everything." We are "limited in every respect" and "find this intermediate state between two extremes reflected in all our faculties"

(94). The ordering structures of creation limit and define us whether we recognized them or not.

We can see with our eyes, but we cannot look directly at the sun, nor can we see x-rays. We hear with our ears but cannot hear sounds either too high or too low in frequency. We can smell with our nose, but most olfactory stimuli escape our attention. We can taste with our tongue, but extremes overwhelm us. We can feel with our skin, but we cannot feel molecules or touch the stars. Every way we experience the world around us is in the intermediate range. The very small and the very large, the very low and the very high escape us. Let us not be arrogant and assume that the situation is any different for either our mind or our heart.

Pascal writes, "We are floating in a medium of vast extent, always drifting uncertainly, blown to and from; whenever we think we have a fixed point to which we can cling and make fast, it shifts and leaves us behind; if we follow it, it eludes our grasp, slips away, and flees eternally before us. Nothing stands still for us" (94). We are not "nothings"; we are not "everythings"; we are simply "some-things" in the middle of the vastness of the universe.

"This is our natural state," he observes, "and yet the state most contrary to our inclinations. We burn with desire to find a firm footing, an ultimate, lasting base on which to build a tower rising up to infinity, but our whole foundation cracks and the earth opens up into the depth of the abyss" (95). And the greatest of the greatest, whether Gilgamesh or Descartes, are consumed.

The path to wisdom lies not through our strength but through our weakness, says Pascal. Recalling the stories of Joseph, Moses, and Jesus, Pascal maintains that "Man is only a reed, the weakest in nature.... There is no need for the whole universe to take up arms to crush him; a vapor, a drop of water is enough to kill him. But even if the universe were to crush him, man would still be nobler than his slayer, because he knows that he is dying and the advantage the universe has over him" (95).

"Thus our dignity consists in thought. It is on thought that we must depend for our recovery, not on space and time, which we could never fill. Let us then strive to think well; that is the basic principle of morality" (93). Our thinking must be with our heart as well as our brain. With the heart we can intuit God and sense our limitations; with our brain we can gather information and measure the creation.

It is within the context of limitation, balancing the logic of the heart with that of the mind, that Pascal makes his final point, namely that the only way to make our "somethingness" authentic is through love. Love of our neighbor for Pascal is inseparable from our love of God. "It is impossible to know the parts without knowing the whole," says Pascal, "as to know the whole without knowing the individual parts" (93). Everything is inseparably related. We cannot dispense with God at the macro-level and expect be happy with our neighbors at the micro-level. We cannot dispense with the intuitions of the heart and expect the products of science to satisfy our soul. We can only love the part to the same degree that we love the whole and the whole to the same degree that we love the part.

In order to be genuinely content as a "something" between nothingness and eternity, we must accept that we can order the world with our intellects through science *and* that we must establish a relationship of love with our Creator and with our neighbors. This brings the polarities of the antinomy together. With science we build our world and push the frontiers of intellectual knowledge. Living with the awareness of God, we become aware of limits, and in the wisdom of limits, love finds true expression. Embracing this antinomy, life becomes whole.

What terrifies our conscious rational selves is that this *logique du coeur* demands that we keep the dictates of reason and the intuitions of the heart in dialectical tension with each other; that we give up our lust for knowledge and for power for their own sake and live within divinely imposed limits, using whatever limited knowledge and power we attain not for ego gratification but for compassionate living. It necessitates that we recognize that we are not the center of the universe; God is. This results in the awareness that living harmoniously with all beings in the spirit of reverence for our Creator, not seeking power for-and-of-itself in order to dominate others, is the true goal of human existence.

The *logique du coeur* demands the crucifixion of the ego. Our mind entices us to disobey the ordering principle of creation in the spirit of pride, while the intuition of the heart whispers in a still, small voice that we must submit to the ordering principle of creation in the spirit of humility. We must yield not to the quest for unlimited knowledge to gain absolute power but to the divine will to recognize limitation and learn compassion. The intuition of the heart calls upon us to offer up our weaknesses so that God's grace can redeem and we can forgive. The wisdom of limits, as the Hebrews discerned long ago, means we are not here to conquer the earth or our neighbors. We are here to do justice, to love mercy, and to walk humbly with our God. Knowledge without faith leads to science;

knowledge infused with faith leads to love.

One can only wonder how philosophy and history would have turned out had Western philosophical and political traditions followed Pascal instead of Descartes. Pascal was essentially ignored. Descartes was hailed as the great genius of the age, and almost without exception, science, philosophy, and much of theology embraced his ideas.

Gottfried Leibnitz, a German mathematician and philosopher, was a contemporary of Descartes and Pascal. Following Descartes, Leibnitz was a deist. He believed that God created the universe to be perfectly coordinated and harmonious. He used a clock for an analogy to describe his concept of the universe created by God that now operates as a great machine without the interposition of God, even as a timepiece, once assembled and set in motion, operates without the assistance of its maker. In this mechanistic view, neither the universe nor humanity needs God; each operates independent of God's influence. God had been required for the original "flick of the finger," to recall Pascal's term, but after creating creation, God apparently went on to other affairs.

Leibnitz used the clock analogy to portray a world in which the individual components have no real contact. They interact as the pieces of a clock do, but they have no *essential relationship.* Each part of the universe, called "monads" by Leibnitz, was a representation of the entire universe. Yet at the same time, Leibnitz taught that, although each monad was distinct from all other monads, each mirrored the universe with a distinctiveness peculiar to itself. Humans are not only mirrors of the created universe but are also, by virtue of intellect or spirit, made in the image of God. For Leibnitz, every human mind is a little divinity and exists on its own. The individual units give nothing to, and receive nothing from each other. Each contains a totality or completeness in and of itself.

This concept has been in many ways the cornerstone of the European intellectual tradition since the Renaissance. It has become the *idée fixe* of Western culture. It has led to the development of a society based on the principles of exclusion and rivalry wherein the individual ego reigns supreme without regard to communal relations. It has resulted in the notion that the most effective means of conflict resolution is more conflict. This mentality in the United States has produced a society of "rugged individualists" with over 200 million privately held weapons.

Although no one of note worked out the political implications of Pascal's philosophy, Thomas Hobbes, an English friend of Descartes' and contemporary of Leibnitz's, laid out the sociological implication of Leibnitz's theories. Hobbes taught in his famous book *Leviathan* that the state of nature is incessant warfare among the parts. Furthermore, Hobbes taught that humans are solitary by nature and have no inherent need to live in social groups. The State, or government, serves essentially to establish a balance among the competing individuals in the collective by simultaneously gratifying and placing limits on their egoism.

Although Hobbes was an active advocate of religious freedom, he argued for a principle that was to become the basis for all subsequent Western authoritarian states. In Hobbes's theory of the State, the authority of all members of the country was to be concentrated in a single representative individual: the will of all the people united in the single will of the monarch.

In social psychology, this concept involves the surrender of certain egotistical ambitions by the citizens, which they transfer to an absolute sovereign. They are indemnified for this loss with the invitation to engage in what psycho-analysts call "projective identification," i.e., projecting all desires and hopes on the monarch and by identifying with what the monarch then proclaims and does. Everyone is recompensed for the restrictions suffered by a monarchy by being able to participate, at least vicariously, in the omnipotence of the monarch. What a deal!

The philosophical plot thickens when one understands that the omnipotence of absolute monarchy can manifest itself only by internal repression and external expansion. Domestic totalitarianism and foreign imperialism are inherent consequences of Hobbes's model of the State. If a snake wishes to become a dragon, it must devour other snakes unceasingly. Peace becomes merely the respite between wars.

Hobbes's views caused quite a stir among his contemporaries, and although widely supported by the nobility of Europe, they did not go unchallenged. Anthony Ashley Cooper, the third Earl of Shaftesbury educated in philosophy under John Locke, disputed Hobbes's pessimistic view of human nature. In his book, *Characteristics of Men, Manners, Opinions, Times,* published in 1711, he advanced the thesis that there was no inherent contradiction between altruism and egoism. He argued that each human being possessed a natural moral sense, which, if developed fully, could lead that individual to contribute to the common good.

There is less to Shaftesbury's ideas than meets the eye, however. He betrayed his aristocratic background by espousing the belief that a conflict between altruism and egoism existed only among the less developed individuals of society. He divided the populace in two groups: the first was typified by the *homo universale* of the Renaissance; the other, by ordinary persons who make up the masses. Further, he sided with Hobbes's view that all power should be concentrated in the hands of the monarch. Although altruism was just as much a part of the human heart as egoism, humans were too unpredictable and would inevitably abuse their freedom. It was the task of political leaders to reason with the masses and get them to do the right thing.

Despite Shaftesbury's inconsistencies, he was one of the few thinkers of the eighteenth century to seriously challenge Hobbes's notion that society was exclusively composed of egocentrics who had no natural relations with each other or the world, and whose natural predilection was toward rivalry and war. Like Pascal, Shaftesbury stood alone, arguing that humans were, by nature, social beings who could rely on their inherent feelings of partnership with humankind to lead them to communal harmony.

Toward the end of the eighteenth century, a virtual consensus emerged among moral philosophers that ethical behavior could not, as Shaftesbury claimed, be based on any *natural* inclinations of the human heart. Ethics, it was agreed, could only arise from the subordination of the individual will to universal norms. In light of what they saw around them, moral philosophers felt that Hobbes's theories were simply more plausible than Shaftesbury's were. Put simply, philosophers took as given our separateness and therefore our selfishness, but having dispensed with the "God hypothesis," had nowhere to turn to discern the redemptive aspects of humanity and history except in the abstractions of philosophical logic.

To accept that humanity's instinctual urges were purely and exclusively egotistical raised a profound question among those who wished, nevertheless, that humanity do good. Without recourse to God, how can individuals be compelled to renounce the unconditional gratification of their egotistical desires in order to ensure the welfare of all? How can selfish persons be persuaded to share?

The most famous attempt to answer this question came from the eighteenth century German philosopher Emmanuel Kant. In his *Critique of Pure Reason,* published in 1781, he set forth his "categorical imperative" in which he offered his own version of the Golden Rule, "Act in such a way that you could will the maxim of your conduct to become a universal law."[3]

Some observers regard this maxim of Kant's moral philosophy to represent the apex of the modern Western intellectual tradition and to be the guiding principle of all moral conduct. But in the light of the Hobbesian context in which he wrote, and in the light of the consequences of Kant's thinking on European thought and politics—especially in Germany—it is perhaps wise to take a closer look at an assertion that appears superficially to be a rewording of Jesus' command to "do unto others as you would have them do unto you." It gives insight into what happens when one tries to mimic the commands of God without actually believing in God.

Kant argues that it is impossible to

3. Immanuel Kant, "Critique of Practical Reason," in Horst E. Richter, *All Mighty: A Study of the God Complex in Western Man,* trans. Jan van Heurck (New York: Hunter House, 1984), 27.

base morality on emotional motives. There is no room for Pascal's logic of the heart. The only act that qualifies as a moral act is one that is performed directly out of a sense of rational *duty*. In the realm of ethics, Kant maintains, humans should rely exclusively on their practical reason, ignoring all other motivations. All natural inclinations stem, ultimately, from physical causes and will inevitably lead to a conflict with duty. Kant defines virtue as "moral disposition in conflict" (28). Self-control, therefore even self-coercion, is integral to all moral disposition, and it is what compels us to do what we would not do naturally.

At this point, questions arise. Where may we find the incentive for moral conduct if such an incentive is not within us naturally? From whence does the motivation for ethical action come when such motivation is contrary to all our natural impulses, emotions, and inclinations? How may we be redeemed from selfishness without grace? Kant's reply is that the true motivation of practical reason is nothing other than the moral law itself.

Now, it is difficult to imagine how an abstraction can be an inducement for selfish persons to share. It is even more difficult to imagine how Kant's moral law can be divorced from any egotistical interest, a point made by his German contemporary, the philosopher Arthur Schopenhauer. Schopenhauer suggested that if we examined moral law from the vantage of the recipient rather than the initiator we would realize that the ideal world is composed of individuals who, obeying Kant's categorical imperative, do deeds beneficial to themselves.

Schopenhauer asserted that Kant's argument boils down to putting the Golden Rule in the negative, i.e., Do not do unto others what you would not want them to do to you. This suggests that one's well-being is the ultimate basis of one's good deeds to others. When the first of Christ's two commands is disregarded, then self-centeredness rather than God-centeredness becomes the basis of love of neighbor.

Kant, who regarded himself as an antagonist of Hobbes, ends up setting forth an ethics compatible with that of Hobbes. Kantian ethics can be seen as a strategic compromise designed to reconcile the inherently conflicted interests of self-seeking individuals in society. His are the ethics of enlightened, rational self-interest.

Kant's moral law makes a person's reason tantamount to divinity. The moral law is actually described as holy; it appears as an abstract surrogate for an infallible sovereign monarch. Kant even speaks of the "solemn majesty" of the moral law. This reverent glorification turns it into a representation of God. Following Descartes, Kant replaces God with human reason, and, therefore, the only referent for value and morality must be human self-interest. Schopenhauer was right: There is no other logical or practical alternative.

The internal contradiction within Kant's moral ethic remains unresolved. Having split asunder the antinomy of head and heart, the essentially formal abstraction of the moral law stands immutably on its throne, cut off from its opposite, intuitive instinct. Although resolved superficially, Kant leaves Western moral ethics trapped in an inner conflict it cannot resolve.

The concepts of the supremacy of reason and human insignificance, logical certitude and instinctual awareness, power and impotence remain split and polarized with no overarching commonality to undergird or to unify them.

Kant negates the cruciform nature of reality by cutting off the opposites from one another, embracing the rational, logical, and dutiful and rejecting the spiritual, intuitive, and covenantal.

Kant's moral ethics, like Hobbes's social philosophy, are representative of an entire historical period. They indicate that, from the sixteenth to the eighteenth century, the ego of European culture was steadily expanding and that the European mind perceived this swelling tide of egocentrism as sufficiently threatening to deny it altogether. Hobbes did this by subjugating all individuals under a monarch governed by self-interest; Kant, by subjugating all personal inclination under self-will governed by a sense of duty.

We can well understand Kant's ethics, as well as Hobbes's theory of the State, as defense mechanisms and as the logical conclusion of that awakening "will to power" initiated by Descartes, the true character of which would be eventually laid bare by Friedrich Nietzche. In the end, Kant and Hobbes only fed the will to unbridled power, though they both thought they were offering a rational way to curb the selfish use of power.

Kant's moral philosophy had a direct social affect. Duty became a virtue in civic affairs; passion, something tolerated only in private life. The political implications of his moral imperative compelled Kant, like Shaftesbury and Hobbes, to attribute ultimate power to the State, not to the individuals and certainly not to God.

In his essay *Idea for Universal History with a Cosmological Purpose,* Kant wrote, "Man is an animal who needs a master if he is to live among others of his species. For there is no question but that he abuses his freedom with respect to others of his kind. And, although, as a rational being, he may desire a law which imposes limits on the freedom of all, nevertheless, whenever he can get away with it, his own self-seeking, animalistic inclinations seduce him to exempt himself from this law. Thus he needs a master who will subdue his personal will and compel him to obey a universally valid will, so that all men may be free."[4]

With statements like these, it was an easy matter for an authoritarian State like Prussia, already embracing the social theories of Hobbes, to turn Kant's ethics into a tool for the exercise of authoritarian control. The authority of the State was simply made synonymous with the moral law. Prussian students memorized Kant's laudation to Duty in his *Critique of Practical Reason*, "Duty! Thou great and exalted name who dost contain nought which is pleasing or ingratiating, but demandest submission... ."[5] It is small wonder that conservative advocates of law and order down to the present day have consistently cited Kant.

Rather than liberating morality, Kant merely takes philosophy and moral ethics the next step forward in the development of our collective "impotence-omnipotence complex." Kant discards the God of the medieval Church and speaks glowingly of human autonomy. The supreme arbiter of the good now becomes the abstractions of the human mind. Kant's philosophy reflects the attempt to conceive of God not only as equivalent to human reason but also as an intellectual or spiritual principle within the self, rather than the embodiment of true power and holiness knowable only by faith through grace.

With Kant, our underlying collective fantasy to have dominion over the earth ceased to be our exclusive desire; now we sought to spiritualize nature and humanity and to soar, like Icarus, into

4. Kant, "Idea for Universal History," in Richter, *All Mighty*, 31.

5. Kant, "Critique," in *All Mighty*, 32.

the heavens. At the highest reaches of philosophy, social ethics, and political theory, we were articulating logical rationales for the raw exercise of power. Having dispensed with God, we had no way to proceed other than to equate ourselves with God.

Another German philosopher and disciple of Kant, Johann Fichte, took the next step in developing the theme of ego self-aggrandizement when he claimed that the ego posited not only itself but also all that was not itself. Kant had taught that one could not know the *ding an sich* (the thing-in-itself). One cannot know objective reality on its own terms exclusively. Everything we know is first filtered through our categories of cognition. Human subjectivity is the prism through which all objective truth flows and is responsible for such things as different witnesses at an accident giving differing accounts about what "really happened." Every individual has his or her unique perceptual filters, emotional biases, and methods of communicating.

In this sense, Kant shared the Hebrew understanding that context shapes content, although the context for the Hebrews was a faith that pointed away from the individual toward God, and for Kant, the context pointed away from God to the individual. For the Hebrews, Truth was God; for Kant, as Kierkegaard was to say later, "Truth is subjectivity."

Fichte, for his part, simply eliminates the "thing-in-itself" that Kant had spent much effort on and asserts that intelligence-in-itself is the only reality. No world exists independently of consciousness; consciousness is capable of apprehending only what it contains within itself.

According to Fichte, consciousness ascends stage by stage. At the highest stage, the human apprehends itself as pure, undiluted, self-determining subjectivity. The mind transforms all incoming data to pure activity. The thinker and the thought become fused; thought and being become one. Intellectual contemplation becomes instantaneously an action performed on oneself: One is the subject as well as object of all one's actions.

Fichte's line of reasoning was given its highest expression by another German philosopher and contemporary of Kant's, Georg Hegel, who argued that categories of intelligence become categories of reality, the final forms of all life. Hegel frequently makes the terms "Idea" or "God" synonymous with "mind" or "spirit." Thus, the German transcendental idealist tradition culminates, at least at the philosophical level, in the human effort to crown itself Lord of Creation. With the transcendental idealist tradition, identification with God was affected by a fusion of God and reason within the human mind. Our narcissistic delusions of grandeur were given ultimate philosophical sanction, for what the Western philosophical tradition had now developed was nothing less than the claim of omnipotence for human thought.

Like Hobbes and Kant before them, Fichte and Hegel argued that the implications of this reasoning lay in a "closed commercial State" in which the government exercises absolute control over trade and production, communicates to the citizenry what their duties are, and ensures that these duties are carried out. However, Fichte did not content himself with offering merely a philosophical rationale for an authoritarian social and political order. Fichte urged his contemporaries to gratify their individual egoism in a collective national egoism. He urged the German people to take charge of the world.

His argument was that certain nations have a higher destiny to rule over other nations in order to lead them toward lofty historical goals. Fichte's claim was that the Germans represented "the national medium of Christian principles." In his *Patriotism and Its Opposite,* published in 1807, he argued that "If the German fails to assume the scientific governance of the world, then, at the conclusion of all manner of vexation and travail, the non-European nations, the tribes of North America, will do so, and will bring to an end the existing order of things."[6]

Only the Germans were capable of creating a truly Christian State, Fichte argued, and it was their historical mission to do so. In so stating, he completes the European appropriation of divine power through identification with God. He reflects this not only in the form of individualistic delusions of grandeur but also in the political theories of expansionist nationalism and theologically sanctioned racism.

We can see in hindsight that below the sublime abstractions of the German Idealists was a stinking cesspool of repressed violence where the will to power and the exercise of force were the true realities. The more lofty their rhetoric, the more repressed their emotions; the more compelling their logic, the more firmly they established the twin notions that the human mind was the ultimate referent for value and that authoritarian power was the only "reasonable" method of governance.

These philosophical reflections were integrally related to a number of political, social, and economic developments, the principal one being the Industrial Revolution. Whereas the Neolithic revolution began in Palestine circa 10,000 B.C.E. and transformed the hunter-gatherer societies of the Paleolithic period into farmers, the Industrial Revolution began in Britain

6. Johann Fichte, "Patriotism and Its Opposite," in *All Mighty,* 34.

circa C.E. 1750 and began the transformation of agricultural societies into centers of industry. This in turn produced a tremendous population explosion in urban centers, where most of the factories were located, and a dramatic increase in literacy, because profitable industry
required effective communication.

The French Revolution of 1798 was as important to
the politics of the Enlightenment as the Industrial
Revolution was to its economics. It served as an historical
catalyst for nationalism, idealism, and rationalism. The
nation-state truly came into its own in and through the
French revolution, as did the motto of the Revolution,
liberté, égalité, fraternité, shouted in the streets of Paris and
carried throughout Europe by Napoleon's conquering
armies. The basis of the French Revolution was the
Enlightenment belief that secular government, designed
by human reason, was the most effective instrument of
social engineering.

It was the philosopher Jean Jacques Rousseau who
expressed the philosophical and political outcome of
Cartesian logic and prepared the philosophical groundwork for the Industrial and French Revolutions of the
eighteenth century. God had long since been dispensed
with and the power of the Church had largely been broken.
Upon this rubble, Rousseau postulated the coming of age
of the human community, governed by itself, predicated
upon reason, and aware of its national identities.

Proclaiming the ideal of the "noble savage" in *Discourse
on the Origin of Inequality Among Men*, published in 1754,
and in *Emily*, published in 1762, Rousseau argued that
human nature was fundamentally good and was only
spoiled by corrupt institutions. In *The Social Contract,* also

published in 1762, he envisioned a society of self-motivated individuals, all instinctively good and spoiled only by irrational governance. His *Declaration of the Rights of Man* redefined society from one of vassals within a Mother Church, obeying the commands of God as interpreted and mediated through the ecclesiastical structure, to one of open societies comprised of free citizens, conversing in rational discourse and governed by democratic processes.

Western Europe spilled forth around the world in the confidence that the economics of industrialism, the idealism of the French Revolution, and the philosophy of the Enlightenment constituted the wave of the future. By the end of the nineteenth century, there was no corner of the world where one could not see some European State's flag fluttering in the breeze. Western missionaries, soldiers, and traders circumnavigated and colonized most of the planet with the good news that Christianity, democracy, and capitalism, as enunciated by the Caucasian race, were destined to lead the world to the glories of civilized living and rational conduct.

The Greek and Renaissance ideal of "man the measure" became the universal watchword; the Enlightenment was held forth as the world's manifest destiny; and scientific materialism was proclaimed as the universal language whereby nature could be understood and harnessed to meet the goals of the human community in its inexorable march of progress.

Amid this euphoria came the German philosopher Frederick Nietzche who intuited that the European obsession with "man the measure" was going to conclude not with civilized rationalism but primitive barbarism. Nietzche's fundamental contribution to Western philosophical thought was his uninhibited revelation of the dark, instinctual, violence-ridden side of the European drive for power. Nietzsche not only confesses, he openly celebrates European culture's usurpation of divine power through self-identification. God is dead! Nietzsche proclaims. Long live the Superman!

Nietzsche's Superman does not recognize the existence of any being superior to himself, not a personal God, not any moral law, not a metaphysical intelligence, not a World Soul. The Superman lays claim to all these himself. The will to power is the strongest of all human instincts; it merits absolute self-affirmation.

Insofar as one can speak of morality within this context, one can only speak of "master morality" as against "slave morality." The transformed power, which was the original cornerstone of Christian ethics, was termed by Nietzche a "slave morality."[7] Teaching love of enemies, the willingness to forgive and suffer for others, and the triumph of meekness was termed an attitude of "weakness." No longer, declares Nietzche. The good arises out of "triumphant self-affirmation" (35). Only untransformed power is good. It is the right and the duty of the strong to rule over the weak. The Superman is the "meaning of the earth." The love of anyone else is merely a failure in self-love.

Nietzche's Superman represents the most complete realization of the post-medieval dream of annexing divine omnipotence to human control. Uncompromising and unfettered by any restraint or guilt, the Superman celebrates himself through a purely narcissistic exercise of limitless strength. He is "a wheel rolling of itself," says Nietzsche (35). Nothing happens *to* him; he *causes* all things to happen. "I am

7. Friedrich Nietzsche, "Genealogy of Morals," in Richter, *All Mighty*, 35.

Zarathustra, the godless one; I myself cook up every morsel of chance in my pot. And only when it is well done do I bid it welcome and permit it to serve as my food. And verily, many a chance came to me with an imperious air; but my will addressed it even more imperiously, and chance sank to its knees in entreaty" (35–6). For Nietzche, even fate surrenders to the human will to power.

In *Genealogy of Morals*, published in 1898, Nietzche celebrates the "exultant monster" that commits rape, arson, torture, and murder with the "blameless conscience of the predator" and then departs "in high spirits and with an untroubled mind" (38). Nietzche's frenzied glorification of reason betrays a secret desire to eradicate anything in himself that he feels may overwhelm him, particularly the intuition that human rationality is heading towards an orgy of violence. Nietzche's madness was that he gloried in this destructiveness; he did not call the alarm to prevent it.

Nietzche's is the old, medieval problem of feeling absolutely dependent and insecure, for which he over-compensates with narcissistic obsession, seeking to eradicate completely all passivity, tenderness, and compassion—all "slave morality." Only the most unlimited egoism can prevent a relapse into gentleness. Only a clear commitment to untransformed power can prevent us from embracing power transformed.

Nietzche understands that we would again become insignificant and small, completely dependent upon God, if we failed to root out all those inclinations that connect us with others. He intuits Pascal's truth that love of God and love of neighbor are intertwined, and he calls for the elimination of both. Only a radical contrast to our former weakness—unbridled barbarism—seems to him capable of breaking the inhibitions created by the Christian command to love God and one's neighbor. He turns medieval dependence into its polar opposite in order to conquer it. Nietzche fights blood with fire.

What emerged in human form to answer the innermost prayers of ancient Jewry was the "Son of Man," the "suffering servant," who led a life of transformed power, whose weakness on the Cross allowed God's opportunity to redeem. By becoming a raging predator, Nietzche imagines he has become free of all Christian "weakness." What emerges out of the Enlightenment is the image, in human form, of a "blond Teutonic beast," a "prowling beast of prey, greedy for victory and spoils" (41–2).

Within a generation of Nietzche, Adolf Hitler masterminded the destruction of Europe and killed six million Jews. At the apogee of scientific and technological advance, at the pinnacle of Western philosophical logic, and led by the industrial democracies and Christian nations of Europe and North America, the twentieth century surpassed every other period in recorded history in brutality, violence, sacrilege, and destructiveness.

Zbigniew Brzezinski, in his book *Out of Control*, published in 1993, brings these points into extreme focus in his discussion of the "global crisis of spirit" that he believes undergirds the current chaos infecting world politics and contemporary society.

"Contrary to its promise," writes Brzezinski, "the twentieth century became mankind's most bloody and hateful century, a century of hallucinatory politics and of monstrous killings.... Never before in history was killing so globally pervasive, never before did it consume so many lives, never before was human annihilation pursued with such concentration of sustained effort on behalf of such arrogantly irrational goals."[8] It is essential to understand that our barbarism has not been the *exception* to our Enlightenment but the *result* of our Enlightenment. Our century has reaped the whirlwind of our attempts to live rationally without the "God hypothesis."

What Brzezinski calls the "politics of organized insanity" characterized the twentieth century. Marxism and Nazism were its starkest expressions, as they "represented politically the most extreme and philosophically the most arrogant effort in human history to attain control over the totality of human environment, to define dogmatically mankind's social organization, and even to condition the human personality. In brief, the architects of coercive utopia allocated to themselves the role that mankind traditionally consigned to God" (32).

By Brzezinski's reckoning, the social engineering of Hitler claimed 17 million lives; of Stalin, 20–25 million; of Mao, 29 million. Altogether, he calculates that internal politics were responsible for killing 80 million individuals during the twentieth century. When one adds to this the 90 million claimed in military conflict, one arrives at a staggering total of 170–175 million lives destroyed senselessly by either military conflict or political idealism. "This," he says, "is more than the total killed in all previous wars, civil conflicts, and religious persecutions throughout human history" (32).

The moral tragedy of our civilization has been that the very philosophical notions we set up so laboriously to replace the "God hypothesis" in order to

8. Zbigniew Brzezinski, *Out of Control: Global Turmoil on the Eve of the Twenty-First Century* (New York: Charles Scribner's Sons, 1993), 4–5.

become "enlightened" have only served to encourage our barbarism. Thus the twentieth century produced technological progress beyond the wildest dreams of our forebears and manifested a morality as base as the crudest of the barbarians we thought our civilization had vanquished. One can only imagine a Hitler or a Stalin of the third millennium when human power and control may well extend to our entire solar system or to our galaxy.

Only consumerism, termed "permissive cornucopia" by Brzezinski, has matched barbarism in the modern era. "Permissive cornucopia" is a term derived from the mythic Golden Horn, which suckled the god Zeus and had miraculous powers to supply whatever the one sucking desired. "The progressive decline in the centrality of moral criteria is matched by heightened preoccupation with material and sensual self-gratification," says Brzezinski. "Unlike coercive utopia, permissive cornucopia does not envisage a timeless state of societal bliss for the redeemed but focuses largely on the immediate satisfaction of individual desires, in a setting in which individual and collective hedonism becomes the dominant motive for behavior" (65).

Permissive cornucopia is, in fact, exactly the opposite of totalitarianism. Instead of brutality, uniformity, discipline, and terror to accomplish a future "workers paradise," there is no coercion at all. Not only is society permissive, it *must* be permissive, for in cornucopian society not only are all desires satisfied but also they are satisfied on a completely individualized basis. Our worship of materialism has given rise to insatiable greed and a culture that officially condemns but, in fact, encourages financier Ivan Boesky's proclamation during the 1980s that "Greed is good." The Golden Horn accommodates everyone who sucks it.

The result is that all desires become equally good, making neither coercion nor self-denial necessary. The problem, Brzezinski points out, is that "a society in which self-gratification is the norm is also a society in which there are no longer any criteria for making moral judgments. One feels entitled to have what one wants, whether or not one is worthy. Thus, moral judgments become dispensable. There is no need to differentiate between 'right' and 'wrong'" (66).

"Instead, for pragmatic reasons of social order, the critical distinction is between what is 'legal' and what is 'illegal'; thus legal procedure, especially the court system, substitutes for morality and for the church as the principal definer of that morality. Religion as the internalized guide to individual conduct is thus replaced by the legal system, which defines the external limits of the impermissible but not of the immoral." Brzezinski calls this "procedural morality" (67).

When the religion and law function normally in society, an inner morality developed by religious training balances the procedural morality of legality. However, in modern Western civilization, particularly in the United States, says Brzezinski, "politics and economics conspire to create a culture inimical to the preservation of an important social domain reserved for the religious. An increasingly permissive culture, exploiting the principle of the separation of church and state, squeezes out the religious factor but without substituting for it any secular 'categorical imperatives,' thereby transforming the inner moral code into a vacuum" (68).

"It is a striking paradox," concludes Brzezinski, "that the greatest victory for the proposition that 'God is dead' has occurred not in the Marxist-dominated states, which politically propagated atheism, but in Western liberal democratic societies, which have culturally nurtured moral apathy" (68).

The result is that civic freedom is increasingly disengaged from the notion of civic responsibility and is equated with promiscuous personal liberty. The "good life" is increasingly defined not as a life of virtue and compassion but as the acquisition of all manner of material goods such that we can enjoy a lifestyle that can satisfy any whim and all desires, and that, above all, can take the waiting out of wanting.

Thus we drift, sustained by little more than the accelerated pace of technological and economic expansion, which we call "progress." Fanatics who use violence with increasing ferocity to accomplish irrational utopian goals buffet us, and promiscuity, which saps our moral core by the ubiquitous bribes of instant and constant gratification, seduces us. The twentieth century added to the Cartesian hubris by proclaiming "I kill, therefore I am," and "I consume, therefore I am."

Our tragedy is that there has been no religious tradition strong enough to keep Europe or North America from succumbing completely to these self-deceptions by offering another understanding of covenant. No one has arisen who could redefine God within a modern framework. The Mother Catholic Church never recovered from its medieval corruption or the Protestant Reformation to become relevant to modernity, although she still holds all the essential traditions required for a holistic approach to life and the world. Pascal, a devout Catholic, was ignored.

Although the Protestants played an important role in breaking the power of the Church, they also have contributed to our predicament. When Martin Luther began the Reformation in 1517, he made two crucial moves that served to feed the Promethean impulse of modern society as well as to deprive it of any mitigating force. In breaking away from the Mother Church with the declaration that one was justified by grace through faith alone, Luther effectively gave each individual in the religious realm what Descartes had given the individual in the philosophical realm. "I am the arbiter of my own faith; therefore I am" summarizes the Reformation.

Protestantism made individual faith and human subjectivity the ultimate and sole source of religious content and value. The essential reason why northern Europeans embraced the Reformation with such enthusiasm was that it gave theological justification for their secular efforts to break the political and economic power of the Church.

Equally important, Luther stripped the feminine component out of religious worship. He believed, with John Calvin and the other early reformers, that the cult of the Virgin Mary was an egregious corruption of the medieval Church. Rather than reform the traditions that had grown up around her, the Protestant reformers abolished Mary from any significant role in the Reformist movement.

The result of this at a psychological level was the generation of the personal empowerment and creativity that have produced the modern world. The Reformation supported the developments of the Industrial and French Revolutions and the advancement of capitalism and democracy. The Reformation and the Enlightenment were responsible for the belief that humanity was the epicenter of a universe in which we could do whatever we wanted if it served the goal of human progress, generally defined as further scientific and technological growth.

The Reformation also produced the alienation that came with the realization that we faced the universe and the unknown alone and without community. Unfettered individualism empowers but it also terrifies. As we saw in the story of the Garden of Eden, alienation is the shadow-side of untransformed power. Protestantism went on to deprive us of the feminine side of our religious ethic, which was necessary to cope with the very alienation it had engendered. There was no Mother Mary to help us in our hour of need. As our alienation deepened, our only recourse was to feed our power drive.

Although the Reformation empowered economic and political freedom and gave rise to capitalism and democracy, it also was destined to culminate in the excesses of twentieth century totalitarianism. The psychologist Erich Fromm was correct in his book *Escape From Freedom* in arguing that an essential connection exists between Luther and Hitler. The Nazis personified the shadow-side of the Reformation even as they personified the shadow-side of the Enlightenment. I would add to this that our massive nuclear arsenals, whatever the political justifications, are, in the end, overcompensations for the vulnerability we feel as we confront the universe alone without our God and without our Mother.

Paradoxically, our need for the Mother has not gone away and neither has our need for worship. We have simply replaced God with rationalism, and Mary, with materialism. Nevertheless, the fervor with which we worship our new gods is as ardently prejudiced as was our medieval devotion to the Church and to a flat earth.

Scientific rationalism and the belief in technological progress dominate the modern world just as completely as the Augustinian world-view dominated the Middle Ages.

The modern world accepts the evolutionary theories of Darwin as genuine, just as the medieval Church accepted the writings of the Church Fathers. There are debates and schools of thought, of course, but few challenge seriously the basic tenets of evolutionary theory or those of scientific materialism. We embrace materialism with as much sincerity as the medieval faithful adored Mary.

Forsaking the God of the Hebrews, what has resurfaced is the religion of the Great Mother, albeit in an unsanctified form. The belief in scientific materialism ("materialism" comes from the root *mater*, which means "mother" and "earth") commands almost unanimous respect and allegiance in the world today. We are still devoted to the Mother, but she is no longer alive and vibrantly active as she was in the Upper Paleolithic period. We have made her temporal, mechanical, and have used her to serve scientific and technological progress.

The most powerful of our contemporary idols is Mammon, the Biblical term for riches derived from the Sumerian-Babylonian goddess Mammetun, Mother of Destinies. Mammon shares the same root word with "mammary," "mammal," and "mother." The Bible calls upon the believers to choose between God and Mammon. The medieval Church decried Mammon as the epitome of commercial greed. John Milton, the greatest of the Puritan poets, depicted Mammon as one of the fallen angels before creation. In *Paradise Lost,* first published in 1674, Milton describes the great battle between the forces of Satan and the hosts of God after they threw Satan from Heaven. During one battle, the armies fought around a hill belching forth sulfur. It is here that Mammon, one of Satan's angels, enters the fray. Milton notes that when

Mammon had been in heaven, he always had:

> a downward bent, admiring more
> ...the riches of Heaven's pavement, trodden gold,
> Than aught divine or holy else enjoyed
> In vision beatific: by him first
> men also, and by his suggestion taught
> Ransacked the Center, and with impious hands
> Rifled the bowels of their mother Earth
> For Treasures better hid. Soon had his crew
> Opened into the Hill a spacious wound
> And digged out ribs of Gold. [9]

Mammon comes from the earth. He symbolizes an obsession *with* the Mother while having no sense of reverence *for* the Mother. When we forsake the Creator we do not cease to worship, we simply idolize what is created: the riches of the earth. Forsaking God, we rape our mother and seize her gold to fashion money.

"Money" was first minted in the Roman temples to the goddess Juno Moneta, the goddess of advice and admonition, hence the terms "money" and "monetary." The first coins were made of gold and other precious metals, such as silver, bronze, and copper. Money has been around ever since and has taken on an increasingly important role in society and politics. Today, capitalism is the prevailing global ideology. In the age of globalization, it has become a universal religion. The ardent English Protestant Adam Smith first articulated its virtues in 1776, with the publication of *The Wealth of Nations*. In it he argued that, in the absence of any prevailing morality, the only thing that

9. John Milton, *Paradise Lost, Norton Critical Editions* (New York: W. W. Norton, 1975), bk.1, lines 680–90.

remained for individuals to do was to pursue wealth in a self-interested way. This, he believed, was the "great Good." In effect, Smith did in economics what Luther had done in theology and what Descartes had done in philosophy: apply the norm of individualism and human subjectivity, "I acquire wealth; therefore I am." The Enlightenment transformed Mammon from devil into the global god.

Today, money is disconnected even from the earth. We are no longer on the gold standard, and money is not tied to any earthly commodity. It now circulates around the globe, filled with an almost breath-like spirit, subject to inflation and deflation, giving life and causing disruption to all it infuses. It has become a global god.

The Hungarian born financier George Soros writes in *The Alchemy of Finance*, published in 1988, that dollars are not lifeless units but, taken as an aggregate, constitute a lifelike organism governed by internal laws and regulations, the understanding of which can make one very rich. He himself has won and lost billions trading currencies on the world market. Like blood, money circulates, animating the economy and trade. Monetary assets are liquid, and like mother's milk, operate to satisfy consumers according to the laws of supply and demand. Even as in times past when the unfettered Mother Goddess could devour her young, so now the pursuit of money consumes our soul.

Therefore, at the turn of the millennium we find ourselves in the best of times and the worst of times. We have gained the whole world, and we have lost our soul. We have forgotten that by negating God and refusing to revere the Mother we condemn ourselves to serving Mammon. Modern philosophy, modern theology, and modern economics have all bowed down before this altar.

Rather than joining with Pascal in seeking to establish a new relationship with God, we have joined with Descartes in seeking to usurp the powers of God. The philosophical and theological tradition of the West endorsed this Cartesian development and gave logical and moralistic rationales for the raw exercise of power and unfettered accumulation of wealth.

The God of the Hebrews has been replaced by an unsanctified Mother Goddess; faith, borne of grace, has been replaced with reason mediated through subjectivity; and the belief in redemption in history by the will of God has been replaced by a scientific notion of technological progress by human effort alone. The result has not been the Promised Land but a world dominated by relentless technological development, unparalleled barbarism, and insatiable consumerism.

As paradoxical and nonsensical as this may seem, all these advances, all these corruptions are being held in the depth of the purposes of God who, despite our barbarism and consumerism, is inexorably working divine judgement on our blindness and arrogance, such that out of the wrath of judgement will come the fullness of redemptive love, even as the Resurrection came through the darkness and the horror of Golgotha, as the figure hanging there cried out, "My God, my God, why hast thou forsaken me?"

CHAPTER 14

Nuclear Weapons and the Holocaust

Words move, music moves

Only in time; but that which is only living

Can only die. Words, after speech, reach

Into the silence. Only by the form, the pattern,

Can words or music reach

The stillness, as a Chinese jar still

Moves perpetually in its stillness.

Not the stillness of the violin, while the note lasts,

Not that only, but the co-existence,

Or say that the end precedes the beginning,

And the end and the beginning were always there

Before the beginning and after the end.

And all is always now.[1]

THE ENLIGHTENMENT ENDED WITH THE Holocaust and Hiroshima. As such, these events stand as referents for our time, the cornerstones, if you will, of value. They

1. Eliot, *Collected Poems*, 194.

conclude the past even as they lay the groundwork for the future. They brought life to the point of death and ignited the fires of renewal. The Holocaust was followed by the establishment of the State of Israel and the ending of the Diaspora, thereby ushering in a whole new era in the profoundly symbolic history of Jewry. The advent of nuclear weapons brought to a close the era of nation-states and challenged the human community, particularly those of us living in the West, to examine finally our relationship to and obsession with power.

What the Holocaust was for Jewry, Hiroshima portends for humanity. Both events, horrible beyond words and yet transformational beyond imagination, can, if interpreted deeply and in light of the cruciform structures at work in the Exodus and the Cross, set the stage for new and bold definitions of meaning and hope. The Holocaust, like the Black Death, swept European Jewry into ovens of fire. Ironically, the Nazis began where the flagellants had left off: They placed their most lethal death factories in Poland, where King Casimir had welcomed the Jews fleeing from the west six centuries before.

Nuclear weapons, like the Black Death, came suddenly, without warning, only it was not a disease from the East but a technological device from the West. Its effects were equally repugnant: nausea; vomiting and a general absence of hunger; diarrhea mixed with blood; fever and an overall sensation of bodily weakness; purple spots on various parts of the body caused by bleeding under the skin; ulceration and inflammation of the mouth cavity and the throat; bleeding in the mouth, gums, throat, urinary tract, and rectum; loss of hair; and an extremely low white cell count.

Similarly, radiation sickness, as contagion six centuries

before, was essentially unknown. Dr. Hachiya, Director of the Hiroshima Communications Hospital, was not certain of the true nature of the disease until he attended a lecture by two outside consultants nearly a month after the bombing. At first, he had thought Hiroshima had suffered a germ warfare attack.

The net effect of the Holocaust and of Hiroshima, like the Black Death, was a complete disruption of any sense of normalcy. As the survivors of the atomic bombings—called *hibakusha* in Japanese—experienced it, the atomic attack exploded the boundaries of self. The phrase used repeatedly by many of them was *muga-muchu,* meaning "without self, without center." The *hibakusha* experienced a shattering breakdown of faith and trust in the larger human community supporting each individual life and in the structures underlying and framing human existence. The nuclear age has essentially been about the replacement of the natural order of living and dying with an unnatural order of death-dominated life.

It is reasonable to think that the prospect of the death of humanity itself would produce early and serious efforts at disarmament. Simple survival instincts seem to mandate this. Yet, despite the specter of mutual assured destruction, the testing and threatened use of nuclear weapons has continued at an unrelenting pace for over five decades. The capacity to destroy has become a global obsession.

The nuclear arms race only abated somewhat with the visionary leadership of Mikhail Gorbachev, combined with the dissolution of the Soviet Union. Though the United States was left without a credible enemy, the arms race has not stopped. The arsenals, though marginally diminished, remain, and the threat of nuclear proliferation continues to threaten global security. The cornerstone of national security of every nation possessing nuclear weapons remains the continued possession of and willingness to use these weapons.

In 1998, India and Pakistan detonated nuclear devices and are developing delivery capabilities, joining the United States, Russia, Britain, France, China, and Israel. There are nearly fifty other nations with varying degrees of nuclear capacity.

Because the threat of more Hiroshimas remains, experiences that would enable us to break out of our collective reliance on nuclear weapons are important to examine. In this regard, I would like to stress several psychological aspects, specifically two psychological patterns: non-resistance and a sense of mission. I examine these responses because they not only give us insight into the way out of our own predicament, they also shed light on how the ancient Jews and the medieval Europeans were able to open up amid their respective crises. As we shall see, they are essential components to embracing the feminine impulse within, ameliorating our destructive inclinations.

Psychological non-resistance involves submitting to forces one recognizes cannot be overcome. It suggests an encounter with ultimate mystery that must be absorbed rather than fought, assimilated rather than rejected. To use Jungian terminology, it is a psychological movement in which the ego learns slowly and painfully to open up to the Self in order to receive what the Self has to offer: an active and positive feminine response to destructiveness, which is the key to transformation.

In his book *The Search for Meaning*, Victor Frankl discusses this phenomenon among certain Holocaust survivors. He and his entire family were imprisoned in death camps where everyone, save he and his sister was killed. Though he escaped death, he was subjected to unspeakable tortures. One day, sitting naked, beaten, and alone in a cell, Frankl experienced an epiphany—"the last of the human freedoms," as he called it—in which he realized that although the Nazis could control every aspect of his external life and his pragmatic choices, they could not control his inner life or his inner responses. There is a vast gap between stimulus and response, where self-awareness, imagination, conscience, and individual will can be found. This "interiority" is, for Frankl, what makes us human.

Indeed, Frankl was able to transform the horrors he was experiencing outside of himself into an equally profound inspiration in the interior of himself. It was as if he were able to transform the darkness that surrounded him in the camps into a lightness of being inside his soul.

Frankl survived the death camps by refusing to abandon a search for meaning even as he was surrounded by the negation of meaning. As he studied other survivors he came to see that the ones who survived the most holistically were those who somehow in their suffering were able to connect with a sense of interior meaning, often by simply spending time in acts of imagination that transcended the terrors the Nazis perpetrated on them. Retreating to this inner sanctum, untouchable by even the worst tortures, allowed them to be free of their torturers. Wiesel experienced something similar, though he puts it somewhat differently. "In those times," he says, "one climbed to the summit of humanity simply by remaining human."[2]

2. Elie Wiesel, in a speech at the inauguration of the Holocaust Museum, Washington, D.C., March, 1993.

An insight into this process as experienced by the Hiroshima survivors can be gained by examining the Japanese word for resignation, *akiramu*, used to describe how they came to terms with the experiences they endured. *Akiramu* means "way of nothingness," a means of blending with and being acted upon by the numinous forces and events surrounding us. It connotes the idea of an active inner encounter with powerful forces, not a passive submission. *Akiramu* embraces the destruction rather than rejects it, thus activating transformation rather than guilt, empowerment instead of despair.

Everyone involved in the Holocaust or in the Hiroshima and Nagasaki bombings was psychically mutated as they were thrust from normal to death-dominated life. The critical point lay in whether, as a response to this shattering experience, they closed themselves off or opened themselves up, whether they reacted in a distorted way through denial or in a positive way by allowing the full power of the destructive forces to penetrate the depth of their beings, thereby transforming their souls.

Most closed themselves off, with the resulting guilt, paranoia, and death identification so common among survivors of horrendous events. Nevertheless, a few, like Frankl and Wiesel, opened themselves up and gained mastery of themselves and the ability to help others achieve meaning. For each alternative response, the path lay through "the way of nothingness." The choice individuals made after finding themselves on this "way" determined whether their final destination lay in paranoia or meaning, nihilism or integration.

Perhaps the most outstanding example of this positive formulation among *hibakusha* is that of a Hiroshima city official responsible for the wartime distribution of food and provisions. Finding the City Office in flames when he arrived immediately after the bomb fell (he was 3,000 meters from the epicenter at the time of the explosion), he quickly set up a temporary headquarters in an adjacent building that remained standing.

From there he worked, ate, slept, and traveled throughout the city, helping to deal with the dead and to care for the living. Learning that the mayor was dead and knowing that the other officials, many of higher rank, were incapable of effective response, he took over the reins of power without hesitation. He was later to recall:

> They say I shouted at and directed the deputy mayor and other officials who were my superiors. I did not know I was doing this, as I was working like a man in a dream.... I cannot say how much I devoted myself to the work, but I do know that for the year I was doing it, I simply was not aware of whether I was living or not.[3]

He made it his mission to make Hiroshima "a city of brightness," to develop "a bright and forward-looking city population," because he was acutely aware that "this experience should not be just confined to us. It is a great and significant experience—it should be shared with the world".[3]

He did this despite enormous personal problems and challenges. His personal experience of the psychological sufferings characteristic of *hibakusha* was intrinsic to his leadership. While carrying out the enormous task of locating goods and distributing them throughout the city, he

3. Robert J. Lifton, *Death in Life: Survivors of Hiroshima* (New York: Simon and Schuster, 1967), 211–2.

had little time for contact with his immediate family, even when his own father-in-law lay dying. The father-in-law died alone, causing the official extraordinary feelings of grief and death-related guilt.

Furthermore, he was terrified, as were the other *hibakusha*, of being struck down by the "invisible contamination" of radiation sickness. Rather than becoming morbid or neurotic, however, he simply continued to direct the distribution efforts, but instead of traveling all over, he remained in the central office.

This city official lived out what the late mythologist Joseph Campbell defines as the classic pattern of the hero: He answered the "call," the "summons," of the atomic bomb, which was simultaneously an "awakening of the self" and a "road of trials." Even in the death of his father-in-law, there can be found a symbolic "atonement of the father" in which the official reasserted his paternal bond and then transcended it. Finally, he and his fellow survivors exhibited "the freedom to live." In this sense, he is a classic example of transformed power. By absorbing rather than repelling the death immersion of the nuclear attack, he was transfigured and was able to embark on his deeply human quest.

His ability to draw upon his tradition, as a resident of Hiroshima, while simultaneously being able to embrace the fact of the atomic bomb, which had transformed him into a *hibakusha*, is significant. This profound interweaving of powerful forces, old and new, light and dark, empowered him to make the type of boldly innovative decisions and stratagems necessary for the city's survival. Furthermore, it permitted him to experience personally and publicly the entire gamut of survivor-conflicts, enabling other *hibakusha* to share in and identify with his death immersion and his rebirth.

This process allowed the man and the other *hibakusha* who identified with him to move beyond a preoccupation with either life before the bombing or with the devastation of the Bomb itself. Instead of directing their will towards protecting themselves or towards assigning blame for their plight, they asked the question, What is needed? In this spirit of service, they were able to act creatively. This posture engendered initially an enlargement of their sense of self through absorption of the Bomb experience and then a transcendence of the bomb experience through an articulation of a vision of "a city of brightness."

The official continued to be plagued by the guilt of having survived when others had died, his father-in-law in particular. Nonetheless, this guilt did not prevent him from reaching the depths of an even fuller humanity. Indeed, his example is one that inspired the lives of many *hibakusha* and offered to the whole of Japan a model of the possibilities inherent in a receptive attitude in the face of an overwhelming encounter with death.

This situation is similar to the Jews in the aftermath of the Holocaust. The horror of their experience gave rise to calls for justice and revenge upon the perpetrators. The Nuremburg trials were the result, marking the first time in history when the international community asserted collectively that there is a moral code that takes precedence over national policy and military command, and that each citizen is responsible to remember and obey this morality, even if this means disobeying their superiors.

More deeply, world Jewry experienced and interpreted the Holocaust within the depths of Jewish tradition, a tradition galvanized over two thousand years before by their prophets who, at the nadir of persecution and despair at the hands of the Roman and Greek overlords, knew that the God of Israel lived and would ensure their deliverance, no matter how desperate their situation. In that very act of faith, world Jewry was empowered to embrace a higher sense of mission and move beyond Nuremburg and the demands of justice to establish the State of Israel and experience renewal.

Although Jews had been returning to Palestine since the late nineteenth century, it was in the aftermath of the Holocaust that they intensified this migration and moved forward to take the "Promised Land." They ended their Diaspora, begun two thousand years before, with the destruction of Jerusalem and their martyrdom at Masada. Three years after the death of Hitler, the State of Israel was established. In moving from mass death at the hands of the Nazis to mass migration to Israel, the Jews drew upon the ever-present power of their Exodus from Egypt some three thousand five hundred years before, still vitally alive in the depth of their communal and personal memory and still shaping their trust in God, their life in community, and their hope for the future.

As I stated earlier, contemplating such interconnections is a staggering enterprise, one that shatters all our simple categories within which we understand God, humanity, and the world. To do so is to experience a shuddering, emanating from the depth of our being, and a deep sense of vulnerability, which opens us up to the realization that the same awful purpose at work in these immense movements of history is at work in each individual life. At a minimum, intellectual knowledge is not enough. The demand is that we immerse ourselves in the experiences themselves, allowing their "invisible contamination" to permeate our very soul. Refusing to do this, we condemn ourselves to denial, guilt, psychic numbing, and destructiveness. Embracing these memories, we allow their redemptive impact to transform our life.

As the Holocaust rekindled the flame of Jewry and catalyzed the establishment of the State of Israel, Hiroshima's and Nagasaki's precious contribution to the world is our organic knowledge of the atomic bomb experience, which serves as an organizing principle of humankind's struggle for survival.

The fact that the Second World War was followed by the Cold War indicates that this has not been a straight-forward or linear process. For the most part, the world has cut itself off from the important connection of these horrific events to the whole pattern of human survival. The tragedy of the post-war period is that, when drawn into the experience of death immersion, we rejected rather than absorbed the blast, and in our rejection, we identified with death and became obsessed with destructive power, thereby propelling ourselves into the Age of Overkill.

In the United States particularly, where there has not been a single utterance on record from any President, senior military, or senior public official in the spirit of *akiramu*, there is an almost morbid fascination with violence and destructiveness. Not only does it possess the most sophisticated arsenal of nuclear weapons while actively seeking to deny this power to others, the United States spends more on national defense than the other 184 nations of the world combined. The United States is also the largest seller of weapons internationally. Domestically, private American citizens possess over 200 million weapons, making the United States the most massively armed and lethally violent nation on earth. The U.S. television and movie industries spew out violence, mayhem, and chaos to a populace that, if statistics are to be believed, spends more time in front of televisions than in the workplace.

One of the few historical parallels to this obsession with violence and the capacity to destroy was the popular Roman entertainment of crowding into coliseums and gleefully watching gladiators struggle and hack each other to death and wild animals rip apart and devour defenseless humans. Barbarism in Rome was called sport. Today we call it entertainment.

Along with this overwhelming presence and lust for violence there has simultaneously and synchronistically been an immense renewal of the human spirit among those individuals for whom *akiramu* has been a living reality. The sense of mission displayed by a few *hibakusha* reverberated worldwide and led to the creation of myriad peace and citizen action groups in almost every nation on earth. For the first time in history, ordinary citizens realized en masse that their governments were unwilling, if not incapable, of dealing constructively with the nuclear crisis and that human survival mandated individuals to take personal responsibility for international affairs.

Beginning in the 1950s, peace groups challenged initially belligerent governments and an uncaring public to take seriously the facts and consequences of nuclear weapons and the ancillary technology of nuclear power. The peace movement and antinuclear power movement gained momentum separately and together during the 1960s and 1970s and were integral to and indispensable in the decisions made by the political leaders from the 1980s to end the Cold War. Mikhail Gorbachev, the architect of the ending of the Cold War, has stated on numerous occasions that he was emboldened to act as decisively as he did because of the presence of the peace movement in Western societies. The success of the peace and antinuclear movements gave dramatic meaning to the observation of the sociologist Margaret Mead that "when the people lead, eventually the governments will follow."

More broadly, the world has experienced the liberation of women, initially and most dramatically in the nation that first dropped the Bomb. Nothing is as threatening as the annihilation of humanity. Nothing is as fundamental as the relationship between the sexes. In order to change the balance of power in this relationship after millennia of male dominance, the basis for every transaction in human society must be altered. The fundamental transformations taking place around the world in economics, politics, society, and religion are and will continue to be radically affected by the liberation of women.

It is not a coincidence that such a fundamental liberation is taking place at exactly the same time as the world has developed the technology of absolute annihilation. The capacity for complete destruction has triggered at the deepest psychosocial level of our collective consciousness an equally fundamental revolution in human relations. Embracing this revolution is, in the end, the only secure and lasting guarantor of human survival.

Not only are women on the rise throughout the global social structure and active in every discipline, they are transforming every area of endeavor as they gain equality. Even in the realm of male sexuality, particularly in the gay movement, there have been transformations due to the impact of feminism, for liberation in one sector has profound implications in all others.

What is occurring is a huge shift in gestalt. The liberation of women is not one trend among many; it is a central and decisive trend. The beginning of gender equalization has been the gateway for democratization throughout Western culture and around the world. As Hiroshima and the advent of nuclear weapons signaled the end of the old industrial order of nation-states, the liberation of women will play a central role in any renaissance or reformation leading to a new era.

CHAPTER 15

THE FEMININE

Time past and time future

Allow but a little consciousness.

To be conscious is not to be in time

But only in time can the moment in the rose-garden,

The moment in the arbour where the rain beat,

The moment in the draughty church at smokefall

Be remembered; involved with past and future.

Only through time time is conquered.1

AN EXAMINATION OF WOMEN'S LIBERATION on the political and economic levels of life has been brilliantly described by a panoply of feminist writers over the past four decades, from Simone de Bouvoir to Betty Friedan. In this chapter, I want to concentrate on the feminine itself, which underlies this liberation, and to do so in a manner that carries forward the themes of non-resistance and a sense of mission. The feminine is an eternal archetypal force, psychological in nature; feminism is a recent historical phenomenon, political in nature. In this sense, feminism is as vulnerable as any other movement to the seductions of power-for-the-sake-of-power. Feminism

1. Eliot, *Collected Poems*, 192.

and the feminine are thus interrelated but not synonymous.

The feminine underlies feminism; indeed the feminine is the wellspring of feminism but is far broader in scope and depth. Conversely, feminism draws from the feminine but has a number of explicitly masculine characteristics as well. The task here is to explore the feminine in its psychological dimensions rather than feminism in its historical dimensions. My intent is to connect women's liberation with previous manifestations of the feminine, particularly with Mary and Sophia.

As the city official of Hiroshima and Victor Frankl exemplified, the feminine is deeply embedded in all of us. It is an archetype of the psyche available to all human beings everywhere. We are all survivors of Hiroshima; we are all survivors of Auschwitz. We must all discover the feminine and cruciform structures within if we are to discern the patterns and energies of the psyche that empower transformation.

Whether symbolized by Sophia, by Mary, or by the peace and feminist movements, certain psychological modes of being that influence and are accessible to all human beings are operative in "the feminine." These modes of being are oriented by a certain awareness, a certain way of relating to life, of assimilating reality and forming judgments. The feminine symbolizes particular aspects of spiritual or psychic reality, applicable to women and men, although in different ways. The feminine is activated in times of extreme crisis, and its activation signals and ushers in a new order.

The feminine thus serves as a gateway to a deep and transformational experience of the psyche's cruciform structures. The feminine, in this sense, is an archetypal aspect of the psyche. As an archetype, it cannot be known in and of itself. It can be understood, however, through images and myth and through the behavioral and emotional responses that the archetype arouses in us.

The psyche is structured in polarities of opposites whose interactions vitalize human psychic life. Invariably, we are attracted to one end of the polarity and eschew the other. Though it may seem "other" when we encounter this opposite polarity, we find that it is fully bound up with not only the pole we have already embraced to its exclusion but also with what we are seeking to become.

What Jung called the "individuation process" at the psychological level of our being is the struggle toward wholeness, whereby we engage with the opposites within and are thereby drawn into the maturation process of recognizing and reconciling our indwelling polarities. Our Self is gradually revealed out of a series of successive reconciliations, and this is what nourishes our wholeness. In this process, we become coherent individuals, not just a scattered collection of various influences and impulses. Coming to terms with the cruciform character of our psychic depth allows us to deal more creatively with the polarities and contradictions of everyday life. Indeed, integration of the cruciform dimensions at any level, whether the commonsensical, the psychological, or the spiritual, contributes to its integration on all levels.

Many symbols that come to meet us through the psyche are symbols of male-female polarity. "This primordial pair of opposites," writes Jung in his book *Psychology and Alchemy,* "symbolizes every conceivable pair of opposites that may occur: hot and cold, light and dark, north and south, dry and damp, good and bad, conscious and unconscious."[2] On a symbolic level it can be said that the psyche uses the biological differences between male and female to convey the reality of psychic opposites. Thus, the sexual elements of our being have a spiritual function. The opposite sex conveys the fact of "otherness," that opposite pole of reality that is integrally related to us and yet seems completely distinct from us. In this sense, the feminine symbolizes and best represents certain modes of consciousness and spirit.

The whole person is consciously aware of and related to his or her feminine and masculine aspects. Therefore, masculinity and femininity cannot be described in *isolation from* one another, only in *relation to* one another. They can be described as two modalities, two profoundly interrelated archetypal principles of the human psyche whose complementarity and polarity can be found not only in the interaction *between* the sexes but also in the interaction *within* each individual.

The wholeness of an individual revolves around the axis of fully developed and interrelated masculine and feminine elements. The polar structure of the psyche is the source of this interrelation and the framework for its movement. The libido, the life energy that is generated from the tension of the opposites, flows continually from one pole to another, differentiating the ego from its unconscious state by bringing the distinct elements that must be reconciled to the surface of consciousness.

2. Carl Jung, "Psychology and Alchemy," in *Collected Works,* trans. R. F. C. Hull (London: Routledge and Kegan Paul, 1967),12:144.

Wholeness is a potential that we experience while we are still limited and partial. Wholeness does not mean the absence of polarity but its clash and reconciliation. Indeed, to lose contact with the polarities of psychic life can cause regression into an unconscious state (psychosis) or the splitting of one pole from the other (neurosis). This is what happens when we reject rather than assimilate historical traumas, such as the Holocaust or the atomic bombings of Japan. Whatever we reject lessens who we are and what we can become.

Wholeness is the enlarged state where the feminine is still feminine and the masculine is still masculine, but both cohere in a dialectical relationship, giving rise to an integration of the personality. Our challenge is to grow into a conscious relationship with the masculine/feminine polarity within, just as we must continually interact dialectically with the Holocaust and Hiroshima to prevent them from ever happening again. We can only keep the pledge "Never again!" by never forgetting the experience. We will never forget only if we integrate the past event into the present reality and keep it alive within us in a creative, life-affirming rather than life-denying way. The Holocaust and Hiroshima will never happen again historically only if we keep them creatively alive psychologically.

After several thousand years, during which Western culture developed in increasingly masculine and patriarchal ways, separating the opposites from each other and subordinating the feminine under the masculine, a great reversal is taking place. Just at the point when Western culture, having succumbed almost completely to the illusion of separateness, has fashioned the instruments to destroy the world, feminine consciousness has burst forth to compensate for this one-sidedness and has initiated a process of renewal by affirming the reality of the whole.

Only an incorporation of the healthy feminine into the collective culture will suffice to transform Western civilization and guarantee human survival in the face of the technological capacities to annihilate it. Unconsciously, the culture recognizes this. Consciously, however, the culture is still too one-sidedly masculine and too gripped by a distorted feminine to hear clearly the healthy feminine voice. Understood in this way, the struggle for women's rights and the search for non-patriarchal, feminine modes of being are not simply a political platform for feminist activists. They are a human concern vital to each individual and should be studied and understood as completely as possible. Because of the weapons we are wielding, our survival depends upon it.

The feminine principle has two aspects: an elementary, or static, aspect and a transformational, or active, aspect. The elementary, static aspect of the feminine principle is represented classically as a receptive, dark, moist, and all-encompassing world of formation that holds fast to every-thing created within it. As the fertile darkness of nature that renews life perennially, the static aspect of the feminine gestates new drives, fantasies, images, and intuitions in the psyche. As such, it is associated with the unconscious and the dark mysteries of God.

Like nature, the static aspect of the feminine has an inert, essentially indifferent quality that is impersonal and non-individual. This static quality of the feminine is the very basis of the conservative, stable, and unchanging character of the feminine that predominates in motherhood. It is the aspect that Sophia personifies as the ordering principle of creation and that Mary personifies as Queen of Heaven.

The elementary, static aspect of the feminine is symbolized

also in the Great Mother, or Mother Goddess, who bears, nurtures, protects, and releases life. Common symbols for the static aspect of the feminine include fruit with an abundance of seeds, a plenteous cornucopia, the belly as a containing vessel, and various images of depth, such as, caskets, nests, cradles, or coffins. Representative animal symbols include the owl, with its uterine-shaped body, and the shellfish, with its womb-shaped curvature.

The positive aspect of the static feminine generates emotional responses associated with security, hope, and vitality. The behavior that communicates this positive effect expresses confidence, security, and optimism in one-self, and a protective solicitous concern for others, convey-ing trust and affirmation. The most important aspect of the Great Mother is an attitude of unconditional acceptance. Hence the adage A mother is someone who dreams great dreams for you, yet accepts the dream you decide to follow, and always loves you just the way you are.

In its negative expression, the static aspect of the feminine is described symbolically as ensnaring, fixating, overbearing, leading one from light into darkness, and dragging one beyond one's depths to be swallowed up. This negative aspect of the feminine appears as undifferentiated and collective, as a devouring and castrating force indifferent to individual growth and development.

This negative quality is depicted symbolically as the Devouring Mother, who eats her children alive, or as the Gorgon's head, which paralyses anyone who gazes at it. Negative animal images include the bear with its suffocat-ing hug and the octopus and the spider with their ensnaring tentacles. It is what the Holy Mother Catholic Church of the Middle Ages became and what the Black Death shattered.

Balanced against the static aspect of the feminine is its dynamic, transformational aspect. It is a dynamism classically described in Plato's *Phaedrus*: a divine madness of the soul that invokes primeval forces within that move us beyond our limitations and the conventions of society to higher levels of being and deeper levels of understanding. It is this dynamic, transformational aspect of the feminine that inspired the official in Hiroshima to envision a "city of brightness," Victor Frankl to discover the "last of the human freedoms," and Elie Wiesel and other survivors of the Holocaust to be transformed rather than destroyed by being immersed in death. This dynamic, transformational aspect is at work in much of the feminist movement.

Such a transformation can range from a momentary sense of being taken beyond oneself to a profound enlargement of one's personality. The dynamic feminine leads us to move beyond ourselves to interact with others in emotional and physical relationships. This role was performed by the archetype of Mary in late medieval society. The Black Death shattered the hold of the devouring Mother Church and allowed the transforming power of Mary to spring forth to provide healing and comfort to those suffering. The positive, transformational aspect of the feminine, personified by the resurgence of Mary, broke through the negative static aspect of the feminine, personified by the medieval Catholic Church.

The positive emotional effects of transformation are the feelings we all experience when we are caught up in a creative process, being inspired and compelled to give ourselves to something of life-affirming value. This positive quality of the dynamic aspect of the feminine is expressed when we gain new insights by willingly risking exposure to forces beyond our control and by adopting an attitude of courage and expectation instead of reticence and dread. Thus, Sophia called upon all who heard her voice to come unto her and know the "fear of the Lord." What followed Sophia was the Christ; what followed the adoration of Mary was the Reformation. What is following the liberation of women is a transformation of human relations.

The negative transformations that can result from the dynamic aspect of the feminine are lunacy and madness, instead of ecstasy and inspiration; drunkenness and promiscuity, instead of maturity and growth; and journeys into the dark recesses of one's unconscious, rather than into the light of clarity and insight. Symbols associated with negative transformations include the spells of evil witches; the evil succubus who steals one's soul and sucks it dry; and the devilish temptress, such as, Delilah or Jezebel, who drives us irresistibly toward our doom.

This negative aspect of the feminine filled the flagellants. They prayed to the Blessed Virgin to inspire them, yet what came was not creative inspiration but a frenzy that led to their excesses against the Jews and to their own self-mortification. The word flagellation comes from the flagellants who "flagellated" themselves as they marched along the roads singing hymns to Mary, congratulating them-selves on their willingness to suffer even as Christ suffered.

This negative aspect of the feminine affects us all. The emotional difficulties that indicate negative transformation include a sense of being powerlessly dragged down into a state of confusion and a feeling of being helplessly possessed by an obsessive jealousy that transforms one into a nasty, suspicious individual. Patterns of behavior revolve around degeneration into modes of being that reduce consciousness rather than enhance it. One may sink into a sullen melancholy that spoils a social situation because one suddenly feels sorry for oneself and expects everyone else to make life easier. One loses the ability to meet others half way. Warmth can become sentimentality; irritation, rage; and nostalgia, depression. One can be driven into behaving either self-destructively or destructively toward others.

Put abstractly, one could say that feminine consciousness has to do with intuition. Symbolically, this is represented by the heart, because it is peculiarly attuned to unconscious processes. This is to be understood as distinct from masculine consciousness, which separates itself from the unconscious into something discrete and separate. Masculine consciousness has to do with intellect, which is represented symbolically by the head, because it is peculiarly attuned to conscious processes. Each of these modes of being is found in both sexes, although each finds its most direct expression in its corresponding sex.

The feminine quality of understanding begins with perception and intuition. Ideas "seize" us; they "arise" from our unconscious without being willed or logically thought out. We say, "it suddenly hit me," and become more aware of meaning than of facts, more aware of organic growth than of mechanical chains of causation. This process is activated by the static mode of the feminine; in order to be seized, we have to be open, as the official in Hiroshima and Victor Frankl demonstrated.

This way of understanding usually takes place when we are not making a conscious attempt to reach a solution. It comes in the stillness of daydreaming, in the relaxation at twilight, and it is symbolized by the moon reflected in a pond, shining in the darkness, reigning over fertility and growth on earth. Darkness, then, rather than the burning rays of the sun, characterizes feminine understanding and the mysterious processes of the unconscious where creative activity germinates.

Nighttime is for sleeping, a time when consciousness is enfolded into unconsciousness. Approximately one-third of our life is spent in what is essentially an unconscious state, allowing us time for recovery in dreams, time for the wounds of our soul as well as our body to be regenerated and healed. The intellect has little to say during these times. The moon, the darkness, the unconscious speak only the language of the heart, Pascal's *logique de coeur*.

Enfolding consciousness into unconsciousness, allowing intuition to master intellect, darkness to lead our light, brings something new into consciousness. This bringing forth of the new is the work of the transformational, dynamic mode of the feminine. It reaches out to complete a process in the conscious that was begun in the unconscious. Unlike the masculine approach, which acts with the intellect to register, analyze, and classify facts, the feminine quality of understanding conceives a content, allows it to germinate, and then brings it forth into the world. In the masculine way of understanding, more information is acquired; in the feminine way, a transformation is experienced. Thus the apocalyptic Jews experienced Sophia in their prophecies, and Saint Bernard, Saint Francis, and Saint Bridgett experienced Mary through mystical trances and visions.

This difference in modes of understanding implies a difference in processes. The feminine accepts a conception, carries it, assimilates it, and allows it to ripen within, much as a pregnant woman carries within her womb the seed of life until the infant is birthed. Feminine activity is a way not of controlling but of submitting to a process that is simply happening of its own accord. We cannot expect transformation by being actively masculine in relation to the will of God; we can only be transformed if we are in a receptive, feminine posture toward the Spirit. *Only* in our feminine aspect can we pray truly and deeply, "Not my will but thine be done."

As the moon reflects the sunlight, feminine consciousness turns to and reflects unconscious processes, guides itself by them, and gathers them into itself. In this way, activity remains intensely personal because the person involved is transformed by the activity being submitted to. It is a quality of activity that one receives and responds to with one's whole being, a quality that is essential to religious experience particularly. We must be open to the spirit and be willing to be transformed by it, subordinating our ego to a larger process.

Feminine understanding and activity engender a qualitative, as opposed to a quantitative, sense of time. The feminine experiences time as dynamic rhythms and cycles, in contrast to static sequentiality and mathematics. The moon, with its own cycle of fullness and emptiness, symbolizes feminine time and represents the mysterious, unconscious, and feminine rhythms of growth and fertility, birth and death, ascending and declining.

What happens within depends on what happens without, and vice versa. Will-power and reason do not avail in the feminine posture of openness to the numinous. The person simply waits, attuning himself or herself, watching for the qualitatively "right" moment. When one is out of synchronization with the "fullness of time," a quick intellect becomes coercive, an open heart becomes lethargic or despondent, and the ensuing activity becomes inappropriate. Feminine time is, therefore, inseparably interconnected with feminine activity and understanding. The great, central events of the Exodus and the Crucifixion and the impact of other events, such as, the Renaissance, the establishment of the State of Israel, and the liberation of women, have all been transformational in human history and in consciousness because they emerged not by a masculine act of will but in the feminine fullness of time.

It must be emphasized that the masculine impulse has equally static and transformational aspects and equally positive and negative dimensions. The static aspect of the masculine applies the intellect to understanding the world, whereas the transformational aspect of the masculine commands and implements the plans of the mind. When used positively, this allows for the accumulation of knowledge, the development of mathematics, science, and technology, and the establishment of large-scale social organizations— all expressions of physical and intellectual power. The masculine is like the sun bringing light to life, allowing the human mind to dissect and analyze the world in order to use the resources of nature for human benefit.

When utilized negatively, masculine consciousness commands simply in order to control, wills simply in order to subjugate, and makes distinctions simply in order to exploit. The combination of a piercing intellect and the will to power is like the scorching sun at midday, where because there is no shade, the plants wilt and the animals run and hide.

The feminine is not "better" than the masculine, even as intuition is not superior to intellect, or the moon, superior to the sun. Each has its proper place in the order of things. Problems arise when we split off these opposites from one another, as our civilization has done by embracing a masculine, intellectual, and conscious mode of being to the exclusion of almost all else. This has led to unparalleled destructiveness and to the development of weapons and mentalities capable of destroying the world.

The feminine comes in times of crisis, because when society or the individual has ceased to live in accordance with the ordering principle of creation, the static aspect of the feminine is required to open us to the spirit again. The dynamic aspect of the feminine is essential to lead us forth on the path of transformation. Survival in times of crisis depends on the willingness of consciousness to be led by the unconscious, the intellect to be led by intuition, the sun to be led by the moon.

The feminine is the gateway to the spirit world, to the divine summons to examine our violation of limits and hence to the abuse of our power that produced the crisis. Only the feminine can accept a transformation of power by learning again the wisdom of limits. This is why Eve, rather than Adam, engaged in the dialogue with the serpent in the Garden and why Mary, rather than Joseph, was called to obedience by the angel. Only with a feminine spirit can we access and be affected by the transformational powers of the psyche and the grace of the Spirit.

The feminine compels us to examine our relationship to power and thus leads us to take seriously our shadow dimensions. The feminine aspect of spiritual transformation involves the process of searching out and accepting those parts of oneself that one normally despises and rejects. It is the force that binds us to events, such as the Exodus or the Crucifixion, the Holocaust or Hiroshima. It is what allows us to "Never forget!"

As we saw earlier, this is related to what St. Paul calls the "foolishness of God." The feminine affirmatively seeks in the destructiveness threatening it the beginning of the transformation of the destructiveness into creativity. The feminine searches out the vulnerable, shadowy aspects, intuiting the goal not to be perfection, which is to vanquish the shadow, but wholeness, which is to integrate it. Transformation not dominance is the result. It seems foolish, for it requires submission to all those things that the powerful and the worldly-wise, operating by the strength of the negative masculine, counsel us to reject and to deny.

The feminine style of transformation is to seek the meaning hidden in the center of concrete happenings; it goes deeply into the "dark" of personal events and emotions where we find extraordinarily intense responses. It is the darkness that quickens the transformational power of the feminine. Thus, Sophia was activated by the Greek and Roman violence against ancient Jewry; the adoration of Mary, by the Black Death; the establishment of Israel by the Holocaust; and the peace and feminist movements by the atomic bombings of Japan.

To follow this "foolishness" of the feminine in such times requires high degrees of courage and tenacity, for what we discover in the dark may often initially be in conflict with how we are behaving in the light; what we may discern with the heart may contradict the facts of our head. Here again the primary symbol is the crescent moon that points downward and shines in the night.

This quality of feminine consciousness that allows things to happen in their own time is responsible for the understanding that the transformation of the ego is achieved through sufferance, through the willingness of the ego to accept that the Self, not the ego, is the center of the psyche. Feminine consciousness is the essential ingredient in the "crucifixion of the ego at the hands of the Self," to use Jung's phrase. Feminine consciousness is the key to individuation. This explains why Christ, who was decisively authoritative in his ministry, became utterly receptive in the face of the Cross. "Not my will but thine be done" were his words just before he received the kiss of Judas in the Garden of Gethsemene.

It is precisely in this receptive orientation of the ego to the Self that the union of opposites is achieved. In employing the intuition of the heart rather than the logic of the head, in being a part of a process rather than seeking to control events by will, and in flowing in a rhythm of time rather than ordering time in order to control it, an interiority, a receptivity, an openness is created, which allows the life process to instill a deeper sense of the wisdom of limits within those of us who live in a world obsessed with breaking all limits.

Feminine consciousness offers itself as an empty vessel to Spirit. Our existence on earth allows the Spirit to act in and through us as we learn to set aside the needs of our individual will and our ego and accept that our purpose on earth is to be part of a greater whole, a greater Will. Earthly materiality thereby becomes a temple of divine presence.

Thus Mary, in a posture of obedience in the Spirit, could say, "Be it unto me according to thy word" and thereby be filled by the Spirit. Her Annunciation is paradigmatic of all annunciations of the heart, whether they are becoming quiet so that an inspiration can burst forth or learning patience so a process can come to organic fruition in the "fullness of time." Feminine consciousness allows itself to be "impregnated" by the Spirit. Religious penetration is like physical penetration: It seeds the flesh, changing us as we change it. Out of receptivity comes fulfillment. Out of Mary's obedience comes the birth of "the Christ." Mary the Virgin becomes Mary the Mother.

The ego cannot create this new attitude or reality; rather, it learns to receive it in ever-deepening humility and, in receiving, nurtures the new contents growing within as a mother, her child. For the feminine, the spirit is always "other," and the relationship to it is always intimate, concrete, sensual, never abstract or impersonal. The result transforms the bearer and the borne.

Patriarchal consciousness finds all of this confusing and threatening. The modern world emphasizes the manipulative, rational, and formulating capacities of consciousness—essentially the masculine in its negative aspects. We have been taught to relate to the world through the head, seeking control, rather than by balancing the head with the heart in the pursuit of harmony within a greater whole. Our educational institutions prepare us for social responsibility by giving us facts, refusing to teach values other than the virtues of competition and dominance. Our intellect achieves its clarity through dividing the world into discrete, definable units and by maintaining independence from and even opposition to intuition. We have become cut off from the principles of the feminine world of the unconscious and have built a world predicated almost entirely on negative masculine principles.

The positive feminine refuses such subordination and is, in fact, *activated* by such one-sidedness. In the face of the negative masculine, the positive-static and transformational-feminine creates unity through yielding to and embracing the destructive aspects of the masculine in the spirit of *akiramu*. A feminine posture in times of crisis thus becomes the key to survival. Whereas masculine consciousness sees antinomies and seeks to split the opposites, feminine consciousness embraces antinomies, intuiting the inner connections between those opposites, which the masculine wants to divide and conquer.

Splitting the opposites is the key to masculine power, and when this power is used for negative masculine goals of domination, exploitation, and control, nothing but violence, hatred, and discord results, no matter what technological and scientific advances have been made in the process. This further explains my statement in the Introduction that the more technology we have, the more destructive we become. This is because the cornerstone of modern civilization is the masculine in its most negative aspects.

In the thick of this, the feminine begins to move, as Sophia or as Mary or as feminism. In moving, it brings the opposites together again, initially in the spirit of *akiramu*. It submits to the full force and violence of masculine destructiveness, but does so by embracing the destructiveness, thereby assimilating all the negativity. The feminine is not the whole, but it is the *insight* into the whole and, as such, the *gateway* to the whole. By intuiting the whole and the unity of opposites, the feminine can absorb the force, energy, and power of masculine destructiveness, which dominates and separates; can transform it into a force, energy, and power that serves and unifies; and can suffer for others rather than demand that others suffer. Only in the feminine can untransformed power become power transformed.

The supreme irony is that we rarely embrace this feminine posture except in times of acute crisis. For the most part, masculine modes of being, particularly in their negative aspect, give us sufficient control over nature and our fellow humans that we tend to resist any acknowledgment of the feminine until we are compelled to do so for survival's sake. We tend to equate masculine consciousness with "normal" consciousness, feminine consciousness with being "weak."

Even when we are confronted by the destructive results of our negative masculine misuse of power, our masculine impulses continue to say, "This is not us, this is 'other,' something to be fought and rejected." The feminine whispers at that very moment, "Embrace the darkness, submit to its disintegrating powers by tapping into a deeper connection with the whole, of which the darkness, as the light, is but a part. There you shall experience the transformational power of God." Thus Moses could return to Egypt, Jesus could receive the kiss of Judas, and Wiesel could endure the hanging of the youth and remain human. This is the guidance of the feminine in her deepest, most profound and mysterious aspect.

In its highest expression, the feminine spirit transcends earth and sky, not to disappear into abstractions but to be transformed through specific acts and moments. It is a process symbolized by a flower. The feminine spirit remains always attached to the earth, to history, to individuality. Like the flower, it keeps its roots in the earth, for the earth is the Mother. The downward directed path of the feminine is, therefore, the path of the lowly manger, the everyday air, the common soil of ordinary experience in which one receives and achieves transformation.

The flower is the supreme visible form of Sophia; it is why Beatrice calls Mary a rose. In the East, the Buddha is classically depicted as being seated on a lotus blossom, its roots emanating out of the slime and mud at the bottom of the pond, its stem rising up through the water, its petals opening up to the sky. This image is represented by the Biblical theme of God working through our earthiness and our weakness to effect the divine will. It is why the Exodus is always connected with the Promised Land, and the Resurrection is always framed by the Cross. The alchemical process that connects the one with the other is quintessentially that of the feminine.

On the surface, the feminine seems only to be a simple mother with child. However, inside, as the earliest figurines of the Mother Goddess depict, she contains every child, even the "Son of God." This is hinted at in all the depictions of Mary. She is the Mother of God; she contains God within her. Michelangelo's *Pietà*, sculpted within a generation of the Black Death, reflects this. The frail broken body of "the Christ" lies dead upon Mary's lap. Jesus has been laid upon her as the Man of Suffering, destroyed by the wisdom of the world; Mary is depicted as Mother of Tears, completely enveloping him in the "foolishness of God."

The *Pietà* represents the highest expression of the feminine modality of being. It expresses the wisdom of the heart, the wisdom that arises in and through a genuine relationship with others. It is a wisdom bound to the earth, to organic growth, to living historical reality in all its light and dark dimensions. Therefore, the ancients said of the feminine, whether depicted as the Mother Goddess,

Sophia, or Mary, that she was the ordering principle of creation, which brought all aspects together into alignment with the will of the Creator. She relates intimately with human beings, wooing them to her that she might transform their souls and thereby their relationship with power, particularly in times of the excesses of power. Hers is a wisdom of intuition and of compassion, arising through natural relatedness and teaching humankind the limits of power. This is why power aligned to the ordering principle is power transformed. Without alignment, it seeks to conquer; in alignment, it seeks to serve.

Knowing the ordering principle of creation, which the feminine represents, offers us a moral basis for knowledge and a moral limit to power. The positive and transformational aspects of the feminine within all of us are jointly the gateway to the individuation of the psyche and the grace of the Spirit. The feminine is not that wholeness or that grace; it is what opens, leads, and connects us with the grace of the Spirit. The feminine infuses knowledge with faith and transforms power through crucified wisdom.

CHAPTER 16

FAUST

For our own past is covered by the currents

    of action,

But the torment of others remain an experience

Unqualified, unworn by subsequent attrition.

People change, and smile: but the agony abides.[1]

T HE EPIC OF GILGAMESH DISTILLED THE contradictions of humanity at the inception of civilization. The story of Faust encapsulates the predicaments of humanity after we attained civilization, after we arrived where Gilgamesh thought he wanted to go. By putting the consequences of the negative masculine tendencies of modern culture and the transformational power of the feminine into poetic form, Faust's story is our story; his tragedy, our tragedy; his transformation, our way through the night. Published in segments by Johann Goethe in the late 1700s, it ranks as one of the greatest literary achievements of Western civilization.

    Faust's tale begins as the epic of Job: The Lord has called the divine counsel. In attendance is the devil, Mephistopheles. The Lord asks Mephistopheles to consider Faust, "my serf."[2] "Though now he serves me but in clouded ways," says God, "Soon I

1. Eliot, *Collected Poems*, 209.

2. Johann Wolfgang von Goethe, *Faust*, trans. Walter Arndt, ed. Cyrus Hamlin (New York: Norton & Company, 1976), line 298.

shall guide him so his spirit clears" (308).

> "You'll lose him yet!" retorts Mephistopheles,
> "I offer bet and tally,
> Provided that your Honor gives
> Me leave to lead him gently up my alley!" (312–4).

God quickly agrees. Their ensuing conversation portrays the devil as infinitely complex and cunningly wise. Goethe understands the insights of the early Hebrews concerning our antinomial experience of God, that the Eternal creates the good and the evil, the weal and the woe of life. Goethe was acutely aware of the cruciform nature of reality and surmised that its origin and its unity took place in the divine Pleroma, though none of the characters in his tale were thereby absolved of any responsibility for their actions.

Mephistopheles makes sport of God's creation. He ridicules human beings' propensity to take a serious interest in anything that exists in creation, especially when the object of their interest gives them confidence in their own individual strength. In this sense, Mephistopheles and God agree. Supreme wickedness and divine wisdom concur in recognizing the vanity and weakness of all created things. God comments that "Man ever errs the while he strives" (317). "Yes," agrees Mephistopheles, and then says of Faust: "Dust shall he swallow, aye, and love it, Like my old cousin, the illustrious serpent" (334–5).

Mephistopheles proclaims this truth to disgust humankind with what is good; the Lord proclaims it to elevate us above what is evil. Goethe understood the contingency of life, that humanity is frail and limited, even if in our pride we seek to attain heights far beyond our capacity. The relationship of Faust and Mephistopheles is clearly reminiscent of Eve and the serpent, although, given the rise of patriarchy, the protagonist is a man gripped by the power of the intellect rather than a woman.

We also see in Faust the point eloquently demonstrated in the story of Joseph that, although the devil uses creation to denigrate humanity and seduce us to do evil, God uses creation, even the evil that Satan intends and that we commit, to work the good. All the evil intentions of the Satanic side of the universe, all the frailties that humanity has been heir to as fallen beings since Adam have served the holy purposes of God, who weaves all the strands together—the good and the evil—into a purpose that redeems. God allows evil into the divine court because God uses evil for a divine purpose.

Mephistopheles, as the serpent of old, is "wise above all creatures." Given the Age of Enlightenment he lived in, Goethe's Devil is also a very civilized. Throughout his relationship with Faust, the Devil handles ridicule with dexterity, sensibility with sarcasm. He is awkward without being timid, disdainful without seeming arrogant. It is in the presence of women that he is the most insecure. He ridicules creation because he is terrified of the ordering principles of Sophia inherent in creation. He affects something of tenderness with women, because it is only in their company that he needs to deceive in order to seduce.

Mephistopheles seduces in order to elicit and to encourage the passion of others. He himself cannot even imitate love. Seduction is the only activity possible for him, filled as he is with hopeless cynicism. Thus, Mephistopheles is the renegade of creation; he is condemned to futility by his own will, seeking to deceive others into sharing his alienated state. His ultimate goal is to lead humanity to violate the ordering principles in creation. He does this by offering humanity power over creation.

For his part, Faust exemplifies all the weaknesses of the human condition: He has the desire for knowledge but suffers the fatigue of labor; he yearns for success and knows the futility of mere pleasure. "I'm too old to be content with play," he says, "too young to be without desire" (1546–7). As such, he presents us with a perfect figure of a changeable and volatile being whose sentiments may be grand but are still even more ephemeral than the short existence of which he complains.

Faust has far more ambition than he has strength; yet he is filled with such an inward agitation and thirst for knowledge that he resorts to all manner of sorceries to escape the hard but necessary conditions imposed upon human life by the structures inherent in the world and by his own mortality. Like Gilgamesh, he longs to conquer death, but he is civilized enough to know it cannot be done. Instead, Faust lusts simply for knowledge, to taste eternity somehow before his inevitable demise.

Like Adam and Eve, Faust knows his limits but feels compelled to transgress them. Aware of his mortality, he has only one desire: to know everything in order to exercise absolute power. To use Pascal's terms, he is a "something" whose only ambition is to be "everything." The more aware he grows of his age, the deeper his craving becomes for the limitless. In this regard, Faust personifies the negative aspect of the masculine archetype.

It is in a state of exhaustion, after spending the night in incantations, that he meets Mephistopheles for the first time. He is not afraid but promptly calls Mephistopheles "Lord of Flies," a literal translation of the Hebrew

Baal-zebub (2 Kgs. 1:2). He then inquires further concerning this Devil before him, to which Mephistopheles replies, "Part of that force which would do ever evil and does ever good" (1335–6). Even the Great Deceiver knows that all his evil intents and machinations are used by the divine Spirit for good. Despite this, Mephistopheles says:

> [I am] the spirit which eternally denies!
>
> And justly; for all that which is wrought
>
> Deserves that it should come to naught;
>
> Hence it were best if nothing were engendered.
>
> Which is why all things you have rendered
>
> By terms like sin, destruction—evil, in brief,
>
> Are my true element-in-chief (1338–44).

Like Eve with the serpent, Faust finds this reply intriguing. Just before Mephistopheles' entry, Faust had been in communication with an earth spirit who had given him insight into the age-old recognition that the universal is only to be found, and can only be manifested, in the particular. Each point of existence is a microcosm of the macrocosm of the Totality. Therefore, to see connections *between* things is to discern the reality *inside* a thing. Faust had long pondered the mystery and the paradox of the One and the Many.

What Faust yearns for, however, is participation in reality as known under *earthly conditions*, not as known from an eternal, mystical standpoint. He is desperate to move from intuitions concerning reality to actually experiencing the depths of reality. Faust is far more interested in power on earth than he is in insights into heaven. The Spirit he had summoned before his fateful meeting with the devil was an earth spirit in the thick of life, "weaving the living garment of God" and weaving it as interdependent opposites. It tells Faust:

> In tides of living, in doing's storm,
> Up, down, I wave.
> Waft to and fro
> Birth and grave,
> An endless flow
> A changeful plaiting,
> Fiery begetting,
> Thus at Time's scurrying loom I weave and warp
> And broider at the Godhead's living garb (501–9).

Faust is enchanted by the cruciform nature of reality the spirit describes. Indeed, it is precisely because he had felt a rising courage to bear the "weal and woe" of the world that he had summoned the spirit in the first place. Why is everything comprised of opposites? Why does death beget more life? What connects a speck of dust with the farthest star? How is the One related to the Many? How do the Many come from the One?

Faust is seeking more insight into these mysteries when Mephistopheles appears. Faust demands of the Devil pleasures that will *never* satisfy and that will turn into new desires. In one of the clearest expressions of hubris and Titanism in all of literature, he proclaims, "I tell you it's not a question of pleasure at all; [it is a] question of unending growth, of unlimited expansion, of total immersion into the opposites of existence." Faust storms against the restrictions of time, space, and causality. He demands to be able to transgress all limits and to throw himself completely into the polarities of the universe, not to escape them but to be immersed completely in them.

These, then, are the conditions of Faust's wager:

Should ever I take ease upon a bed of leisure,
May that same moment mark my end!
When first by flattery you lull me
Into a smug complacency,
When with indulgence you can gull me,
Let that day be the last for me!
This is my wager! (1692–7).

"Done!" exclaims Mephistopheles, and the Pact has begun.

As Goethe understands it, the point of departure for humanity's "Faustian Pact" is the insatiable thirst to behold and to know the inner essence of things. Our perennial obsession is to satisfy an insatiable desire to move beyond the limits imposed upon us in and by existence. Through the parable of *Faust*, Goethe re-creates the Fall of Adam and Eve, who wanted to know what God knew and were willing to break all limits to gain that knowledge. Faust's ultimate ambition is to taste of the tree of the knowledge of good and evil, to know *everything* experientially.

Now the leader, Mephistopheles goads Faust,

Go, spurn intelligence and science,
Man's lodestar and supreme reliance,
Be furthered by the liar-in-chief
In works of fraud and make believe,
And I shall have you dead to rights (1851–4).

Faust's initial release from the limitations of the ordering principle of creation consists in being initiated into the basic principles of devilry. He learns to manipulate reality through magic to gain its secrets. The further his greed for knowledge grows, the more reckless his pride becomes.

Thinking he has accomplished great feats, he begins to idolize himself, only to come crashing down when what he gains evaporates or is destroyed in the very act of being attained. Thinking his new knowledge gives him equality with God, he is only made aware of the deeper dimensions of his vulnerability, of his "nakedness."

Faust's first tragedy is his seduction of Gretchen and her subsequent pregnancy and death. He wants to possess her completely and acquires the means to do so by magic, only to destroy her by violating her innocence. Unwilling to abide by the ordering principles of creation, he seeks control over creation. Gretchen had wanted the union, but Faust's deceit and manipulation turned the union into tragedy. As Faust says, "her transgression was a trusting heart" (4407). Nevertheless, both blame Mephistopheles for the disaster.

We see Gretchen for the last time in chains in a prison cell, clearly deranged. After killing her baby and being caught by the authorities, she awaits execution at dawn. Faust comes to her and begs her to come out. "Out where?" she asks. "To freedom," he replies. "Is the grave out there?" is all she can add (4535–9).

Mephistopheles enters, and in a final burst of lucidity, Gretchen appeals to the merciful judgment of God for help. Dawn breaks, and the executioners come. "She is condemned," says Mephistopheles. "Redeemed!" shouts a voice from above (4611–2).

Here Goethe gives poetic expression to the ancient truth that the active aspect of the feminine opens us to the mysteries of divine grace and transformation and that the negative aspects of the masculine can kill and destroy. Like Sophia, Gretchen comes to Faust in his Titanism and his greed and seeks to teach him the wisdom of limits. He cannot know or obtain everything, but he can love her and have a child with her. Only through the willingness to accept limits can we beget and sustain life. Like Gilgamesh, Faust uses Gretchen to fulfill his lust but cannot relate to her in her positive, transformational aspects. And like Ishtar's killing Enkidu, Gretchen unleashes her negative aspect and kills their son.

We next find Faust asleep at sunrise in a beautiful spring landscape. Ariel, the same spirit of the air as in Shakespeare's *Tempest,* guards Faust's slumber. The song of his elfin host helps to banish from Faust's memory the images of horror and anguish left by Gretchen's tragic end. Faust awakens and communes with Mother Earth. In the depths of his fallenness, grace abounds. Immediately after the death of Gretchen, the feminine comes again in her static aspect as Great Mother, beckoning him to transformation.

As he takes in the Great Mother's resplendence, personified by the morning atmosphere, by the sparkling dewdrops, by the sounds of birds, and by the play of light and shadow across the pastures, Faust experiences the recuperation and healing that comes with forgiveness and rebirth. His reaction to the sunrise, to the dawn's glistening light after the darkness of his tragedy, is to make a commitment to embark on a new course.

The scene now changes to an imperial court where a pleasure-seeking and godless young emperor is confronted by an empire drifting into a state of chaos. A satirical tone prevails in the telling of the numerous woes that are befalling him just at the time when all he and his courtiers want is to be entertained. We are reminded by one of those in attendance that the ancient god being worshipped here is Plutus, Greek for "wealth." There is an ancient connection between Plutus and the Greek god Pluto, the lord of the underworld. For the ancients, riches arose from the earth. Uninterested in the inspiration of the spirit, the emperor and his court are addicted to the treasures of Mammon.

Among these reveries, Faust and Mephistopheles are more spectators than they are participants (although the devil's magic does keep the show going). The emperor asks Faust to conjure up Paris and Helen of Troy, considered symbols of perfect male/female balance. Faust, trusting in the infinite resourcefulness of his companion, promises it shall be done. Faust is fascinated by calling into real life the most beautiful woman of ancient Greece. Filled by insatiable energy again, Faust becomes determined to achieve a sense of union with absolute beauty, although he knows she resides in the shadowy world of Pluto's Hades.

The emperor and his court represent the "wisdom of this world," and it is from the earth that they seek pleasure and meaning. The emperor believes that by going down into the bowels of the earth, from whence all riches arise, he will also find the source of beauty and harmony. Believing he is wise, he does not know that he cannot buy love. Nor does he remember that, although Helen was "the essence of beauty itself," as Homer described her, the war that ensured consumed an entire generation of Greeks and Trojans. Helen's beauty was a fatal beauty, even as Mammon's wealth is a wealth that never satisfies.

Ironically, heavenly forces, not Mephistopheles, accomplish Faust's first encounter with Helen. God is always active, using the seductions of Helen and the insidiousness of Mammon to accomplish the divine will. By a singular act of grace from above, Faust's dream is fulfilled: Helen appears before him in all her radiant splendor. Faust then does what Gilgamesh refused to do with Ishtar: For an instant, he fills the beautiful Helen with his seed. Songs fill the court and the boy Euphorion is born. As the issue of fatal beauty and Titanism, Euphorion, too, is obsessed by attaining the impossible. Bounding aloft from a cliff to try his wings, he plunges to his death, another Icarus. Grief stricken, Helen slips from the embrace of Faust and joins their child in the underworld.

Faust is determined be united with Helen forever. Blinded by his own arrogance, he cannot relinquish the negative feminine and his increasingly morbid attraction with destructive behavior. He is replicating with Helen what he did with Gretchen, but he cannot stop himself. Mephistopheles urges him on, telling him that he can only go deeper into the darkness by asking the Mother Goddesses, who:

> "...sit enthroned in reverend loneliness,
> Space is as naught about them, time is less;
> The very mention of them is distress.
> They are—the Mothers...."
> "The Mothers!" exclaims Faust.
> "Are you awed?" replies Mephistopheles.
> "The Mothers!" Faust repeats.
> "Why, it strikes a singular chord."
> "And so it ought," says the devil.
> "Where is the road to them?" asks Faust.
> "No road! Into the unascended,
> The inaccessible; toward the never-pleaded,
> The never-pleadable. How is your mood?
> There are no locks to probe, no bolts to shift;

By desolations harrowed you will drift.
Can you conceive of wastes of solitude?" (6223–7).

Faust does not understand. He repeats that he wants to get to where the Mothers are. Mephistopheles replies:

...had you even swum the trackless ocean,
Lost in its utter boundlessness,
You still saw wave on wave in constant motion....
There you see Nothing—vacant gaping farness,
Mark not your own step as you stride,
Nor point of rest where you abide (6239–48).

After this enigmatic statement, the devil hands Faust a key, saying "This key will scent the true site from the others, Follow it down—it leads to the Mothers" (6263–4).

Taking the key, Faust says:

"Awe is the finest portion of mankind;
However scarce the world may make this sense—
In awe one feels profoundly the immense."
"Well then," shouts Mephistopheles, "sink down!
Or I might call it: soar!
It's all one and the same. Escape the naming
Of what has formed....
Formation, transformation,
The eternal minds eternal recreation,
Enswathed in likeness of manifold entity,
They see you not, for only wraiths they see" (6275–89).

Goethe gives no details of Faust's encounter with the Mothers, only that it empowers him. Returning to court, he again calls forth Paris and Helen before the emperor. As the assembled courtiers admire her beauty Faust is overcome with jealousy and passion. He reaches out to touch her and is knocked unconscious by the subsequent explosion in which Paris and Helen disappear. Mephistopheles drags Faust off and deposits him in his old study.

Through more of the Devil's magic, Faust is transported to ancient Greece. As soon as he sets foot on that sacred soil, he awakens. He is possessed by only one thought: to find Helen again. His first words are "Where is she?" He is led by the centaur Chiron to the priestess Manto, who guards the approach to the underworld at the foot of Mount Olympus. Manto hears Faust's plea sympathetically and promises to lead him down to the great goddess Persephone, who alone can grant his request.

Persephone releases Helen from the underworld for the third time to unite with Faust for one timeless moment. Their greeting turns into a duet of poetic ecstasy, but their union is once again shattered by the death of their son Euphorion. Helen vanishes forever back into the underworld.

Faust has experienced his third tragedy at the hands of the negative feminine, this time hidden in the bowels of the earth, the kingdom of Mammon. He has not yet learned that the "wisdom of the Greeks" leads not to fulfillment but to emptiness; that idolatry leads not to liberation but to further bondage; and that the quest for the limitless leads not to complete knowledge or absolute power but to further vulnerability and perpetual shame.

Faust is borne into the sky carrying the garments Helen left behind. Goethe here recalls the ascension of the prophet Elijah and the empowering of his disciple Elisha, who watched him ascend to the heavens in a chariot of fire, holding on to Elijah's coat. Soaring with the clouds,

Faust's gaze is arrested by the ceaseless ebb and flow of the tides. They impress upon him the enormous harmonized power of Nature. For the first time, he is given to "see" but not to understand the ordering structures of creation.

Instead of falling to his knees in worship of the Creator, Faust's Titanism is rekindled. He decides to curb the sea in order to reclaim a vast expanse of shoreline with a network of dykes. Failing to unite with the feminine through the wisdom of the earth, he challenges himself to conquer the earth, to have dominion over it by force of will. Having initially been seduced by the desire to *know* all things, Faust now succumbs to the desire to *control* all things.

This is Faust's final act of hubris, an attempt to transform one small bit of chaos into order. In doing this, he recalls God in Genesis, when at creation, "The earth was without form and void, and darkness was upon the face of the deep; and the Spirit of God was moving over the face of the waters. And God said, 'Let there be light' and there was light" (Gn. 1:1,2). Faust becomes enraptured by an ultimate vision of himself bringing "order" to Nature, thereby gaining a place for a fresh start of a free people on virgin soil. His final mission is to bring the ideals of the Enlightenment to a small part of the earth and to create paradise.

Faust seeks to be like God. In his pride, he seeks to impose order on something with an existing internal order. Rather than acknowledge this pre-existent order and seek union with it, saying, "Not my will but thine be done," Faust sees the ordering principle in creation as chaos and boasts, "Not thy will but mine be done."

Faust temporarily succeeds in his project. He first buys some land from the emperor. The worshipper of Mammon sells Faust some earth. Faust expends enormous energy taming this land. Then with the same hubris of those who built the tower of Babel, Faust builds a high tower so that he can watch his fleets gather in the distant harbor. Standing atop the highest parapet, Faust exults. He has reached the heavens.

Only one detail mars his absolute rule. On a high dune landward from his palace dwells a very ancient couple, Philemon and Baucis, with land-rights antedating his own. They are not dazzling like Paris and Helen, nor have they transcended any limits. They are simply a humble couple living in harmony with each other and with the earth. They have accepted the limits of their existence. They live in love.

Watching them going about their humble chores in and around their thatched hut and offering prayers and thanksgiving to God in their tiny chapel, Faust becomes jealous. He offers to buy them out. They politely refuse. Day after day, the tinkle of their chapel bell sounds in his ears as they go in to pray, reminding Faust that he does not possess *everything*. He chafes and upbraids himself for becoming obsessional about possessing the couple's tiny allotment, but his desire only grows.

Mephistopheles returns from a voyage overseas, and Faust confesses his obsession. Faust orders an act of "benevolent violence," but the order for the dispossession of the couple's land ends in catastrophe. The old couple die of fright as their door is being knocked down; a guest who puts up a fight is killed; and, in the scuffle, a fire is ignited, which destroys the hut and the chapel.

As in the Gretchen and Helen tragedies, Faust has been undone by his impatience and his will-to-power. "Too rashly bid, too swiftly done" (11382), he mourns, but once again he quickly puts the past behind him and places the blame on Mephistopheles, even as Adam blamed Eve and both blamed the serpent for their sinful deed.

Faust now contemplates his life from deep within his castle. Four spirit sisters, Want, Distress, Guilt, and Care, approach from without. The first three find their entry barred; they have no power over Faust. Only Care gets into Faust's inner sanctum, although as Want, Distress, and Guilt depart from the castle, they hail the approach of Brother Death.

Possessing all the earth, Faust, like Gilgamesh, now confronts the final barrier. Sensing Death approaching, he protests, "I have not fought my way to freedom yet" (11403). He begins to reflect upon his life, his involvement with the powers of magic, his Pact with Mephistopheles, the tragedy of Gretchen, the effervescence of his union with Helen, and the destruction of Philemon and Baucis. In the aftermath of pride, facing the inevitability of death, regret sets in. "If only I could undo some of the things done," he ruminates.

Care slips into the room, and Faust demands that she remove herself. "I am where I should be," she replies. He is about to resort to magic again to have his way, but he stops. "Restrain yourself," he whispers to himself, "and speak no conjury" (11422). This is the turning point in Faust's life. Though Death is at his door, Faust has for the first time not yielded to impatience and not forced his will through magic. He has taken the first step to reverse the patterns of his responses to life. He has finally recognized the wisdom of limits.

This first step is equivalent to traversing the whole road. Care seizes the opportunity and begins to challenge

Faust to question his will. She echoes Sophia's pleas to
Israel to repent and to acknowledge that the Lord is God.
She begs Faust to understand that grace is sufficient to
transform hubris into humility, bondage into freedom.

Faust remains unmoved. In his final hours, he will not
give in to what he considers neurotic self-doubt. He says
to Care:

> I only sped the whole world through,
>
> Clutched any stray temptation by the hair,
>
> And what fell short, abandoned there,
>
> And what eluded me, let pass.
>
> All that I did was covet and attain,
>
> And crave afresh, and thus with might and main,
>
> Sped through my life; first powerful and great,
>
> But now at pace more prudent, more sedate.
>
> I know full well the earthly sphere of men....
>
> What he perceives, that he may seize,
>
> Let him stride on upon this planet's face,
>
> When spirits haunt, let him not change his pace,
>
> Find bliss and torment in his onward stride,
>
> Aye—every moment stay unsatisfied (11434–52).

Then you must "famish in abundance," Care replies
(11462). Unable to break Faust's self-confidence, she
breathes a spell upon him, depriving him of sight. "Man
commonly is blind throughout his life," she comments,
"My Faust, be blind then as you end it" (11497–8). This
breath of blindness is a transformational act of grace.
When pride went to its death, Faust was struck blind by
the transforming power of the feminine. Like Saul on the
way to Damascus, Faust's eyes were condemned to darkness

so that his heart could "see."

Faust had matched his energies against an entity of the spirit world and been transformed against his will. He maintained the integrity of his conscious will against all the pleas of the feminine spirit to submit to a higher Will and then was forced to meet Death in the spiritual realms beyond the light of consciousness. No mortal can emerge from such a transformation completely unscathed. He must bear a mark of the struggle.

Reacting to Care's spell, Faust says,

The night, it seems, turns deeper still—but shining,
The light within continues ever bright,
I hasten to fulfill my thoughts designing,
The master's word alone imparts his might... (11498–502).

He only earns both freedom and existence
Who must reconquer them each day (11575–6).

Faust is given to understand that only in transformation do we experience inner peace; everything else is human choice governed by uncontrollable passions to know in order to conquer. In that brief instant, Faust "sees" the light for the first time, not the ordinary world by the light of reason but the spiritual world by the light of grace. Deprived of the logic of his intellect, he discovers the logic of his heart, for Care was addressing his heart. Accepting blindness, the ultimate limitation for someone who wanted to see everything, Faust is redeemed. Submitting to the grace of God, he discovers the sanctity of existence and the reality of freedom.

In this state of outward darkness and inward transformation, with Mephistopheles at his side, Faust dies. Good and evil are never separated, even in the moment of the triumph of grace. The devil smiles. "It is finished," he says to his minions, echoing Jesus' last words on the cross. Faust now "stranded lies, a whitened shell." Cynical to the end, Mephistopheles prophesies that the elements, in league with his demons, will ultimately take over and reduce all human effort to nothing. As the spirit that forever denies, the Devil expresses again that wish for ultimate annihilation, which he first expressed during his initial conversation with Faust:

> All over and pure nothing—just the same!
> What has this constant doing ever brought
> But what is done to rake away to naught?
> So it is over! How to read this clause?
> All over is as good as never was,
> And yet it whirls about as if it were.
> The ever-empty is what I prefer (11592–603).

As Mephistopheles moves in to snatch Faust away to the perdition of Hell angels suddenly descend from on high and lift Faust's immortal essence up into the sky. The Devil watches, confused and powerless. The angels, floating into the higher atmosphere, sing,

> Whoever strives in ceaseless toil,
> Him we may grant redemption.
> And when on high transfigured love
> Has added intercession,
> The blest will throng to him above
> With welcoming compassion (11936–42).

As Faust's soul shakes off the dust and ashes of mortality the Virgin Mary, not Helen, hovers above, as Virgin *and* as

Mother. With her are various other women who appear in the Gospels in association with Christ as well as Gretchen, who gladly welcomes Faust's "return to bliss," although she adds that it is "too bright as yet for him to see." The play ends with a Chorus Mysticus:

All in transition
Is but reflection;
What is deficient
Here becomes action;
Human discernment
Here is passed by;
Woman Eternal
Draws us on high (12104–11).

Mephistopheles lost the wager, yet Faust did not win it. To the end, he exemplifies the fallen state of humanity. At no point, either before or after his Pact with Mephistopheles, does he demonstrate anything other than hubris and the insatiable obsession to transgress every limit he comes upon. He dies with the blood of Gretchen, his sons, and Philemon and Baucis on his hands, the price for his Titanism. Nothing can undo these evils, not even grace.

Only when Care touched him against his will was he blinded in order to "see." In our fallenness, we never choose grace. Grace chooses us. Faust comes to the final realization that true redemption and genuine freedom come only when the human spirit is moved by the impulse of divine love, when instead of seeking to control the divine, we are empowered by grace to sacrifice our lust for knowledge and power and to surrender to the divine presence, thereby attaining entry to a higher realm of understanding and of freedom.

Mephistopheles is defeated by grace, against Faust's will. Faust's pride was the occasion for grace. Working through his arrogance and his tragedies, love intercedes by the "awful grace of God." Untransformed power is redeemed by power transformed. Ordinary history is changed suddenly, dramatically, and irrevocably by a "mighty act of God." And it is the subtleties of the feminine that weave the plot and exert the final magic that allows a man blinded by pride to truly "see."

CHAPTER 17

THE ARRIVAL OF
BUDDHISM IN THE WEST

You are not here to verify,

Instruct yourself, or inform curiosity

Or carry report. You are here to kneel . . . [1]

EINSTEIN WAS ONCE ASKED WHAT HE SOUGHT. He replied, "I want to know what the Old One thinks. The rest is detail." Einstein made the atomic bomb possible; he also triggered a revolution in our understanding of the world. Given the previous discussion of the feminine, I suggest that Einstein, in his own way and in his own time, was particularly open to her guidance, for he often talked of intuition as being an inner guide to his abstract calculations. This is not to say he always listened.

As the cosmologist Brian Swimme tells the story, Einstein extended his general theory of relativity of 1914 to include gravitational effects. His calculations revealed that the universe was actually expanding in all directions. This came as a complete shock, for no one in all of scientific history had suspected that the universe was anything but static and constant. The notion of the universe as a vast but fixed space was the very foundation of Newtonian physics and had been embraced by every great scientist Einstein knew, whether Newton, Galileo, Darwin, Herschel, or Curie.

Einstein's calculations revealed that the universe had erupted from a single, ultimate density and was still exploding out-

1. Eliot, *Collected Poems*, 215.

wards. Refusing to believe his own calculations, he inserted into his equations what became known as the "cosmological constant." In so doing, Einstein preserved his attachment to a static universe.

It was only with these altered calculations that he published his study. The Russian mathematical cosmologist Alexander Friedmann worked with these equations and made the same startling discovery: The universe was actually expanding in all directions. He quickly wrote to Einstein with these surprising results, but Einstein refused to be dislodged from his Newtonian world-view. He not only ignored Friedmann's letter, but when Friedmann published his results in 1922, Einstein wrote a note to the magazine calling Friedmann's results "suspicious."

In 1923, when the astronomer Edwin Hubble trained his telescope on Mount Palomar in California towards the stars, he observed that the distant galaxies were, in fact, traveling away form the Earth. Hubble invited Einstein to come and see this astonishing phenomenon. Einstein became convinced that the world-view that had under-girded the entire Enlightenment process was essentially wrong. With this realization, he wrote to Friedmann, acknowledging the accuracy of his own calculations without the "cosmological constant." Toward the end of his life, Einstein recalled this experience and called it the "greatest blunder of my scientific career." This episode calls to mind Jung's observation that "One finds one's destiny on the path one takes to avoid it."

Since then, of course, our understanding of the universe and matter—indeed all of life—has been revolutionized many times over. We have now come to understand that there is not just one universe, static and unmoving, but an infinite number of universes, expanding, contracting, and interacting, with universes coming out of universes in an infinity without limits or end. We also now know there is no such thing as solid matter, as Newton thought, but that matter is comprised of energy configurations. Objective reality has no objectivity.

Moreover, what we thought of as empty space between objects is not emptiness at all but a field of infinite potentiality, a realm of unlimited possibility that cannot be measured but that is nonetheless there. We are coming to realize that the static, materialistic, and quantifiable world of Newton and the Enlightenment has simply dissolved before our eyes, giving rise to an understanding that we are in a universe where the invisible is real, the visible is ephemeral, and all is comprised of a vast web of relations, always changing, not always predictable, and incessantly interactive.

At the apogee of Western scientific endeavors to understand a universe thought to be mechanistic and predictable, scientists have pulled the rug out from under their own feet. The world has become porous, full of mystery, completely relational. One cannot understand any part in isolation; one can only view the part in the context of the whole and the observer along with the observed. Niels Bohr, the originator with Werner Hiesenberg of the field of quantum mechanics, reflected about their discoveries that "We must be clear that when it comes to atoms, language can be used only as poetry."[2]
Physicist Geoffrey Chew, the originator of bootstrap theory, suggests that this new understanding of the universe may be "the foretaste of a completely new form of human intellectual endeavor, one that will

2. Niels Bohr, quoted in *New York Times Book Review,* Sunday, 5 October 1997, 9.

not only lie outside physics, but will not even be describable as 'scientific.'"[3]

Wherever they turn, scientists are meeting mystery, compelling Robert Jastrow, the astronomer and founder of NASA's Goddard Institute for Space Studies, to muse that

> the barrier to further progress seems insurmountable. It is
> not a matter of another year, another decade of work,
> another measurement, or another theory; at this moment it
> seems as though science will never be able to raise the cur-
> tain on the mystery of creation. For the scientist who has
> lived by his faith in the power of reason, the story ends like
> a bad dream. He has scaled the mountains of ignorance; he
> is about to conquer the highest peak; as he pulls himself
> over the final rock, he is greeted by a band of theologians
> who have been sitting there for centuries.[4]

The "band of theologians" include the Buddha, Lao Tzu, Patanjali, and other mystics, still sitting quietly, meditating on the water.

It was a contemporary of the Buddha, Lao Tzu, who articulated the principles of Taoism that all the phenomena of the world are seen as integral to and part of the Cosmic Way, the Tao, whose laws are not handed down by a divine lawgiver but are inherent in the very nature of the Way itself. In the one book he left, the *Tao Te Ching*, one reads:

Humanity follows the laws of the earth
Earth follows the laws of heaven
Heaven follows the laws of Tao
Tao follows the laws of its own intrinsic nature.[5]

This "intrinsic nature" is an integral whole in which all the parts must assemble

3. Geoffrey Chew,
'Bootstrap: A
Scientific Idea?"
in *Science* 161 (23
August 1968): 765.

4. Robert Jastrow,
*God and the
Astronomers* (New
York: W. W.
Norton, 1978), 116.

"without the slightest excess or deficiency," as Chen Shun, another great Taoist sage, wrote. We are in a vast web of relations in which everything, including humanity, must find its natural place. Furthermore, as the Buddhist scholar Lama Anagarika Govinda describes it, "The external world and the inner world are two sides of the same fabric, in which the threads of all forces and of all events, of all forms of consciousness and of their objects, are woven into an inseparable net of endless, mutually conditioned relations."[6]

It was Einstein, perhaps the greatest scientist of the Enlightenment, who made Western science receptive to this ancient perception from the East. The descriptions of reality made by him, by Heisenberg, by Bohr, and by a host of others since have sounded more like the Buddha than like Descartes, more like Lao Tzu than like Newton. Western science was opening the door to the Eastern mystics at the time when Einstein was developing equations that lead to the atomic bomb and Heisenberg was offering his scientific genius upon the altar of the Nazis.

In our darkest hour, when the entire metaphysical tradition of Western civilization had collapsed into an orgy of bloodletting and cruelty beyond measure, the serene insight of the Orient that all is part of an interdependent whole came wafting through the souls of the very scientists most trained to exclude it as a possibility.

Reflecting on the havoc his generation had brought upon the earth, Einstein wrote that "the religion of the future will be a cosmic religion. It should transcend

5. Lao Tzu,
Tao Te Ching, trans.
Ch'u Ta Kuo (New
York: The Buddhist
Lodge, 1937),
chap. 25.
6. Lama Anagarika
Govinda,
*Foundations of
Tibetan Mysticism*
(London: Samuel
Weiser, 1974), 93.

a personal God, avoid dogma and theology, covering both the natural and spiritual. It should be based on a religious sense arising from the experience of all things natural and spiritual as a meaningful unity. Buddhism answers this description.... If there is a religion that can cope with modern scientific needs, it would be Buddhism."[7]

Toynbee, the historian, and Einstein, the scientist, intuited the great truth that the present generation has seen the end of the primacy of Judeo-Christianity and the end of the legitimacy of Western scientific materialism. Both traditions are predicated on the metaphysic of dualism. Judeo-Christianity and much of Greek philosophy are constructed upon a dualism that divided heaven from earth, God from humanity, intellect from feeling, the "chosen ones" from the damned. So, too, is our scientific world-view. Newton and Descartes depicted a sterile and mechanistic universe without spirit, movement, or meaning. Scientists, along with most of Western culture, have believed science can decipher life as simply as an engineer can dismantle and discern the workings of a watch.

Then came Einstein, Heisenberg, and the new physics; then came Auschwitz and the atomic bomb; and then came the establishment of Israel, the liberation of women and the concomitant peace, civil rights, and environmental movements, and, most profoundly, the arrival of Buddhism to the West. All these factors have contributed to the beginnings of a new cosmology and spirituality, one that over time will compel Western civilization to understand more clearly the normative truth of the Buddha's great doctrine of *anatta*: There is no separate self; everything is part of an

7. Lama Surya Dass, *The Buddha Within* (New York: Random House, 1997), cover page.

interconnected and inseparable whole. The world is indeed burning. Arising out of the ashes of the old order, like a Phoenix, are the ingredients of a new cultural framework, a new world-view, that can ensure that the global civilization we are now constructing will, with all its contradictions, be predicated upon a metaphysic of interdependence and wholeness.

If we embrace this emerging integral vision, the opportunities are as immense as the consequences are dire if we do not. Our choices over the next several decades will determine whether globalization comes to mean the continued rapacious exploitation of planet and people by global corporations and governments, or some form of global governance in which all the major stakeholders are welcomed to the table to reason together concerning common challenges. This will be determined to a large degree by whether we continue to view the earth as simply dirt beneath our feet, or as a living ecosystem in which we must find our rightful place. It will be determined, too, by how we view ourselves: whether simply as consumers in a material world, or as highly complex beings with deeply spiritual dimensions that must be integrated into our other dimensions in order to attain wholeness.

What we cannot say any longer is that there is no viable alternative to patriarchy or scientific materialism or free market capitalism. There is. It is our great historic challenge to turn from the negative aspect of the masculine, wreaking such havoc upon our planet and our civilization, and under the guidance of the feminine, allow the Spirit to lead us along a gentler more integrated path.

CHAPTER 18

WANDERING IN SINAI

We shall not cease from exploration

And the end of all our exploring

Will be to arrive where we started

And know the place for the first time.

Through the unknown, remembered gate

When the last of earth left to discover

Is that which was the beginning;

At the source of the longest river

The voice of the hidden waterfall

And the children in the apple tree

Not known, because not looked for

But heard, half-heard, in the stillness

Between two waves of the sea.

Quick now, here, now, always—

A condition of complete simplicity

(Costing not less than everything).

And all shall be well and

All manner of thing shall we well

When the tongues of flames are in-folded

Into the crowned knot of fire

And the fire and the rose are one.[1]

W E MUST END WHERE WE BEGAN: WE HAVE been delivered from Egypt, but we have not yet reached the Promised Land. We are wandering in the wilderness of Sinai. We have reached the end of our beginning, but have not yet begun the beginning of our end. We are between worlds.

Egypt we know all too well: the onslaught of the Greeks and Romans upon the Jews; the scourge of the Black Death upon medieval Christendom; the nightmare of the Holocaust and scourge of nuclear weapons upon the living.

We also know signposts on the way to the Promised Land: the birth of Christianity after the rise of Sophia; the inception of the Renaissance following the Black Death and adoration of Mary; the creation of the nation of Israel after the Holocaust; the liberation of women in the aftermath of Hiroshima; and the arrival of Buddhism to the West. We glimpse the Promised Land through each beginning arising out of the ashes of the old order, generating new challenges, new opportunities, and new crises.

Wandering in the wilderness of Sinai is the time of anomie between the old

―――――――――
1. Eliot, *Collected Poems*, 222–3.

and the new, a time of hope and alienation, expectation and confusion, anticipation and dislocation. The old is spent but not yet gone; the new is arriving but not yet here. Sinai bespeaks a time of turbulence and fluidity as creativity and chaos mingle, leaving the past behind and shaping the coming future. The world is now in the wilderness of Sinai. Seen from the realm of Spirit, we are between the times and will always be until the end of time.

Civilization stands at the end of an era and for the next several decades will undergo the "travail pains of the Messiah," to recall the words of the apocalyptists as they grappled simultaneously with the destructiveness of the Greeks and Romans and with the hope inspired by Sophia. For the first time in human history, the world is being enveloped by a single global civilization, which is drawing in and reframing every society, every nation, and every belief. This magnetic pull is being resisted by all sectors, even as they are being drawn in by it.

Everywhere, individuals are participating in the throes of globalization and the emerging integral culture as well as clinging ever more firmly to their particular tribe, nation, culture, or group. Against the insecurity of the unknown, most are clinging to the known. Though compelled by the future, most are content to remain with the past. Thus our institutions are bending, groaning, indeed, breaking up as time, values, and allegiances split apart and face each other as from opposing sides. Anchored in single traditions, we are being drawn into a world of multiple identities, from the local and ethnic to the regional, national, and global.

At the beginning of the twenty-first century, at the turn of the third millennium, we are poised in the space between worlds and are drawn by but have not yet embraced the global civilization we are being born into, leaving reluctantly the traditions that have brought us to the present. Past and future, death and life, curse and promise are filling the present moment and rending the world asunder.

The Jews wandered for forty years in the wilderness of Sinai. It took time for those who still yearned for the leeks and garlic of Egypt to die off and a new generation, who remembered the time in Egypt only through the ritual of the annual Passover, to emerge. Even Moses died in Sinai. We should expect no less of our generation. Transitions take time. As the snake sloughing off its old skin or a chick emerging from the egg, the pace cannot be forced or hurried. Life has its own momentum, its own ways, and its own wisdom. We will only emerge from the wilderness in the fullness of time, at the end of the age.

We must therefore remain sober and realistic. The next phase of human development will continue to reap the whirlwind of our God complex. Our Faustian Pact has not yet played out. We will continue to make incredible advances in science and technology and use our new-found powers for primitive, mostly selfish ends. The cruciform patterns of history destine us to re-enact new manifestations of our fallenness even as we continue laboriously to become more civilized. As with Faust, our hubris condemns us to unimaginable destructiveness and greed and yet "in our despair, against our will, comes wisdom by the awful grace of God."

The paradox of the next stage in human development is that the global culture we are building will be the product of our idealism and our accomplishments as well as our corruption and our weakness. This is where and how the Spirit works in and through history. Redemption, when it comes, is born in weakness and is considered foolishness by the strong; nevertheless, it triumphs through grace, shattering the edifices erected by human pride. The stories of Joseph, Moses, and Jesus all dramatize the singular fact and Biblical theme that our salvation is delivered out of crisis, in the middle of scandal, through acts of "foolishness."

That we are in a world shaped increasingly by technology and by an ethic that celebrates unfettered materialism and its concomitant permissive cornucopia; that we are beset by pervasive violence and the fanaticism of various tyrants; that there is abundant moral decay and a pervasive crisis of spirit; and that within this context the exquisiteness of Eastern mysticism and the dynamism of gender parity is emerging should renew a sensitivity to the truths that civilization was founded upon, as well as ignite a faith that the hand of God is pervasively present, fashioning out of our limitations the divine purpose of redemption.

We can look to the democratizing impulse generated by the liberation of women, to the metaphysics of holism from the East, to the efforts of the environmental movement to instill again a reverence for the earth, to those technical and scientific advances that have improved the human condition, even to the dramatic progress made combating and eliminating many deadly diseases as signs of hope amid tragedy. This is the alchemy of history: The crushing together of the opposites that are dying—even dead—can be used to bring forth life, renewed in hope by the mercies of grace. Lead can be turned into gold. It was ever thus; it will ever be thus.

We can achieve this transformation only by being

willing to suffer through the metamorphosis, even as the loud cries and the agonies of the mother accompany all births. This is to say that, on the historical level of things, humanity's immediate future will be remarkably turbulent. It is only out of this maelstrom that the next phase of our deliverance will come. It is only out of the ashes that the Phoenix rises and a global culture will take shape.

Whatever the new world-order in the next century may be, the institutions will have changed but the fundamentals of human nature will have not. Human nature, with its lust for complete knowledge and absolute power, will fill the next historical epoch with all the contradictions and opportunities for redemption that have characterized our past. This is why we need to be drawn continually into the realm of the Spirit. In the future, as in the past and present, the alchemy of transformation will take place by the sheer grace of the mysterious purpose of the Eternal, turning the baseness of our depravity into vessels shaped by divine grace.

In the farthest future we can imagine, our relationship with our Creator will be as central as it was in the deepest past we can remember. This relationship profoundly focused and established in the Exodus and the Cross, exquisitely understood by the Buddha, will enable us to embrace the earth, the cosmos, and each other more wholly. It will empower us to discern our rightful place in the scheme of things, our "somethingness" in the midst of the All in All.

Human history is a relentless march of "progress" only in a technological sense. Our gadgets may improve, but our propensity toward the transgression of limits and thus our perennial need for redemption by grace remain the same. Everything we think, say, and do in our ordinary reality is still under challenge from the ordering structures of creation. The cruciform structures inherent in our psyche and in the Spirit will continue to govern the patterns of history. All progress remains under constant judgment; all redemption is an act of grace. To keep this tension on the knife edge without cynicism or optimism is the essence of spiritual realism, which is born of judgment and grace. Judgment without grace becomes corrosive cynicism; grace without judgment becomes facile optimism.

We can know, with Eliot, that the next phase of history will be another painful interaction between the fire and the rose. The immense upheavals in the environment will compel a new relationship with nature; the breakdown in the nation-state and the emergence of global communication, global politics, and global economics will necessitate a new sense of humanity as a single yet diverse community; and the inadequacies of the current religious institutions will generate a new spirituality, which will fill old wineskins with new wine.

The communities being shaped today, those of the darkness and of the light, will themselves become institutions. The perennial human struggle for civilization will take place on a higher plane, though for the same purpose: to discern those ordering principles of creation that guide us to live more resonantly with the whole and more authentically as a part. We can live transcendently in the future only because we carry it in our memory from our past.

We know this, because there is a cruciform structure in Eternity, in nature, and in our own inner depth. We know that inherent in creation is an ordering principle, which beckons us to "do justice, love mercy, and walk humbly with our God." We also know that we are obsessed with gaining absolute knowledge in order to wield absolute power. All the violence, all the injustice, all the exploitation in the world is rooted, in the end, in what is described in the third chapter of Genesis: Although we know the limits of our nature and our life, we are compelled to violate these limits out of an inner compulsion for more knowledge in order to exercise increased power. Our disobedience perennially distorts our exercise of freedom.

Yet it is in the depths of our predicament that we come to know that our Redeemer lives, that the violation of limits will engender the wisdom of limits, that the Exodus will lead to the Promised Land, that the Black Death will generate the modern era, that the Holocaust will be followed by a return of Israel, and that nuclear weapons will spawn a global transformation of values between men and women and will release the feminine spirit upon the world. The darkness activates the feminine, generating the light. Life is ever the same; life is ever changing; life is forever cruciform.

The Messiah comes not as a conquering hero but as a suffering servant; not as a hurricane but as a still, small voice; and not as a destroyer but as a giver of life who is destroyed as the gift is given. The darkness assaults this seeming weakness: Untransformed power can only respond with untransformed power. In the face of this, the Messiah bends, breaks, and dies, assimilating the darkness in a supreme act of forgiveness. This obedience, this giving up of one's will so that "thy will be done," ignites a new world.

EPILOGUE

A STORY TOLD TO ME DURING A DISCUSSION on these matters exemplifies the essence of the wisdom of limits and the humility of transformed power. It concerns the philosopher Moses Mendelsohn, and is, I believe, a true story. I present it here, as the theologian Philip Turner told it to me.

Mendelsohn was a philosopher who lived in the time of Kant. Though he was of humble origin, he achieved considerable prominence. His father decided that, since his son had done well, it would be right for him to marry. In the manner of that time, Moses' father made the arrangements. An agreement was reached that Mendelsohn should marry the daughter of one of the Lessings. She was young, beautiful, and accomplished. This caused quite a stir, not only because of Mendelsohn's humble origins, but also because he was a man noted for his extreme ugliness. Indeed, he was so ugly he was known as the "Jewish Socrates."

The engagement had something of the archetype of the beauty and the beast about it. As in the fable, the couple had never met. A party was arranged. Mendelsohn arrived early and immediately began an intense philosophical discussion. He was so caught up that he did not notice that his fiancé was late in arriving. When she came finally, she stepped into the room unnoticed, took one look at Mendelsohn, and fainted. She was quickly carried out. Mendelsohn noticed nothing and continued his discourse.

When the young woman came to some minutes later, she gazed at her father and said, "No, I won't do it."

By this time, Mendelsohn was aware that something was wrong and asked his father if there was some difficulty. His father answered, "What can I say my son? She says no."

Young Mendelsohn thought for a moment and answered, "My father, I quite understand, but I ask one favor. I would like permission to see her alone for ten minutes." His father said it would be difficult, but he would do what he could. He managed to arrange a meeting. After a courteous bow, Mendelsohn said, "I want you to know that I understand, but I should like permission to tell you a story."

"The story concerns my soul before I was born—just when I was on the way with my guardian angel to earth. Even then, I knew that for each soul there is another one intended. I asked my guardian angel if I could look upon the soul of my intended. At first, he refused, but I asked him to give me one good reason why not. He could find no reply, so he reluctantly agreed. I went right away and looked upon the soul of my intended and do you know what? She was the ugliest woman I have ever seen. I went back and said to my guardian angel, "No, I won't do it!"

He said, "But you must."

I thought for a moment and then said, "Yes, I'll marry her but only on one condition."

"What's that?" said my angel.

I answered, "My condition is that I take her ugliness."

THE AUTHOR

DR. JAMES A. GARRISON, JR. WAS BORN OF Baptist missionary parents in Szechuan Province, China, in 1951. From 1953-1965, he lived with his family in Taiwan. His early experiences set the stage for a life of engagement in international issues and social activism. By the time he began university, he had traveled in over forty countries worldwide and was active in the anti-Vietnam war and environmental movements.

As a Ph.D. student at Cambridge University (1975-1982), Dr. Garrison became engaged in the citizen diplomacy movement to reduce the nuclear tensions between the United States and the Soviet Union, founding two organizations dealing with the nuclear power and nuclear weapons issues: The Radiation and Health Information Service; and East West Reach. In 1980, he published his first book on the issue, *The Plutonium Culture;* followed in 1982 by *The Darkness of God: Theology After Hiroshima;* and in 1983 by *The Russian Threat.*

Throughout the decade of the 1980s, Dr. Garrison refined his skills at facilitating private discussions among leaders across national boundaries and disciplines. From 1986-1990, he directed the Esalen Institute Soviet American Exchange Program, that engaged in private sector diplomacy with Soviet counterparts in a variety of sectors. In 1991, he founded the International Foreign Policy Association in collaboration with Georgian President Edward Shevardnadze and former Secretary of State George Schultz, focusing on providing humanitarian relief for children in the former Soviet republics. In 1992, at the behest of Mikhail Gorbachev, Dr. Garrison founded and became the President of the Gorbachev Foundation/USA.

These two organizations set the stage for the establishment, in 1995, of the State of the World Forum, a San Francisco based non-profit institution created to establish a global network of leaders, citizens and institutions dedicated to discerning and implementing those principles, values, and actions necessary to guide humanity toward a more sustainable global civilization. With President Gorbachev as its Convening Chairman and Garrison as its President, the Forum has convened leaders from all over the world to its annual and regional Forums in San Francisco, Moscow, Washington, D.C., New Delhi, Islamabad, Guanajuato (Mexico), Brussels, Belfast, and Monterrey (Mexico).

Additionally, the Forum has launched and directed a number of action oriented strategic initiatives across a spectrum of areas, including nuclear weapons elimination; the environmental impact of endocrine disrupting chemicals; nurturing the whole child; coexistence and community building; and bringing information affluence to the developing nations of the world.

Dr. Garrison's degrees include: B.A. World History, University of Santa Clara; M.T.S., History of Religion, Harvard University; and Ph.D., Philosophical Theology, Cambridge University. He has written six books concerning the historical and theological implications of the advent of the nuclear age. He lives with his wife Claire and two sons, Luke and Zachary, in Mill Valley, California.

INDEX

Adam, 60–3, 72
Aeschylus, xxxix
Amos, 57–8
Anatta, doctrine of, 53
Antiochus Epiphanes, 93
Apocalypse, xxxiii, xxxvii,
  80–116
Aryans, 22, 26, 45
Barabbas, 171
Bâton de commandement, 4–5
Bernard, St., 213
Black Death, xxxv-xxxvi,
  191, 198–203, 207–9,
  212, 218, 223–4, 294
Brzezinski, Zbigniew,
  259–63
Buddha, 52
Catal Huyuk, 14–6, 22
Civilization, 36, 43, 61
Cooking, 33

Cross, the, 156, 160,
  164–5, 172, 177–8
Crucifixion, xxxii, 172,
  176–7
Cruciform nature
  of reality, xxvii
Dante, 216–7
Descartes, René, 227–9,
  234
Disciples, the, 158–67,
  175
Einstein, Albert, 331, 335
Enkidu, 31–8
Enlightenment, liii-liv
Eve, 60–3, 67–77
Evil, 68–9, 93, 100, 103,
  107, 327
Exodus, xxxii, 58, 87
Faust, 309–29
Female figurines, 9, 17

Feminine, the, 287–308
Fichte, Johann, 252–4
Flagellants, 206–7, 295
Frankl, Victor, 274–5
Freedom, 100–3, 346
Garden of Eden, 61–2,
  66, 75, 102
Garrison, James, 353–4
Gilgamesh, Epic of, 29–44
Globalization, xxiv, 341,
  343, 345
God, xl–xliii, 57–75,
  85–93, 102–15, 117–21,
  123–9, 182
Gorbachev, Mikhail,
  273–4, 283
Great Mother, 1–28, 32,
  42, 46, 266–7, 293
Greeks, 91–3, 189
Havel, Vaclav, xxiv–xxv
Hegel, Georg, 253
Helen of Troy, 318–21
Hiroshima, xxxii, 271–4,
  276–9
Hobbes, Thomas, 244–5
Holocaust, 271–6, 279–81
Hosea, 87–9, 127
Hubris, 37, 42, 68, 263
Humans, Early, 1–2, 14
Ishtar, 31–2, 37, 42
Jesus, 19, 97, 107, 141,
144, 146, 157–72
Jews, 55–60, 81–9, 139
Job, 117–21
Joseph, 179–81
Jung, Carl, xxvii, 97
Just Men, 111–3,
  158–72
Kant, Emmanuel, 247–52
Lao Tzu, 334–5
Lascaux, 8
Leibnitz, Gottfried, 243–4
Levy, Rabbi Yom Tov,
  111–2, 114
Limitations, 239, 241–2
Luther, Martin, 264–5
Mammon, 266–9
Mary, cult of, xxxvi,
  213–24
Mary, Mother of God
  143–52
Mendelsohn, Moses,
  349–50
Mephistopheles, 309–29
Monotheism, 21, 59
Moses, 56, 85, 169, 182–3
Nietzche, Fredrich,
  257–9
Nuclear weapons, xxxii–
  xxxiii, xxxv, 272–84
Papal corruption, 192–8,
  222

Paradox of the human condition, 239
Pascal, Blaise, 235–43
Path to wisdom, 241
Patriarchy, 27
Paul, the Apostle, 108–10, 176, 178
Peace movement, 282–3
Pietà, the, 306
Pilate, Pontius, 170–1, 184
Power, xxvi–xxvii, xxix–xxx, 177–8
Reformation, 264-265
Rousseau, Jean Jacques, 255–6
Satan, 67, 92, 117–8
Schwarz-Bart, André, 111–2
Serpent, 66–70, 72, 74

Sexuality, 32–3, 42
Shadow, 93
Shaftesbury, Earl of, 245–7
Siddhartha, 49–52
Sophia, xxxiv, 124–41, 190
Ten Commandments, 98
Titanism, 62, 68
Torah, xlix, 62
Toynbee, Arnold, 91
Transformation of power, 157, 165, 172, 176, 184, 346, 349
Troubadours, 214–5
Urbanization, 25
Vedic tradition, 46–8
Wealth, 268
Wholeness, 290–1
Wiesel, Elie, 110, 275
Yahwist, 63–75

Printed in the United States
87164LV00003B/31/A

9 781931 044004